DESIGNING ORGANIZATIONS

Information and Organization Design Series

series editors
Richard M. Burton
Børge Obel

ORGANIZATIONAL LEARNING: Creating, Retaining and Transferring Knowledge, by Linda Argote

STRATEGIC ORGANIZATIONAL DIAGNOSIS AND DESIGN (2nd Ed.), by Richard M. Burton and Børge Obel

INFORMATION, ORGANISATION AND TECHNOLOGY: Studies in Organisational Semiotics, edited by K. Liu, R. Clarke, P. Andersen, R. Stamper

COORDINATION AND COMMUNICATION USING SIGNS: Studies in Organisation Semiotics 2, edited by K. Liu, R. Clarke, P. Andersen, R. Stamper

DESIGNING STRESS RESISTANT ORGANIZATIONS: Computational Theorizing and Crisis Applications, by Zhiang Lin and Kathleen M. Carley

STRATEGIC ORGANIZATIONAL DIAGNOSIS AND DESIGN: The Dynamics of Fit (3rd Ed.), by Richard M. Burton and Børge Obel

ORGANIZATION STRUCTURES: Theory and Design Analysis and Prescription, by Helmy H. Baligh

ORGANIZATION DESIGN: The Evolving State-of-the-Art, by Richard M. Burton, Bo Eriksen, Dorthe Døjbak Håkonsson, Charles C. Snow

DESIGNING ORGANIZATIONS: 21st Century Approaches, edited by Richard M. Burton, Bo H. Eriksen, Dorthe Døjbak Håkonsson, Thorbjørn Knudsen, Charles C. Snow

Edited by

Richard M. Burton
Bo H. Eriksen
Dorthe Døjbak Håkonsson
Thorbjørn Knudsen
Charles C. Snow

Designing Organizations
21st Century Approaches

Springer

Editors
Richard M. Burton
Duke University, NC
USA

Bo H. Eriksen
University of Southern Denmark
Odense, Denmark

Dorthe Døjbak Håkonsson
University of Southern Denmark
Odense, Denmark

Thorbjørn Knudsen
University of Southern Denmark
Odense, Denmark

Charles C. Snow
Pennsylvania State University, PA
USA

Series Editors
Richard M. Burton
Duke University, NC, USA

Børge Obel
University of Southern Denmark

ISBN: 978-0-387-77775-7 e-ISBN: 978-0-387-77776-4
DOI: 10.1007/978-0-387-77776-4

Library of Congress Control Number: 2007943139

Printed on acid-free paper

9 8 7 6 5 4 3 2 1

springer.com

Acknowledgments

We are grateful to the many individuals at the University of Southern Denmark who helped to make the conference both a professional success and a delightful experience. Further, we thank the Danish Social Science Research Council for its financial support.

Ms. Beverly James has shepherded this book from early drafts to the finished product. All of us –authors and editors-are very appreciative of her help and dedication.

Contents

Editors' Affiliation

Richard M. Burton
Duke University, NC, USA

Bo H. Eriksen
University of Southern Denmark

Dorthe Døjbak Håkonsson
University of Southern Denmark

Thorbjørn Knudsen
University of Southern Denmark

Charles C. Snow
Pennsylvania State University, USA

Contributing Authors

Torben Andersen
The Technical University of Denmark, Center for Technology, Economics and Management, Denmark

Harry Boer
Aalborg University, Center for Industrial Production, Denmark

Richard M. Burton
Duke University, Fuqua School of Business, USA

Lex Donaldson
Australian Graduate School of Management, Sydney NSW, Australia

Bo H. Eriksen
University of Southern Denmark

Kirsten Foss
Copenhagen Business School, Denmark

Dorthe Døjbak Håkonsson
Aarhus School of Business (CORE), University of Aarhus, Denmark

Kaisa Henttonen
Lappeenranta University of Technology, (TBRC), Lappeenranta, Finland

Frances Jørgensen
Aarhus School of Business (CORE), University of Aarhus, Denmark

Per Krogager
Tvilllum-Scanbirk, Masco Corporation, Denmark

Jørn Flohr Nielsen
University of Aarhus, School of Economics and Management, Denmark

Børge Obel
Aarhus School of Business, University of Aarhus, Denmark

Henrik Bendixen Sørensen
University of Aarhus, School of Economics and Management, Denmark

John Parm Ulhøi
Aarhus School of Business (CORE), University of Aarhus, Denmark

Sladjana Vujovic
Aarhus School of Business (CORE), University of Aarhus, Denmark

Charles Williams
Duke University, Fuqua School of Business, USA

Editors' Introduction

In May 2006, a number of international scholars within the area of organization design met at a conference hosted by the University of Southern Denmark. The goal of the conference was to stimulate new design ideas and approaches appropriate for the 21st century. This book, which contains the papers presented at the conference, is a companion to *Organization Design: The Evolving State-of-the-Art*, the scholarly volume published from the first conference held at the same university in May 2005. In both conferences, the participants held wide-ranging discussions about design issues and then developed their papers into the two scholarly volumes.

The present volume presents new approaches to organization design with an emphasis on what they imply for both theory and practice. It is divided into four parts. In Part I, Donaldson and Williams examine how contingency theory compares and contrasts with institutional theory and evolutionary theory. Chapter 1, by Donaldson, discusses the basic tenets of contingency and institutional theory and then compares them. Contingency theory, according to Donaldson, focuses on an internal organizational fit for efficiency purposes whereas institutional theory refers to an organization's external fit with its environment. The two theories suggest quite different design recommendations to achieve superior organizational performance, creating a dilemma for the executive who wishes to make informed design decisions. In Chapter 2, Donaldson explores this dilemma further and arrives at a proposed resolution. By using money as a common consideration, the differing design recommendations can be resolved to yield a meta-fit and thereby give the executive decision maker direction for action. In Chapter 3, Williams examines a different organization structure fit – that suggested by a comparison of contingency and evolutionary approaches. Both approaches are built on information processing and behavioral concepts of the firm. Yet, the causal relationships between structure and strategy are substantially different. Contingency theory examines structural adaptation whereas evolutionary theory focuses on strategic issues such as market entry and exit as well as viable pathways to high performance. From the executive decision maker's standpoint, evolutionary theory with its longer-term view is not as focused on short-term efficiency considerations as contingency theory typically is.

In Part II, important process issues in organization design are considered, including rational emotionality and psychological climate, asymmetric collaboration, asymmetric adaptability, and the process of strategic human resource management. In Chapter 4 Håkansson, Obel, and Burton examine the influence of affective events and employee emotions on psychological climate and then explore the implications of climate for organization design. The authors argue that the concept of bounded rationality does not capture the full effect of cognition on information processing and decision making, and they point out that executives must adapt to the organizational climate while at the same time recognize that their actions affect employee emotions and the longer-term psychological climate of the organization. Nielsen and Sørensen, in Chapter 5, examine collaboration in newer, 'less-organized' networks and in alliances between organizations. They argue that these relationships are often fragile in that they are based on more than asymmetric information, and they develop a taxonomy of interface arrangements across organizations. The authors offer seven propositions about the design of inter-organizational collaborative relationships rather than detailed design recommendations. In Chapter 6, Jørgensen and Boer examine change and adaptation in a longitudinal study of a Danish production facility which installed a matrix organization to deal with a highly turbulent environment. When a calmer environment ensued, the facility returned to a functional organization structure, but many problems emerged. The new knowledge and skills that had developed among the staff pushed the organization back towards the matrix, suggesting an asymmetric adaptation and path dependency to contingent relationships. That is, the current organization design, as well as employee experiences and skills, are themselves contingency factors. In Chapter 7, a case study by Andersen and Krogager, the authors examine the human resource management system of a Danish medical company. The practical issue faced the company was how to make the human resource department and its various divisions a central and important function in the organization. Andersen and Krogager develop a quantitative metric for human resources that measures its return on investment. One design implication of this case study is that good metrics can and should be developed so that the human resource department can play a stronger role in both the short-run and long-run management of an organization.

Part III explores the difficulties associated with stimulating and producing innovation in organizations. In Chapter 8, Vujovic and Ulhøi take an information-processing view of innovation and argue that the process should be more open to cooperation and knowledge sharing. They develop four archetypes of the innovation process classified according to type of user involvement and the organizational level at which cooperation with external sources takes place, and they emphasize the importance of clarifying the strategic purpose of innovation. Henttonen, in Chapter 9, investigates tensions in the innovation process. Using a dialectic approach in her case studies, she finds that firms tend to pursue exploitation (innovation in existing businesses) while hoping for exploration (innovation via new businesses). The implication for practice is a need to examine what the firm is actually doing with respect to innovation and comparing that with what the firm wants to do. Thus, in both of the chapters on innovation, the authors emphasize the importance of goals and strategies in the design and management of the innovation process.

In Part IV, the focus is on firm performance. In Chapter 10, Foss discusses product modularity and lead time, showing how the improvement of lead time for new product innovations affects job tasks and information structure in the organization. She argues that modular design can improve lead time, but it requires a well-specified product architecture which is not easily altered. For the executive decision maker, this implies evaluating the trade-off between speeding up the innovation process versus limiting its outcomes due to the use of the modular approach. Eriksen, in Chapter 11, investigates in a large sample of Danish firms whether strategic planning improves firm performance. He finds that a formal, centralized planning process improves firm performance but not in decentralized organizations. The misfit between centralized planning and decentralized operations highlights the need for executives to carefully align processes, structures, and strategies in order to achieve strong firm performance.

Richard M. Burton
Bo Eriksen
Dorthe Døjbak Håkonsson
Thorbjorn Knudsen
Charles C. Snow

October 2007

PART I: CONTINGENCY, INSTITUTIONAL, AND EVOLUTIONARY THEORY

Chapter 1

THE CONFLICT BETWEEN CONTINGENCY AND INSTITUTIONAL THEORIES OF ORGANIZATIONAL DESIGN

Lex Donaldson

Australian School of Business, University of New South Wales, Address: O & M, Australian School of Business, University of New South Wales, UNSW Sydney NSW 2052, Australia.

Abstract: The contingency theory approach to organizational design states that the structure that fits the contingency produces beneficial outcomes for the organization. This chapter argues that institutional theory also implies that there is an institutional fit that produces beneficial outcomes for the organization. The argument is that contingency fit produces internal effectiveness, whereas institutional fit produces external legitimacy and support. Contingency and institutional theories tend to conflict by prescribing different structures as their fits. The chapter shows that these differences are widespread and the fits can be completely different structures. Hence the organizational designer may be placed in a dilemma.

Key words: Conflict, contingency, institutional, organizational design, fit, effectiveness, legitimacy, external support.

1. INTRODUCTION

Structural contingency theory specifies the structure that will be the optimal organizational design – by fitting with the contingencies. Institutional theory has the concept of a fit of the organizational structure to the institutional environment that has beneficial consequences for the organization, in terms of external legitimacy and support. The chapter seeks to establish the institutional fit and its beneficial outcomes as being analogous to the fit and beneficial outcomes of structural contingency theory. This leads to recognition that institutional fits are pertinent considerations in organizational design. The question then arises as to

R.M. Burton et al. (eds.), *Designing Organizations*, doi: 10.1007/978-0-387-77776-4_1,

whether the institutional fits complement, or conflict with, the contingency theory fits. This chapter argues that they tend to conflict. Sometimes the structure that is the institutional fit conflicts considerably with the structure that is the contingency fit. Thus, for an organization, contingency fit and institutional fit will often be conflicting structural choices for the organizational designer.

Traditionally, the study of organizational design (Burton and Obel, 2004; Burton, DeSanctis, and Obel, 2006) has been influenced by structural contingency theory (Pfeffer, 1982). However, institutional theory is a popular theory of organizational structure and is probably the major contemporary theory for the academic study of organizational structure (Scott, 1995). Does institutional theory have implications for organizational design? The present chapter will argue that the institutional theory approach may be used to yield implications for organizational design. Moreover, the theories are complementary only where the structural fits derived from contingency and institutional theories are the same. The analysis shows that this is the rare case. More usually, there will be a conflict between the prescriptions that can be drawn from the two theories, so that if one theory is fulfilled, the other would not be. Thus, the prescriptions from contingency theory may have to be revised in the light of an institutional theory analysis. Therefore, a sound and fully comprehensive organizational design analysis would have to supplement the contingency analysis by an institutional theory analysis. The present chapter raises this issue and seeks to point the way towards the kinds of analyses that might be made. In that way, it is conceptual and exploratory. Elsewhere we have critically discussed institutional theory, especially regarding its lack of integration with structural contingency theory (Donaldson, 1995). The present chapter is a modest step towards their rapprochement on the topic of organizational design.

As is well known, the contingency theory approach to organizational design strongly emphasizes the consequences for performance of structural fit (or misfit) (Donaldson, 2001). In contrast, institutional theory usually operates as a discourse quite removed from structural contingency theory and organizational design (DiMagio and Powell, 1983, 1991). Nevertheless, it can be seen that institutional theory contains arguments that have implications about the structure that fits or misfits the requirement of the institutional environment. The chapter seeks to draw out these ideas, and show how institutional theory can lead to an analysis of organizational design and its consequences, which parallels that from contingency theory. Thus, we can speak of institutional fit (or misfit) and its consequences in a similar fashion to that of contingency fit (or misfit). However, contingency theory and institutional theory posit different effects or outcomes of structure. Contingency theory deals in the outcome of structure on internal effectiveness. Institutional theory deals in the outcome of structure on external legitimacy and support.

The analysis reveals where conflicts will exist between the contingency and institutional theories and the magnitude of the conflicts, that is, how much difference there is between the structures that fit the contingencies and the structure that fits the institutional requirement. In particular, a source of the conflict is the fact that, in contingency theory, the fitting structure varies with the contingencies, whereas the fits derived from institutional theory are typically not contingent, and so not changed by the contingency variables, such as organizational size. Therefore, there are widely varying contingency fits versus a singular institutional fit.

2. INSTITUTIONAL THEORY AND ORGANIZATIONAL DESIGN

Organizational design is the body of knowledge and techniques that seeks to offer useful advice to organizations about their structures (and other aspects) needed to attain their goals (Burton and Obel, 2004; Burton, DeSanctis, and Obel, 2006). It draws upon theories of organizational structure that yield knowledge of the effects (outcomes) of different structures. Structural contingency theory is such a theory (Donaldson, 2001), and it is used in the literature on organizational design to prescribe structures (Khandwalla, 1977; Burton and Obel, 2004). In contrast, institutional theory is a sociological theory that seeks to explain organizational structures, rather than to offer prescriptions (Scott, 1995). Institutional theory explains the structure that an organization adopts as being conformity with cultural codes that thereby leads to legitimacy and support from external organizations. Therefore, institutional theory could also be used prescriptively, in that, knowing which structures will attain legitimacy and external support for an organization, could lead to valid prescriptions being offered about organizational design.

The theory itself is at a high-level of abstraction, dealing with isomorphic processes (DiMagio and Powell, 1983). Nevertheless, it sensitizes the researcher to identify the structure that is the model with which organizations tend to conform in an organizational field. Conformity results in legitimacy and external support, according to institutional theory (DiMagio and Powell, 1983, Scott, 1995). Therefore, an understanding of institutional theory leads the researcher to identify the effects of conforming, or failing to conform, which thereby could inform organizational design.

Thus, we need to discuss in turn the following issues about institutional theory, its explanation of causes of structure, its ideas about the consequences of structures, the relation to organizational design, and conflicts between institutional and contingency theories about organizational design.

2.1 Causes of structure in institutional theory

Institutional theory is a sociological theory of organizations that explains processes through which structures of organizations are adopted. Institutional isomorphism is the process through which organizations become more similar to other organizations within their organizational field, through mimetic, normative and coercive isomorphisms (DiMagio and Powell, 1983). Thus the emphasis is upon the causes of structure. Institutional theory contains many causal mechanisms that are used to explain why an organization adopts a structure. Institutional theory might explain that the organization adopted the structure because it was taken-for-granted by its managers who were not able to think of any alternative (DiMagio and Powell, 1991). Again, institutional theory might explain that the organization adopted the structure because most other organizations had adopted that structure, i.e., mimetic isomorphism (DiMagio and Powell, 1983; Fligstein, 1985). Yet again, institutional theory might explain that the organization adopted the structure because the high-status organizations in its field had adopted it. Once again, institutional theory might explain that the organization adopted the structure because its managers were in a state of causal ambiguity and so any signal from powerful external groups that favoured a particular structure pushed them towards adopting it. Once again, institutional theory might explain that the organization adopted the structure because its consultants (i.e., professional organizations) favoured that as a positive role model (DiMagio and Powell, 1983). Again, institutional theory might explain that the organization adopted the structure because its auditing firms (i.e., professional organizations) required this to approve its audit, i.e., normative isomorphism (DiMagio and Powell, 1983). Yet again, an organization might adopt a structural feature because that was legally required and backed by punitive sanctions, i.e., coercive isomorphism (DiMagio and Powell, 1983).

Thus, institutional theory can be used to explain why a certain structure is adopted. This is the way in which institutional theory has mainly been used to date: to explain the social processes that lead to adoption. There is no necessity that the adopted structure is the most effective in terms of internal operations. The structure adopted could be ineffective. Likewise, the isomorphic processes could push an organization to adopt a structure that fits its contingencies (e.g., size), but they could also push it to adopt a structure that misfits its contingencies. Thus the structure adopted is not necessarily rational. It is primarily symbolic – as "ritual" (Meyer and Scott, 1983), or "myth and ceremony" (Meyer and Rowan, 1977). The structure may accord with a cultural code or ideology of rationality, but its adoption is because of conformity to that ideology, not because it is actually rational. Thus, institutional theory is essentially sceptical about rational organizational design. To date, this is the main relationship between institutional theory and organizational design. However, institutional theory does postulate consequences and, indeed, benefits of adopting structures, and this has pertinence to organizational design. It is this more neglected aspect that we wish to address herein.

2.2 Consequences of structure in institutional theory

As we have seen, institutional theory is primarily about causes of structure, but it does contain ideas about consequences. The adoption of the normatively "right" structure by an organization has positive consequences for it. Conformity by an organization to the model of "correct" structure that prevails in its organizational field leads to legitimacy and support from external organizations. Such supports include accreditation, professional approval, grants and loans (DiMagio and Powell, 1983). Conversely, failure to conform to legal requirements imposed by the state can lead to sanctions (DiMagio and Powell, 1983), so that conformity can be considered here to confer the benefit of freedom from these sanctions, as another kind of external support.

Thus, there is a concept of institutional fit that is analogous to contingency fit. Contingency fit is that level of the structural variable that fits the level of the contingency variable and so produces the highest level of internal effectiveness for the organization (Donaldson, 2001). Institutional fit is that level of the structural variable that fits the institutional environment of an organization, i.e., the structure that is the model structure which is approved as legitimate for organizations within an organizational field. Institutional fit produces the highest level of legitimacy and, hence, external support for the organization.

In institutional theory, one process whereby the organization conforms is by some of its members (e.g., managers) deliberately conforming to gain the advantages of legitimacy and external support. Thus, such action is conscious and calculating. Hence, organizational actors are seen, on occasion, as acting calculatively, with an eye to securing beneficial consequences, by adopting the right structure. More generally, extant organizations might be structured to secure beneficial consequences of institutional conformity through survival processes, such that, organizations which in the past had *not* been structured in this way, as a result, failed and so were disbanded (Hannan and Freeman, 1989). Thus, by conscious choice or differential survival, organizations can become structured in ways that make them conform to their institutional environment and so receive beneficial outcomes from their environment.

2.3 Organizational design and institutional theory

Organizational design seeks to assist managers attain more effective organizations. Therefore, securing any benefits of conformity is a pertinent consideration to be entered into the calculus along with the more traditional benefits from contingency fit. In this way, institutional theory has a capacity to contribute to organizational design.

As regards organizational design, however, there is a difference in specificity between contingency and institutional theories. Structural contingency theory gives detailed prescriptions, e.g., an organization in an unstable environment with high levels of market and technological change is best fitted by an organic structure (Burns and Stalker, 1961). Institutional theory lacks such detailed guidance as to which structure fits the institutional environment. Instead, it holds that there is a general process, institutional isomorphism, whereby organizations adjust to accord with the normatively approved type for their organizational field (DiMagio and Powell, 1983). Thus, the approved structural type may be specific to an organizational field. It requires knowledge of that field to know its approved structural type. Thus, institutional theory does not allow deductions from its core premises to define the approved type, rather, the theory is an approach or perspective, that sensitizes the analyst to inquire into the approved structural type within a field. Once that approved structural type has been identified, then institutional theory can be used to predict that there will be benefits from adopting it. Hence institutional theory may be used to prescribe that adopting the institutionally approved structure as the organizational design will lead the organization to receive the benefits of legitimacy and external support.

Clearly, using institutional theory in this way is compatible with rational organizational design. However, this is not to claim that all of institutional theory is consistent with rational organizational design. There are some mechanisms of conformity in institutional theory that are not consistent with the process of rational organizational design. These include unconsciously following a way of thinking, so that a structure is adopted without thought of alternatives, i.e., it is taken-for-granted. This is not compatible with organizational design which features comparison of alternatives and selection based on consequences. Thus, in writing about the organizational design implications of institutional theory, we are selectively applying elements from the theory that lend themselves to the organizational design project.

3. DIFFERENTIAL OUTCOMES OF CONTINGENCY AND INSTITUTIONAL FITS

Both structural contingency theory and institutional theory deal in outcomes, and it is these outcomes that are the focus of this chapter, consistent with the interest in organizational design. Each theory yields prescriptions; the organizational design issue is how to bring them together in an overall prescription, or meta-prescription. This raises the issue of whether structural contingency theory and institutional theory lead to complementary or conflicting prescriptions, and the implications for organizational design.

Both contingency and institutional theories are sociological functionalist theories in that they explain structures (at least partly) by their beneficial consequences (Merton, 1968). For institutional theory, the benefits of legitimacy and external support provide reasons for adopting and retaining a structure, though some adoption and retention may be due to other causes, such as unreflective conformity to cultural codes.

Both contingency and institutional theories postulate a fit or matching between structure and some other factor. For contingency theory, the fit is of the organizational structural variable to the contingency variable. For institutional theory, there is an analogous fit between the actual structure of the organization and the structure that is institutionally approved.

Contingency and institutional theory both posit a fit that leads to beneficial outcomes. However, the nature of the benefit differs between the two theories. Structural contingency theory posits that structures that fit the contingencies produce more internal effectiveness. Effectiveness essentially means attaining goals (Parsons, 1961). Therefore, for a business firm, effectiveness typically involves sales growth, profitability and such financial measures of success. For a hospital, effectiveness might involve providing high quality treatment at low cost. The effectiveness from fit comes about because of superior internal operations, such as better decision-making and more efficient use of resources.

In institutional theory, organizations are shaped by the wider institutional environment, i.e., organizational field, in which they are located. The institutional environment of an organization typically involves other organizations such as competitors, suppliers, customers, professions, regulators and governments. These organizations influence the focal organization. In institutional theory, conformance produces benefits to the organization such as legitimacy, accreditation, financial support and survival (DiMagio and Powell, 1983). These benefits typically flow through a process whereby the conformity by the focal organization is witnessed by outsiders, who in return bestow the benefits. Thus, the process involves adherence by the focal organization to cultural codes or beliefs held by people in the organizational field.

Hence, institutional theory posits beneficial outcomes, but differing in type and origins from those of contingency theory. Contingency theory posits as the beneficial outcome, the effectiveness that is generated internally from the fit of structure to contingency. Institutional theory posits as beneficial outcomes, the legitimacy and support that come externally, as a result of conformance to cultural codes and norms. Thus two dimensions of outcomes can be distinguished: internal effectiveness and external support.

3.1 Complementary or conflicting theories?

Clearly, the predictions of the two theories differ about the type of beneficial outcomes, however they are potentially complementary. An organization might simultaneously adapt its structure to the contingencies, to gain the benefits of high internal effectiveness, while also conforming to the externally approved model structure to gain the benefits of high external support. There are two ways in which this compatibility could be attained: identical prescriptions about the best structure, or segmentation, meaning that the theories dealt with different aspects of structure.

Identical prescriptions. The structural contingency theory and institutional theory processes are compatible, if the structure that fits the contingency also fits the approved external model. In other words, the structural solution favoured by the two theories is identical.

Segmentation. Compatibility between structural contingency theory and institutional theory is feasible, even if they differ, if the aspects of structures that fit the contingencies are different from those that fit the external model. Then the structural domains of the two theories are separate, so that there is no overlap and no conflict between them.

Thus, the logic of our analysis leads to the realization that, in these two ways, the two theories can be compatible. Where structural contingency theory and institutional theory are complementary, the organization simultaneously has both high internal effectiveness and high external support, i.e., it enjoys both benefits. In organizational design terms, there is a structural design that enables the organization to enjoy the best of both worlds.

Beguiling though this idea of complementary may be, a deeper analysis shows that it is unlikely. More specifically, there are grounds for rejecting both the pathways to complementarity: identical prescriptions and segmentation (i.e., separate structural domains). Each pathway will be critically discussed next. Their rejection leads to recognition that structural contingency theory and institutional theory are usually conflicting in their structural prescriptions.

4. REASONS FOR THE CONFLICT BETWEEN CONTINGENCY THEORY AND INSTITUTIONAL THEORIES OF ORGANIZATIONAL STRUCTURE

4.1 Critique of identical prescriptions

In order to better understand why identical prescriptions are infeasible, it is necessary to identify some other differences between structural contingency theory and institutional theory. Structural contingency theory holds that there are many fits. In contrast, institutional theory says there is one structural model that is approved in an organizational field, i.e. , there is only one structure which is the institutional fit. An organization could be in institutional fit and also be in contingency fit. But many contingency fits are also institutional theory misfits. Therefore the prescriptions of contingency and institutional theories usually differ.

In structural contingency theory, the effective structure varies according to the contingency, which it must fit. In the Cartesian version of structural contingency theory (Donaldson, 2001), the fit is itself a continuum with many points of fit sequentially along the fit line, e.g., between size and formalization (Child, 1975; Keller, 1994). Figure 1 shows the fits between the size contingency and the formalization structural variable. In the configurational version of structural contingency theory, the fits are discrete in space and fewer (Van de Ven, and Drazin, 1985). In both versions of structural contingency theory, however, there is more than one fit point of structure to contingency.

In an organizational field, the externally approved model, that is, the institutional fit, would be only one level of the structural variable. In contrast, there would be many structural levels that fitted the various possible levels of the contingency variable of an organization. One of these structural levels that fitted the level of the contingency variable might also be the institutional fit. However, the other structural levels that fitted the levels of the contingency variable would not be the institutional fit – they would be institutional misfits. Thus, most contingency fits would be institutional misfits.

For a set of organizations with varying contingency levels, the structural levels that were fits would vary. For organizations in contingency fit, only a few would have structures whose contingency fits matched the externally approved model institutional fit. An organization might happen to have a structure that simultaneously fitted both the contingency and the institutional requirements. But this would be a rare case. Most organizations would not fit both requirements. Instead, those organizations in institutional fit will tend to be in some degree of misfit with the contingency. Hence the contingency fit and institutional fit will mostly conflict.

Figure 1 depicts the differing fits of structural contingency and institutional theories, respectively. The structural variable is formalization and takes five different levels, ranging from 20 to 100 per cent.

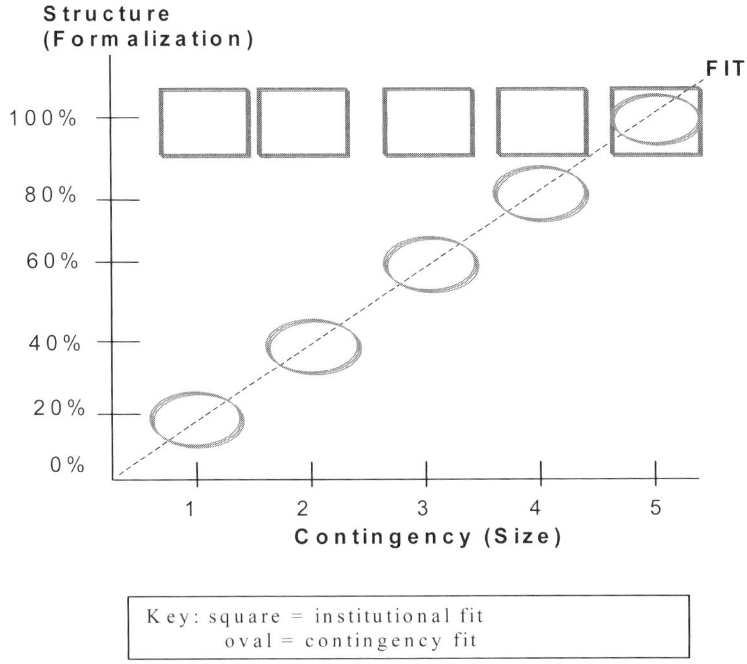

Figure 1. Conflict between institutional fit and contingency fit

The contingency variable is size and ranges from 1 to 5. Structural contingency theory fits (shown as ovals) are defined as existing on the diagonal line running from the origin to the top-right hand corner. The institutional theory fit (shown as squares) is defined as being at the maximum level of the structural variable. The institutional theory fit holds for all the five values of the contingency variable. The contingency and institutional theory fits converge at the point where contingency level is 5 and the structural level is also 5, so that this point is both a contingency theory fit and an institutional theory fit. Thus, an organization at contingency level 5 can be in fit both with contingency and institutional requirements.

For all other levels of the contingency variable, however, the contingency fit and institutional fit are different points. The institutional fit is always structural level 5. In contrast, the structural levels that fit the contingency variable are less than structural level 5, for levels 1 to 4 of the contingency variable. For contingency level 4 the fitting structure is 4, for contingency level 3 the fitting structure is 3, and so on. Hence, the lower the contingency level, the more that the contingency fit diverges from the institutional fit. At contingency level 1, the fitting structure is formalization of 20 per cent, which is 80 per cent different from the institutional fit of 100% per cent. Thus, the contingency and institutional theory fits diverge for four out of the five contingency levels (1 to 4). Hence the fits prescribed by the theories are mostly in conflict.

As an example of the difference between contingency and institutional fits of the same aspect of organizational structure, consider bureaucratic structure. Weber defines bureaucracy as a single type of structure. Institutional theory discusses Weberian bureaucracy as this single type of structure, towards which organizations around the world are converging, because that is the legitimate structure in the Western cultural account (DiMaggio and Powell, 1983). In contrast, structural contingency theory holds that bureaucratization is a variable (Pugh, Hickson, Hinings and Turner, 1968), and that its optimal level is that which fits the size of the organization (Child, 1975). To be in institutional fit, that is, conform to the Weberian model, an organization would need to be highly bureaucratized. Thus, a large organization that is highly bureaucratized would simultaneously fit the size contingency and the institutional requirement. However, the many other structural fits to the size contingency would not fit the institutional requirement. For example, an organization of medium size with medium bureaucratization would be a structural contingency theory fit, but would not be an institutional theory fit, because it was insufficiently bureaucratized to be a Weberian bureaucracy. Again, structural contingency theory would prescribe that a small organization should be low on bureaucratized, that is, be substantially unbureaucratic, even though in a Western culture, where this violates the legitimate, culturally imbued, highly rationalized, institutional model. Hence, structural contingency theory sees a wide range of fits to degrees of bureaucratization, whereas institutional theory sees only a high level of bureaucratization as being the fit. Therefore, only large, highly bureaucratic organizations will simultaneously fit the size contingency and the institutional requirement. Many other, smaller organizations that are less bureaucratic, are in institutional misfit, even if they are in contingency fit.

Another example of difference between fit in contingency theory and institutional theory is "strategy and structure". Structural contingency theory holds that the optimal structure fits the corporate strategy, that is, the level of diversification (Chandler, 1962). A functional structure fits an undiversified strategy, while a divisional structure fits a diversified strategy (Donaldson, 1987; Hamilton and Shergill, 1992). Therefore there is no one structure that is prescribed as being appropriate for all organizations. In contrast, an institutional theory study reports how management of a business firm adopted a divisional structure in order to appeal to the beliefs of outsiders who saw it as the right structure (DiMaggio and Powell, 1991, p. 70). This illustrates how outsiders can influence an organization towards adopting a structure, even though it may have been a misfit (if the company was undiversified). Hence, structural contingency theory sees a broader range of structures that can fit variations in strategy, whereas institutional theory sees there being a model structure for an organizational field. Structural contingency theory sees functional, divisional and matrix structures all as possible fits to the various levels of strategic diversification, whereas institutional theory sees that, within an organizational field, divisional structure is the model structure. Thus, structural contingency theory and institutional theory typically yield conflicting predictions.

4.2 Critique of Structural Segmentation

The potential tension between the requirements of contingency and institutional theory can be avoided if the structures required to fulfil each apply to different aspects of the organization. Then, adopting a structure that fits the contingencies in one part of the organization, is compatible with adopting another structure that meets the institutional requirements in another part of the organization. Thus, the organization can simultaneously adopt structures that allow it to maximize both internal effectiveness and external support. For this to hold, there need to be certain aspects of structure that are appropriately shaped only by the contingencies and certain other aspects appropriately shaped only by the institutional pressures.

The loose coupling variant of institutional theory (Meyer and Scott, 1983) holds that conformity pressures work on aspects of the organization that are visible to outsiders, while the operating core deep in the organization may act in ways that are quite different and not in conformity. Thus, institutional pressures would be expected to be greatest at the apex, such as boards of directors, CEO and head office, rather than at lower levels, such as production workers in a plant. Indeed, loose coupling theory states that the operating core is structured in a different way from the apex so that the core can operate effectively (Meyer and Scott, 1983). From the structural contingency theory viewpoint, such structures, to be operationally effective, would need to fit the contingencies that apply to them. Thus, the structures of the operating core would need to fit the contingencies of the operating core: its size, task uncertainty and so on. In this way, adoption of the institutionally approved model for the organizational apex would produce maximum external support, while, simultaneously, adoption of the structure for the operating core that fits its contingencies would produce maximum effectiveness. Hence, by segmented adaptations, both contingency and institutional requirements could be met, maximizing both internal effectiveness and external support. However, there are grounds for doubting such structural segmentation.

Some institutional pressures may focus on the operating core, for example, governmental safety regulations that apply inside the plant. Then the institutional adaptation occurs for more than just the apex. There is probably some trend over time for the scope of institutional pressures to be expanding, in that the range of structural variables subject to institutional pressures is increasing. The mass media take an interest in more and more internal aspects of organizations, thereby bringing them into public scrutiny and comparing them with the societally approved models of these structures. Similarly, coercive isomorphism is increasing in scope, in many industries and nations, as governments extend the range of their regulations to include more topics, e.g., equal employment opportunity and pollution. Thus the operating core does not seem immune from institutional fit effects.

Similarly, the apex of an organization does not seem immune from contingency fit effects. There are theoretical arguments and empirical evidence that there are structural contingency fits for the apex that affect internal effectiveness. For example, the board of director, the "jewel in the crown" of the organizational apex, has been viewed as being an ornament of mainly symbolic value. Yet research has shown that board structure needs to fit contingency factors, such as the environment, in order not to adversely affect internal effectiveness (Boyd, 1995; Rogers, 2005). Thus, board structure cannot be assigned as being only in an institutional theory segment and not in a contingency theory segment. Board structure is surely an aspect of the organization that is far removed from the operating core of the corporation (e.g., the plants), but even here we see that there are requirements not only from the institutional environment but also from the organization's contingencies. The fact that such a publicly visible feature of the apex is subject to structural contingency effects, suggests grounds for caution in pursuing the idea of structural segmentation.

Overall, the case has yet to be made convincingly that contingency theory and institutional theory each apply only to different aspects of structure. Instead, they make predictions about the same structural variable. As seen, these prescriptions tend not to be identical, but rather are usually for different structures. Therefore structural contingency theory and institutional theory are, in the main, conflicting theories of organizational design.

5. OUTCOMES FROM CONFLICTING STRUCTURAL PRESCRIPTIONS

Because structural contingency theory and institutional theory are mainly conflicting in their structural prescriptions, usually an organization could maximize either internal effectiveness or external institutional support, but not both simultaneously. Choosing the contingency fit maximizes internal effectiveness, whereas choosing the institutional fit maximizes external support. Hence, in choosing a structure, internal effectiveness will be traded off against external institutional support. This presents the organizational designers with a choice. Adopting a structure that fits the contingencies usually entails adopting a level of the structure that to some degree misfits the institutional requirements, so that external support suffers. Conversely, adopting a structure that fits the institutional requirements usually entails adopting a level of the structure that to some degree misfits the contingencies, so that internal effectiveness suffers.

For instance, for a large corporation that is listed on a stock exchange, its board of directors is a structure that attracts public scrutiny, so that corporations strive to be legitimate by adopting the institutionally approved structures. It is considered legitimate to have a majority of directors be non-executives, who are independent of management, so that they can exercise control over management on behalf of the outside shareholders. This board structure accords with the model of "good governance" that is widely held in the community (Kesner and Dalton, 1986). This could lead to external support, in that outside investors wish to purchase the shares, driving up the share price. Thus, a company having the "right" board structure could increase its share price. This, in turn, confers benefits of more valuable shares for existing shareholders. It also makes capital raising cheaper for the company. Also, a higher share price benefits its managers, through social approval and making their share options more valuable. However, a board composed of a high proportion of non-executive directors misfits certain levels of a contingency variable, producing lower internal effectiveness, that is, less profitability (Rogers, 2005). Thus, it may be that, in some corporations, having a higher proportion of non-executive directors leads to a higher share price but lower profitability. This illustrates the possible conflict between institutional and contingency prescriptions, so that either external support (share price) or internal effectiveness (profitability) can be maximized, but not both simultaneously. Hence, there is a trade-off between choosing a board that maximizes either share price or profitability. The organizational designer must sacrifice price or profitability. This poses a dilemma for the organizational designer.

In this chapter we have sought to make a theoretical argument, but it has been at a high level of abstraction. How this applies to each aspect of structure and organizational situation is a matter for detailed theoretical and empirical work. In that sense, the present remarks seek to suggest an agenda for a possible body of future work.

6. INFORMING THE THEORY OF ORGANIZATION DESIGN

This chapter has sought to enrich the theory of organizational design, by introducing into it considerations from institutional theory. While institutional theory is a major contemporary theory of organizational structure, it is not usually drawn upon in the discourse about organizational design. We have sought to show that, although institutional theory does not set out to offer prescriptions about how to design better organizations, it does contain implications for organizational design. Institutional theory holds that organizations which adopt structures that conform to the institutional environment of the organization and prevailing cultural codes, thereby gain legitimacy and external support. These benefits for the organization mean that there is incentive for organizations to be designed so as to gain them, through adopting structural features that confer legitimacy. This entails conformity to the socially approved model of structure within an organizational field. These benefits are analogous to the superior organizational performance that structural contingency theory posits as the outcome from fit of structure to contingency. However, the structures that are fits in institutional theory are only sometimes the same as the structures that are fits in contingency theory. Often, the fits conflict. In this way, the institutional theory considerations have been brought together with the traditional organizational design theory of contingency theory, providing a more comprehensive formulation of the design problem.

7. INFORMING THE PRACTICE OF ORGANIZATION DESIGN

Articulating the institutional theory of organizational design leads to recognition of how organizations can benefit from crafting their structures to fit prevailing institutional norms, so that they secure greater support from external parties. This source of benefit parallels the benefits of internal organizational effectiveness, which results from fitting the structure to the contingencies. It leads to the recognition that the structure that best fits the external norms may not always be the same structure that fits the contingencies. This means that the organizational designer faces a trade-off.

If the external support benefits that flow to an organization from attaining institutional fit are more valuable to it than are the internal effectiveness benefits from attaining contingency fit, then the designer should prefer to attain institutional fit, despite some contingency misfit and so some sacrifice of the internal effectiveness benefits. Conversely, if the internal effectiveness benefits that flow to an organization from attaining contingency fit are more valuable to it than are the external support benefits from attaining institutional fit, then the designer should prefer to attain contingency fit, despite some institutional misfit and so some sacrifice of the external support benefits. If the value to an organization of internal effectiveness relative to external support is ambiguous, then the organizational designer is in a dilemma, not knowing whether to recommend the adoption of an organizational design that fits the contingency or the institutional requirements, because it is unclear which fit is in the organization's best interests.

8. CONCLUSION

Consequences flow from the fit of structures to both contingencies and institutional requirements, producing distinct benefits of each. Contingency fit produces internal effectiveness. Institutional fit produces external legitimacy and support. Therefore, there can be a concept of institutional fit producing certain beneficial outcomes that is analogous to the familiar concept of contingency fit producing its beneficial outcomes. Hence, in considering the best design for an organization, the institutional fit may need to be considered alongside the more traditional contingency fit.

The organizational design implications of contingency and institutional fits tend to conflict. While sometimes the contingency and institutional fits will be the same level of a structural variable, that situation will tend to be rare. The wide range of the contingency fits usually makes sub-optimal the singular fit (within an organizational field) of the institutional model. If contingency and institutional fits each applied to different aspects of structures, then they could be complementary, but recent research tends to point to both contingency and institutional fits applying to the same structural domains. Therefore, fit to the contingency will tend to be to the detriment of fit to the institutional requirement, and vice-versa. Structures will rarely simultaneously maximize internal effectiveness and external support. The contingency and institutional theories tend to conflict in their implications for organizational design. Hence, giving a role to institutional theory in organizational design, while leading to a more fully informed decision, could lead the designer into a dilemma.

REFERENCES

Boyd, B., 1995, CEO Duality and firm performance: A contingency model, *Strategic Management Journal,* **16**:301-12.

Burns, T., and Stalker, G. M., 1961, *The Management of Innovation*, Tavistock, London.

Burton, R. M., DeSanctis, G. and Obel, B., 2006, *Organizational Design: A Step by Step Approach*, Cambridge University Press.

Burton, R. M. and Obel, B., 2004, *Strategic Organizational Diagnosis and Design: The Dynamics of Fit*, Third Edition, Springer/Kluwer Academic Publishers.

Chandler, A.D. Jr., 1962, *Strategy and Structure: chapters in the history of the American industrial enterprise*, M.I.T. Press, Cambridge.

Child, J., 1975, Managerial and organizational factors associated with company performance, Part 2: A contingency analysis. *Journal of Management Studies*, **12**: 12-27.

DiMaggio, P.J., and Powell, W.W., 1983, The iron cage revisited: institutional isomorphism and collective rationality in organization fields, *American Sociological Review*, **48**: 147-60.

DiMaggio, P.J., and Powell, W.W., 1991, *Introduction*, In Powell, Walter W. and DiMaggio, Paul, eds. *The New Institutionalism in Organizational Analysis*, University of Chicago Press, Chicago.

Donaldson, L., 1987, Strategy and structural adjustment to regain fit and performance: In defence of contingency theory, *Journal of Management Studies*, **24 (1)**: 1-24.

Donaldson, L., 1995, *American Anti-Management Theories of Organization: A Critique of Paradigm Proliferation*, Cambridge University Press, Cambridge.

Donaldson, L., 2001, *The Contingency Theory of Organizations*, Sage, Thousand Oaks.

Fligstein, N., 1985, The spread of the multidivisional form among large firms, 1919-1979, *American Sociological Review*, **50**: 377-91.

Hamilton, R.T., and Shergill, G.S., 1992, The relationship between strategy-structure fit and financial performance in New Zealand: Evidence of generality and validity with enhanced controls, *Journal of Management Studies*, **29**: 95-113.

Hannan, Michael T. and Freeman, John, 1989, *Organizational Ecology.* Cambridge, MA: Harvard University Press.

Keller, R.T., 1994, Technology-information processing fit and the performance of R&D project groups: A test of contingency theory, *Academy of Management Journal*, **37**: 167-79.

Kesner, Idalene F. and Dalton, Dan R.,1986, Boards of Directors and the Checks and (Im)Balances of Corporate Governance, *Business Horizons*, September-October, 17-23.

Khandwalla, P.N., 1977, *The Design of Organizations*. New York: Harcourt Brace Janovich.

Merton, R.K., 1968, *Social Theory and Social Structure*, The Free Press, New York.

Meyer, John W. and Rowan, Brian, 1977, Institutionalized Organizations: Formal Structure as Myth and Ceremony, *American Journal of Sociology,* **83**: 340-63.

Meyer, John W. and Scott, W. Richard, with the assistance of Rowan, B. and Deal, T.E., 1983. *Organizational Environments: Ritual and Rationality,* Beverly Hills, CA: Sage.

Parsons, T., 1961, "Suggestions for a sociological approach to the theory of organizations", in: *Complex Organizations: A Sociological Reader,* Holt, Rinehart, and Winston, Amitai Etzioni, New York, 32-47.

Pfeffer, J., 1982, *Organizations and Organization Theory*, Pitman, Marshfield.

Pugh, D. S., D. J. Hickson, C. R. Hinings and C. Turner. 1968. "Dimensions of Organization Structure." *Administrative Science Quarterly,* **13**: 65-105.

Rogers, M., 2005, *Contingent Corporate Governance: A Challenge to the Theories of Universal Board Structure*. PhD Thesis, Australian Graduate School of Management, Universities of New South Wales and Sydney, Sydney.

Scott, W. R., 1995, *Institutions and Organizations*, Sage, Thousand Oaks.

Van de Ven, A.H., and Robert D., 1985, The concept of fit in contingency theory, in: *Research in Organizational Behaviour,* 7, Edited by B.M. Staw and L. L. Cummings, JAI Press, Greenwich, 333-65.

Chapter 2

RESOLVING THE CONFLICT BETWEEN CONTINGENCY AND INSTITUTIONAL THEORIES OF ORGANIZATIONAL DESIGN

Lex Donaldson

Australian School of Business, University of New South Wales, Address: O & M, Australian School of Business, University of New South Wales, UNSW Sydney NSW 2052, Australia.

Abstract: The previous chapter argued that contingency theory and institutional theories lead to prescriptions for organizational design that often conflict. This conflict could pose a dilemma for the organizational designer. However, this chapter demonstrates that the conflict can be resolved. By rendering the outcomes from both the contingency fit and the institutional fit in directly comparable terms, i.e., money, their joint outcome may be found. Thus, the superior fit – contingency fit or institutional fit – can be identified. This gives the overall optimal structure, that is, the meta-fit. Thereby, the organizational designer will usually be able to make a decisive choice.

Key words: Resolving, conflict, contingency, institutional, organizational design, fit, effectiveness, legitimacy, external support.

1. INTRODUCTION

Organizational design is traditionally guided by structural contingency theory (Burton and Obel, 2004; Burton, DeSanctis, and Obel, 2006; Khandwalla, 1977; Donaldson, 2001; Pfeffer, 1982). The previous chapter has argued that institutional theory also has organizational design implications. While fitting the organization to its contingencies (e.g., size, Child, 1975) leads the organization to receive benefits of internal effectiveness, fitting the organization to the requirements of its institutional environment leads the organization to receive the benefits of legitimacy and

R.M. Burton et al. (eds.), *Designing Organizations*, doi: 10.1007/978-0-387-77776-4_2,

external support (Scott, 1995). Conflict can arise, however, between the organizational design implications of contingency and institutional theories, because institutional theory usually leads to fits with the institutional requirements by structures that are not those that fit the contingencies of the organization (DiMaggio and Powell, 1983). This may seem to prevent rational organizational design. However, the chapter shows that when the different outcomes of contingency and institutional fits can both be valued by a common metric, it is possible to find the optimal design for an organization. While each of the contingency and institutional theories posit different outcomes – internal effectiveness and external support, respectively – from their structural fit, they can sometimes be made comparable by the common metric of money. Then, the relative monetary strengths of contingency fit and institutional fit can be used to find which fit is superior, and so identify which structural design is the most rational for an organization.

Where contingency and institutional fits conflict, the extent to which traditional, contingency theoretical organizational design prescriptions need to be revised depends upon the extent to which the institutional requirement for structure differs from the contingency requirement. This gives the amount of difference between the structure that fits the contingency and the structure that fits the institutional requirement. And the need to revise contingency theory prescriptions depends also on the relative strengths of the contingency and institutional fits on monetary outcomes. This gives which of the differing fits, contingency or institutional, is preferable. The chapter seeks to show that the joint outcome of the two theories can be ascertained by rendering both outcomes in money and calculating their joint monetary effects. The organizational design decision becomes choosing between the fit (contingency or institutional) that produces the best joint outcome. This best overall fit is the meta-fit for the organization.

An implication is that, in certain situations, the optimal design, i.e., meta-fit, is to choose the institutional fit, despite misfitting the contingency. In certain other situations, the meta-fit (i.e., optimal design) is to choose the contingency fit, despite that misfitting the institutional requirements. Which fit type should predominate in organizational design depends upon the relative strength of the outcomes of each fit type. Contingency theory is the more determining of rational organizational designs if the monetary effect of contingency fit is larger than the monetary effect of institutional fit. Conversely, institutional theory is the more determining of rational organizational designs if the monetary effect of institutional fit is larger than the monetary effect of contingency fit. The chapter gives an illustration of a procedure, for valorising the outcomes of each of institutional fit and contingency fit in the common metric of money. This analysis is then used to find the best overall fit, that is, meta-fit. Thus, while organizational design needs to include institutional considerations that often conflict with contingency considerations, nevertheless, it is possible to identify an organization design that takes account of both considerations.

2. RESOLVING THE CONFLICT FOR ORGANIZATIONAL DESIGN

The fit between structure and contingency maximizes the internal effectiveness of the organization, that is, the ability to achieve the gaols of the organization, e.g., profitability of a business corporation (Child 1975; Donaldson, 1987; Hamilton and Shergill, 1992; Van de Ven and Drazin, 1985). Thus, contingency fit leads to profitability, which, in turn, leads to higher dividends. In contrast, institutional fit maximizes conformity to the model of the organization that is approved by the institutional environment, leading the organization to be seen as legitimate (Parsons, 1961) and to receive external support, such as grants and loans (Meyer and Rowan, 1977; Meyer and Scott, 1983). For instance, a business corporation that has a legitimate structure (Fligstein, 1985) is more likely to win the confidence of investors, so that there is demand for its shares that are, consequently, more highly priced. Thus institutional fit leads to higher share price. Hence, contingency fit and institutional fit lead to the different outcomes of dividend and share price, respectively. Given that both dividend and share price are measured in the same metric, money, they may be rendered directly comparable, so the outcomes of contingency and institutional fits can be directly compared in their value to the organization.

In economics and finance, shareholder value is the objective of the corporation and so this evaluation gives the outcome that is in the best interest of the corporation. From the viewpoint of the shareholder, their shares give them two benefits: the appreciation in share price and the dividends. Both share price and dividends are expressed in money, e.g., dollars, and for a shareholder, a dollar increase in share price is as valuable as a dollar increase in dividends, so that price and dividends are directly comparable benefits.

Let us consider, as the structural aspect for analysis, the structure of the board of directors of a business corporation. The proportion of directors who are non-executive directors, and who are therefore in a position to be independent of, and to provide control over, the management, is subject to differing theories of organizational design. Having a high proportion of non-executive directors conforms to community expectations about vigilant monitors who can act on behalf of shareholders (Kesner and Dalton, 1986), so that this is the institutional theory fit. In contrast, contingency theory holds that the optimal proportion of non-executive directors is that which fits the contingency variable of need for control of the management (Rogers, 2005). Hence the institutional fit is a high proportion of non-executive directors, whereas the contingency fit varies as to the proportion of non-executive directors. The prescription derived from the institutional theory is that a high proportion of non-executive directors will maximize share price. The prescription derived from contingency theory is that the proportion of non-executive directors that fits the contingency will maximize dividend. Given that both price and dividend are measured in money, and so are directly comparable, we can see whether the monetary value for the organization is greater from institutional or contingency fit.

Suppose that the institutional fit, the majority non-executive board structure, produces a share price gain of $X. For corporations for which a majority non-executive board structure misfits their contingency, the misfit leads to a reduction in dividends of $Y. If the share price gain of $X is greater than the dividend reduction of $Y, then the shareholder will benefit from the corporation having a majority non-executive board. In this case, external support is more valuable than internal effectiveness. Here, institutional fit is more valuable than contingency fit. However, if the share price gain of $X is *less* than the dividend reduction of $Y, then the shareholder would benefit from the corporation moving into fit with the contingency, by adopting a majority executive board. In this case, internal effectiveness is more valuable than external institutional support. Here, contingency fit is more valuable than institutional fit.

In this way, it is possible to calculate the level of structure that yields the most monetary outcome and so identify the optimal structure, the meta-fit. The joint outcome of a structure is the sum of the effects of its degree of contingency fit on internal effectiveness, and of its degree of institutional fit on external support. Whether the meta-fit is the contingency or the institutional fit depends upon the relative monetary effect of the two fits. Where the monetary effect of the contingency fit is greater than that of the institutional fit, then the meta-fit is the contingency fit. Conversely, where the monetary value of the institutional fit is greater than that of the contingency fit, then meta-fit is the institutional fit. Hence, we can find which organizational design is best overall for the organization.

3. ANALYSIS OF CONTINGENCY AND INSTITUTIONAL FITS AND THEIR JOINT OUTCOMES

Let us give a hypothetical example. There are several purposes of this example. Visually representing the differing contingency and institutional fits helps to bring out the contrast between them. This enables an appreciation of the possible divergence of their structural fits. By showing that substantial structural divergences could hold under a range of scenarios, it bolsters the argument that conflict between the contingency and institutional fits is potentially widespread. The example demonstrates that, by valorising both outcomes in money, their joint outcome may be calculated. This, in turn, gives the overall optimum, or meta-fit. Furthermore, it is seen that the meta-fit is usually clear-cut for each organization, in its contingency circumstance, so that rational organizational design would usually have a single prescription.

Let us use as our hypothetical example the structural effects of boards of directors. The structural variable is the proportion of directors who are non-executives (rather than executives) and varies from 20 per cent to 100 per cent, in increments of 20 per cent (see Figure 1). The contingency variable is need for control of the managers by non-executive directors (who are independent of management and hence able to control them). The contingency variable varies from 1 to 5, in increments of 1. The internal effectiveness outcome is produced by the degree of fit of the structural variable to the contingency variable. Fit is attained where the board structure fits the need for control. The greater is the need for control over management by the board, the higher is the required proportion of non-executive directors.

Structure is on the vertical axis, while the contingency is on the horizontal axis (Figure 1). The contingency fit is a line that runs from the origin (structural and contingency variables both zero) diagonally across to the top right hand corner (structural and contingency variables both maximum) (Keller, 1994). The line is at 45 degrees to the horizontal, so that the fit line is defined such that an increase of the contingency variable needs to be fitted by an equally proportionate increase in the structural level. Specifically, for an organization in fit, each increase of one unit in the level of the contingency variable needs an increase of 20 per cent in the non-executive directors to maintain fit. Being anywhere on the fit line produces the highest level of dividend for an organization. Each step away from the fit line is an increase in the degree of misfit and so causes a decline of dividend in dollars.

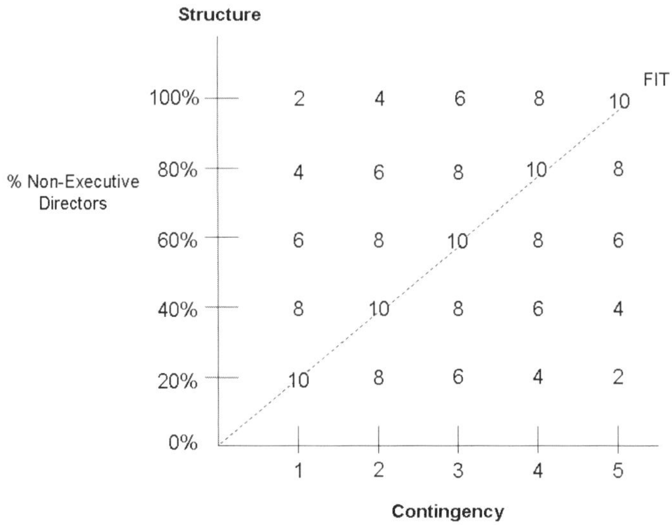

Figure 1. Contingency theory: fit, misfit and internal effectiveness (dividend) – strong effect

The external support outcome is produced by the level of the structural variable, such that each increase of 20 per cent in the proportion of non-executive directors, that is, increase of one degree of institutional fit, produces an increase in the share price of the company in dollars (Figure 2). Therefore, the institutional fit is the maximum structural level. The institutional fits form a line that runs horizontally, because institutional fit is invariant across increasing levels of the contingency variable.

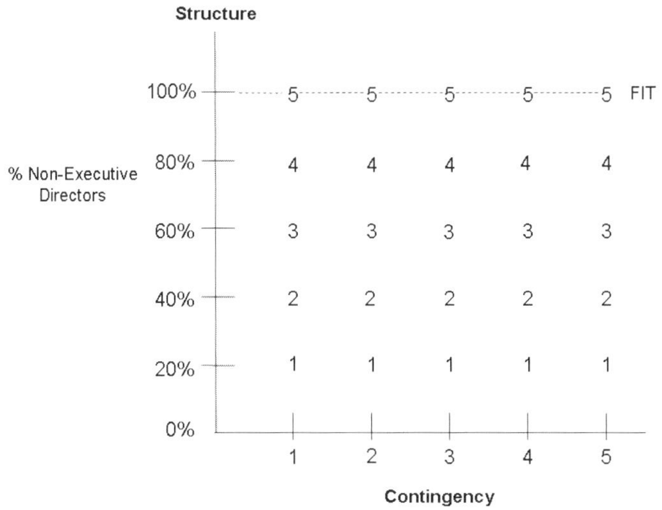

Figure 2. Institutional theory: structure and external support (price) – weak effect

The contingency and institutional theories of fit produce conflicting prescriptions for organizational design. As stated, the contingency fits are on the diagonal (from bottom-left to top-right), whereas the institutional fits are all at the maximum structural level of 100 per cent non-executives. Therefore, the institutional fits tend to diverge from the contingency fits, especially at lower levels of the contingency variable. The lower is the contingency level, the greater is the divergence between the institutional and contingency fits. At the lowest contingency level (1), the institutional fit (100 per cent non-executives) completely conflicts with the contingency fit (20 per cent non-executives). The only exception to this pattern of conflict, is at the highest level of the contingency variable (5), where the contingency fit and institutional fit are the same (maximum) structural level (100 per cent non-executives), so that, in this case, the theories are not in conflict. Overall, for almost all levels of the contingency variable, the contingency and institutional fits diverge, showing that the conflict is widespread. Thus, there is much conflict between the contingency and institutional theories.

These conflicts in structural fits might seem to pose insuperable dilemmas for organizational design, but a resolution may be found by monetarizing each outcome. Then it is possible to identify the optimal design for an organization, that is, to pick either the contingency fit or the institutional fit as giving the superior outcome for the organization. Where the monetary effect of the contingency fit is greater than monetary effect of the institutional fit, then the contingency fit is the optima, that is, the meta-fit for the organization. Where the monetary effect of the institutional fit is greater than monetary effect of the contingency fit, then the institutional fit is the optima, that is, the meta-fit for the organization.

3.1 Monetary Effect of Contingency Fit on Internal Effectiveness Stronger Than Institutional Fit on External Support

Where the monetary effect of contingency fit on dividends is stronger than the monetary effect of institutional fit on price, the optimal organizational design (meta-fit) is to fit the contingency, despite usually being in institutional misfit. For instance, suppose that contingency fit is twice as strong as institutional fit, so that each increase of a degree of contingency fit increases dividend by $2 (Figure 1), whereas each increase of a degree in institutional fit only produces a $1 increase in price (Figure 2). The joint outcome of these two effects is given by the addition of the outcomes – which is shown for each level of the structural and contingency variables in (Figure 3).

For an organization at the lowest level of the contingency variable (1), the highest joint outcome is $11 (= $10 dividend plus $1 price). The point is at contingency level of 1 and structural level of 20 per cent non-executives. It is on the contingency fit line. This is the best overall monetary outcome. Yet it sacrifices $4, by being in complete institutional misfit – rather than being in institutional fit, which would have given $5 in price.

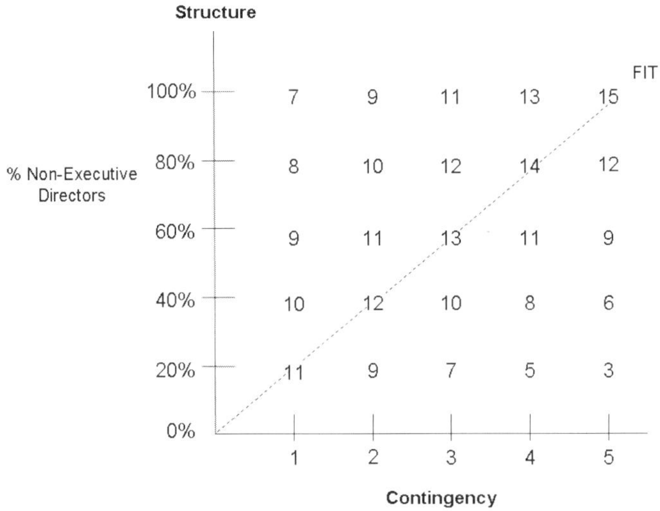

Figure 3. Joint outcomes in money (dollars) where effect of internal effectiveness (dividends) is stronger than effect of external support (price)

Similarly contingency levels 2, 3 and 4, all have as their optimal positions being on the contingency fit line, despite being in degrees of institutional misfit. Contingency level 2 has its best joint outcome of $12 (= $10 of dividend plus $2 of price), at 40 per cent non-executives. This point is on the contingency fit line, but misfits the institutional fit (i.e., 100 per cent non-executives) by 60 per cent of non-executives. The point therefore sacrifices $3 of price. Similarly, contingency level 3 has its best joint outcome of $13 (= $10 of dividend plus $3 of price), at 60 per cent non-executives. This point is on the contingency fit line, but misfits the institutional fit by 40 per cent of non-executives, and therefore sacrifices $2 of price. Again, contingency level 4 has its best joint outcome of $14 (= $10 of dividend plus $4 of price), at 80 per cent non-executives. This point is on the contingency fit line, but misfits the institutional fit by 20 per cent of non-executives, and therefore sacrifices $1 of price. As the contingency level increases, there is a decrease in the amount of difference in the structural variable (the percentage of non-executives) between the contingency fit and the institutional fit, and so a decrease in the sacrifice of price.

Finally, contingency level 5 has its best joint outcome of $15 (= $10 of dividend plus $5 of price), at 100 per cent non-executives. This point is on the contingency fit line, and is also the institutional fit (i.e., 100 per cent of non-executives), and therefore attains the maximum price of $5. At contingency level 5, there is no conflict between the contingency fit and the institutional fit, and it is possible to be in both fits simultaneously. This exception apart, there is always a conflict. However, as seen, the conflict can be resolved – by picking the contingency fit rather than the institutional fit. For every level of the contingency variable, there is an optimal fit, that is, a meta-fit, which is the contingency fit.

This analysis illustrates that, despite the usually conflicting prescriptions of contingency and institutional theories, there is always one fit that is the optimum. For each level of the contingency variable, there is an unambiguous, best solution, i.e., the meta-fit. In this scenario, the meta-fits are always the contingency fits and are almost always not the institutional fits. The reason is that, in this scenario, contingency fit is monetarily stronger than institutional fit.

3.2 Monetary Effect of Institutional Fit on External Support Stronger Than Contingency Fit on Internal Effectiveness

Consider the opposite scenario: where the monetary effect of institutional fit (Figure 4), is stronger than the monetary effect of contingency fit (Figure 5). Again, there is widespread conflict between the contingency and institutional theories. The institutional fits are all at the maximum structural level, while the structural fit to the contingency varies by the contingency. The monetary effect of the institutional fit on price is stronger than the monetary effect of the contingency fit on dividends. Therefore, the optimal organizational design, i.e., meta-fit, is to fit the institutional requirement, despite usually being in contingency misfit. In this scenario, the effect of institutional fit on price is monetarily twice as strong as contingency fit on dividend. Each increase in the degree of institutional fit produces a $2 increase in price (Figure 4), whereas each increase of a degree of contingency fit increases dividend by only $1 (Figure 5). The joint outcome of these two effects is given by the addition of the outcomes, as shown in Figure 6.

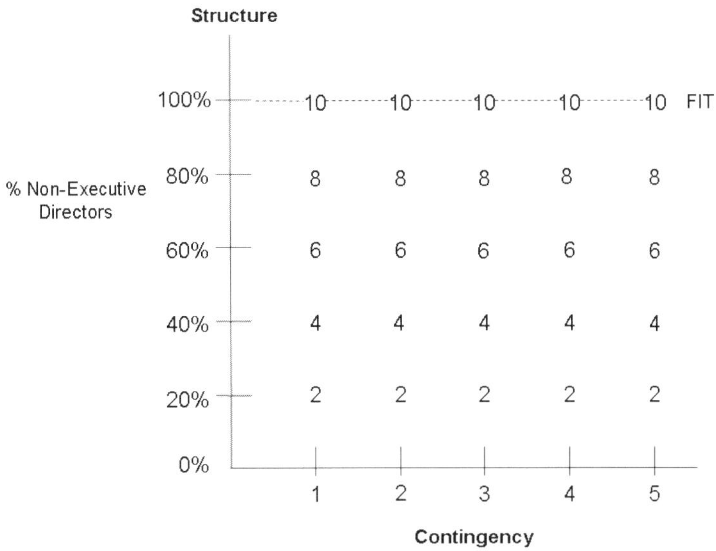

Figure 4. Institutional theory: structure and external support (price) – strong effect

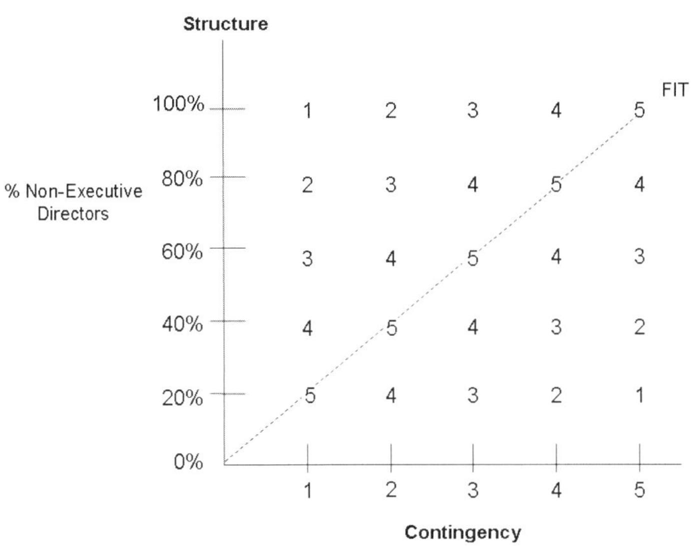

Figure 5. Contingency theory: fit, misfit and internal effectiveness (dividend) – weak effect

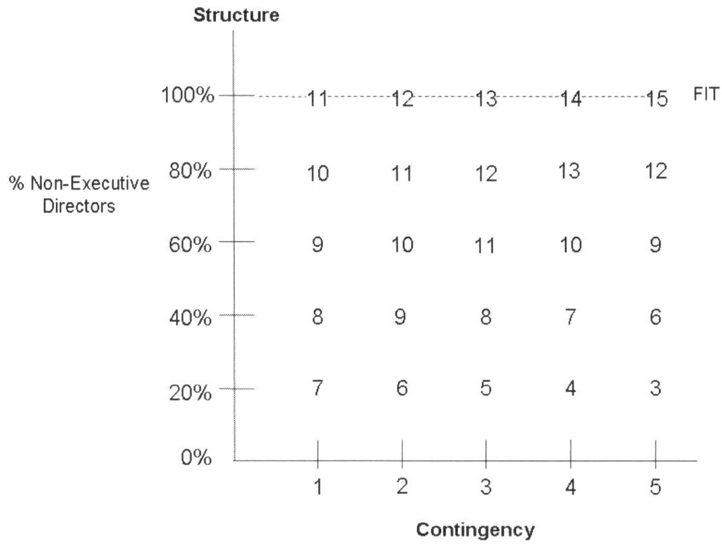

Figure 6. Joint outcomes in money (dollars) where effect of external support (price) is stronger than effect of internal effectiveness (dividends)

For an organization at the lowest level of the contingency variable (1), the highest joint outcome is $11 (= $10 price plus $1 dividend). This comes from being in institutional fit, at the highest structural level (100 per cent non-executives), giving a $10 price. This entails being in maximum contingency *mis*fit, producing a dividend of only $1, thereby sacrificing an additional $4 of dividend that would have occurred had the organization been in contingency fit.

Similarly for contingency levels 2, 3 and 4, the highest joint outcomes, of $12, $13 and $14, respectively, are all produced by being in institutional theory fit, by being at the highest structural level. This always gives a $10 price, but entails them all also being in contingency misfit, so that each point attains a dividend of only $2, $3 or $4, respectively, thereby sacrificing an additional amount of dividend. The sacrifice is less for each successively higher level of the contingency: being $3 for contingency level 2, $2 for contingency level 3, and $1 for contingency level 4.

For contingency level 5, the meta-fit is again the maximum structural level, yielding the maximum possible joint outcome, of $15, because it is both the institutional fit ($10 price) and the contingency fit ($5 dividend).

Overall, the meta-fits are always the institutional fits – which are almost always not the contingency fits. The reason is that the institutional fit is monetarily stronger than contingency fit. Despite conflict between institutional and contingency fits, an optimal fit, the meta-fit, can be ascertained for each contingency level.

Note that, for this, like the previous scenario, the conflict between contingency and institutional fits is greater at lower levels of the contingency variable than at higher levels. This is because the structural levels of the fits are more divergent at lower levels. In these scenarios the institutional fit is the highest level of the structural variable. If the institutional fit was at the lowest level of the structural variable, then conflicts would also arise, but they would be greater for the higher levels of the contingency variable.

The overall pattern is that the relative monetary effects of internal effectiveness and external support determine whether a rational organization fits the contingencies or the institutional requirements, respectively. Where internal effectiveness is stronger monetarily than external support, then it is optimal for the organization to move into fit with the contingency, usually at the sacrifice of some degree of external support. Where external support is stronger monetarily than internal effectiveness, then it is optimal for the organization to fit the institutional requirements, although usually sacrificing some internal effectiveness. The key point for organizational design is that there is an optimal fit. This holds wherever one of the two monetary outcomes is stronger than the other.

3.3 Same Strength Effects of Institutional Fit and Contingency Fit

Above, we have established the general position, which is that where internal effectiveness and external support differ in their monetary effects, then it is possible to find an optimal fit by choosing between the contingency and institutional fits to pick the fit that has the stronger effect. However, for completeness, we need to consider also the situation where both have the same monetary effect. This is something of a special case, which is unlikely in practice, and it has odd results. Because the contingency fit and institutional fit effects are equal, they can offset each other, leading to a range of optima that allow choice of structure. The optimal organizational design, i.e., meta-fit, is to fit *either* the contingency *or* the institutional requirement. Thus, there is harmony between the contingency and institutional theories and both give rational organizational designs. Moreover, where the contingency meta-fit and institutional meta-fit diverge in their structural levels, the intervening structural levels are also meta-fits. Hence many meta-fits exist, allowing much choice.

In this scenario, an organization in contingency fit produces a dividend of \$5 and each decrease of one degree of fit decreases the dividend by \$1 (Figure 5). Equally, the institutional effect is that the institutional fit produces a price of \$5 and each decrease in institutional fit of one degree produces a \$1 decrease in price (Figure 2).

For the lowest contingency level (1), *any* level of the structural variable produces the maximum joint outcome (\$6), as shown in (Figure 7). The reason is that as the structural level increases, the decline in dividend from \$5 to \$1, from increases in contingency misfit (Figure 5), is completely compensated by the increases in price from \$1 to \$5, from increasing institutional fit (Figure 2).

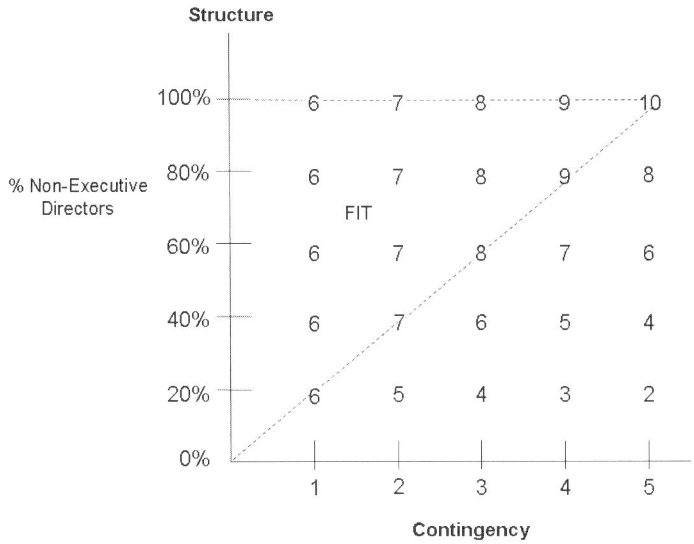

Figure 7. Joint outcomes in money (dollars) where effect of internal effectiveness (dividends) is the same as the effect of external support (price)

Thus, the contingency fit, at 20 per cent non-executive directors, and the institutional fit, at 100 per cent non-executive directors, are both meta-fits. Thus, there is no conflict between the theories. Moreover, the intermediary structural positions (at 40, 60 and 80 per cent non-executive directors) are also meta-fits. Thus, optimal organizational design is not restricted to either the contingency or institutional fits. Hence, here there is equifinality or indifference about level of structure, and the organizational designer could choose any structural level.

Similarly (in Figure 7), for contingency level 2, the contingency fit (40 per cent non-executives) yields the maximum joint outcome, of \$7, as does the institutional fit (100 per cent non-executives), and the intermediary structural levels (60 and 80 per cents non-executives). Similarly again, for contingency level 3, the contingency fit yields the maximum joint outcome, as does the institutional fit, and the intermediary structural level. For contingency level 4, again, the contingency fit and the institutional fit both yield the maximum joint outcome (and there is no intermediary structural level).

Over all the contingency levels, sixty per cent of the points in the contingency-structure space are meta-fits (within their contingency level). Both contingency and institutional fits are always included among the meta-fits. Thus, conflict between the contingency and institutional fits is avoided. For the highest contingency level (5), the optimal position is to have the highest structural level (100 per cent non-executives), which is a contingency fit and also an institutional fit, so that conflict is again avoided. Thus, in this scenario (Figure 7), conflict between contingency and institutional fits is always avoided. However, equality of monetary effects is not likely to be typical.

3.4 Institutional Fit of Intermediate Structural Level

So far, we have treated the institutional effect as being such that the institutional fit, the approved structural model, is the highest level of the structural variable. The relationship between structure and outcome is positive and linear. This is the sort of view implied by institutional theory for Weberian bureaucracy, where the approved model is highly rationalized, in the Western cultural account (Meyer and Scott, 1983). However, other aspects of structure could have different structural levels as their institutional fits. Conceivably, for some aspect of organizational structure, the approved structural model could be at some intermediate level of the structural variable. Thus, we need to consider this possibility.

Again, there would be many conflicts between the contingency and the institutional fits. However, the conflicts are greatest at the extremes of the contingency variable, where the prescribed structures are the most divergent. And, as before, there would a point of harmony between the two theories, but at an intermediate level of the contingency variable.

To explore in detail, consider the following scenario. The institutional fit is at the middle level of the structural variable (60 per cent non-executives) (Figure 8). Thus, the institutional fits are a horizontal line of points at this middle structural level. Once again, the contingency fit is the diagonal line (Figure 5). The horizontal and diagonal lines intersect at the middle level (3) of the contingency variable. Thus, for contingency level 3, the institutional fit is also the contingency fit, so conflict between institutional and contingency fits is avoided.

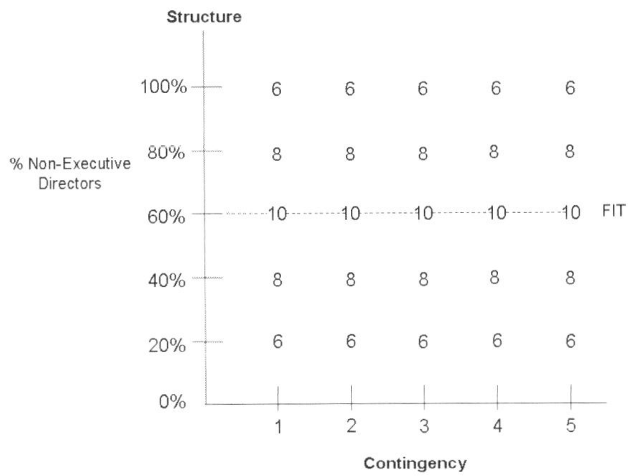

Figure 8. Institutional theory: structure and external support (price) maximum at mid-level of structure

For all other contingency levels (1, 2, 4 and 5) in Figure 8, however, the contingency fit diverges from the institutional fit, so that the fits conflict. The divergence is more so at the extremes of the contingency variable (levels 1 and 5). At contingency level 1, the contingency fit is a structure of 20 per cent non-executives, while the institutional fit (60 per cent non-executives) is a structure of 40 per cent *more* non-executives. Whereas at contingency level 2, there is also divergence, but less so: the contingency fit is a structure of 40 per cent non-executives, while the institutional fit is a structure of only 20 per cent more non-executives than the contingency fit. Similarly, at contingency level 5, the contingency fit is a structure of 100 per cent non-executives, while the institutional fit is a structure of 40 per cent *less* non-executives. Whereas at contingency level 4, there is also divergence, but less so: the contingency fit is a structure of 80 per cent non-executives, while the institutional fit is a structure of 20 per cent less non-executives.

Thus, at almost all contingency levels, the institutional and contingency fits are in conflict, but the conflicts are either side of the middle contingency level. Because the institutional fit is at an intermediate structural level, the conflict between the contingency and institutional fits is greatest at the extremes of the contingency variable. As before, the amount of conflict is a function of the contingency variable, but here it is curvi-linear, not linear. Again, we can resolve the conflict by looking at the joint outcomes to find the optimal fit.

In this scenario, the effect of contingency fit is \$5, which decreases by \$1 for every degree of misfit (Figure 5), while the effect of institutional fit is \$10, which decreases by \$2 for every degree of misfit (Figure 8). The joint outcomes are shown in Figure 9. For each level of the contingency variable, an optimum can be found that yields the maximum joint monetary outcome. Calculating the monetary outcomes allows resolving the conflicts between the contingency and institutional fits for contingency levels 1, 2, 4 and 5. At contingency level 1, the optimal structure produces a joint outcome of $13 (= $10 price plus $3 dividend), at the middle structural level (60 per cent non-executives). At contingency level 2, the optimal structure produces a joint outcome of $14 (= $10 price plus $4 dividend), again at the middle structural level. Similarly, contingency levels 4 and 5 also have their optima at the middle structural level. Thus there is always a meta-fit, with a clear superiority in monetary outcome between the contingency and institutional fits, so that a rational design exists. In this example, the meta-fit is always the institutional fit, usually not the contingency fit, because the monetary effect of institutional fits has been defined as being greater than that of contingency fit.

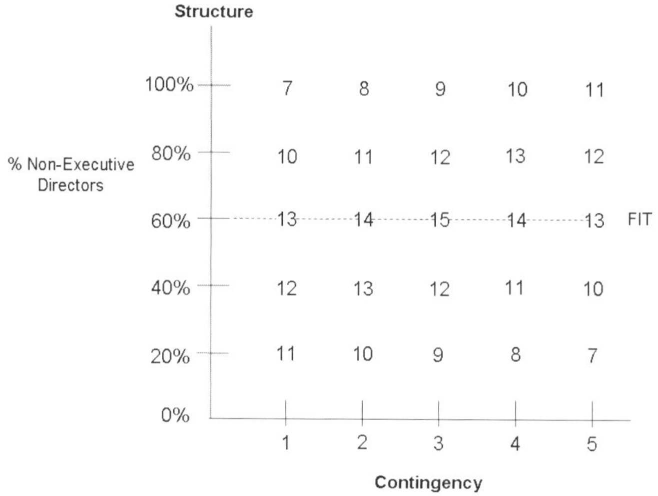

Figure 9. Joint outcomes in money (dollars) where effect of external support (price) is stronger than effect of internal effectiveness (dividends) and maximum external support is at mid-level of structure

In summary, whatever level of the structural variable that constitutes the institutional fit, it will usually be some degree of misfit to the contingency, so that institutional and contingency theory prescriptions conflict. Thus, most organizations will not be able to attain simultaneously the full benefits of external support and internal effectiveness. Nevertheless, if both outcomes can be directly compared in their worth to the organization, the optimal fit, or meta-fit, can be calculated. Then, a rational organizational designer can choose between attaining institutional fit or contingency fit. Whether the institutional fit or contingency fit is optimal will depend upon their relative strengths, such as monetary benefits. Only in rare cases, where the two outcomes are of equal benefit, will both institutional and contingency fits be equally viable options and so leave the best organizational design ambiguous. Thus, there is the potential that organizational design might be enriched and made more comprehensive, by recognizing the benefits of institutional fits, and, through the use of common metrics, evaluating them along with the benefits of contingency fit, leading to better organizational designs.

Thus far, we have treated the level of a contingency variable as a given, which the organization cannot choose and to which it has to adjust its structure. This accords with traditional treatments of contingencies in the structural contingency literature, and is seen most clearly where the environment is the contingency (e.g., Burns and Stalker, 1961), because most organizations cannot control their environments. Evidence exists that strategy (Chandler, 1962), even though an intra-organizational contingency, is the fixed point to which managers adjust organizational structure (Donaldson, 1987; Hamilton and Shergill, 1992). Moreover, for the organizational size contingency, freedom of choice about it would mean that a small organization could choose to become very large, e.g., to go from a dozen employees, to a hundred thousand employees – which is clearly unrealistic. Environment, strategy and size are some of the most important contingencies of organizational structure, and so if there is limited choice over their levels, this is a significant limitation in choice of contingencies of organizational structure. Regarding board structure, the contingency of need for control over the managers is set by the abilities of the managers and whether their motivations support, or conflict with, the interests of the company. To the degree that managerial ability and motivation are givens, then the board cannot choose the level of the contingency variable. Thus, for some contingencies, organizations will not be able to choose their contingency levels, and so many organizations will have the contingency levels that mean that contingency and institutional fits conflict.

Internal effectiveness is wider than just dividend, and external support is wider than just price. Furthermore, there are other possible evaluative criteria besides shareholder value, and some organizations are not for-profit business firms, so that organizational performance criteria may have to reflect other considerations and other stakeholders. If these criteria can provide metrics for directly comparing the value to the organization of internal effectiveness and external support, then the outcomes from contingency and institutional fits can be compared and the meta-fit selected.

In that way, the method for resolving conflict between contingency and institutional fits that has been suggested herein may be generalized.

4. INFORMING THE THEORY OF ORGANIZATION DESIGN

To date, structural contingency theory is the main theory of organizational design regarding organizational structural aspects. Recently, it has been argued that institutional theory also provides some insight about organizational design. Both theories hold that fitting structures produce outcomes that are beneficial for the organization. However, they differ in the types of outcomes that they theorize. Contingency theory holds that structures that fit the contingencies maximize the internal effectiveness of the organization. Institutional theory holds that structures that fit the institutional environment maximize the legitimacy and external support of the organization. These differences make the theories difficult to directly compare.

A way to make the two theories commensurable, however, is to render their differing effects directly comparable, by finding a common metric to measure them. Both internal effectiveness and external support have monetary effects. Therefore the monetary effect of internal effectiveness and external support can be directly compared, so that their superiority relative to each other can be found. This allows identification of the superiority of either the contingency fit or the institutional fit to be established.

5. INFORMING THE PRACTICE OF ORGANIZATION DESIGN

The conflicting organization design prescriptions from contingency and institutional theory make it difficult to decide whether to choose the contingency fit or the institutional fit. Because the fits from the two theories usually diverge, and so are in conflict, this makes the problem of selecting an optimal design potentially serious. However, by using the common metric of money, the value to an organization of being in contingency fit as contrasted with institutional fit may be directly compared. This allows an organizational designer to pick which fit is best for the organization. Thus there is a clear-cut decision for the organizational designer. This holds in the circumstances where the contingency and institutional fits diverge, which, as seen, is the typical situation. In the unusual circumstances where the contingency and institutional fits are the same, then no choice is required of the organizational designer, who has only to embrace that fit.

6. CONCLUSIONS

Contingency theory and institutional theories prescribe different fits and predict different effects. Nevertheless, an overall optimal organizational design may be found by comparing quantitatively the benefits from internal effectiveness with those from external support. This gives the structure that is the best overall fit, or meta-fit, for that organization. These points were illustrated hypothetically for companies whose internal effectiveness outcome from contingency fit is dividend and whose external support outcome from institutional fit is share price. An analysis showed that the contingency and institutional fits almost always diverge, so that contingency and institutional theories frequently lead to conflicting prescriptions about organizational design. When, however, the effects of these fits is expressed in a common metric, money, then the optimal overall fit, or meta-fit could be found, facilitating rational organizational design.

In the analysis, if the structural contingency effect on dividend is monetarily stronger than the institutional effect on price, then the meta-fit is the contingency fit. This holds despite there being a degree of institutional misfit and thus sacrifice of some external support (share price). However, if the institutional effect on price is monetarily stronger than the structural contingency effect on dividend, then the meta-fit is the institutional fit. This holds despite there being a degree of contingency misfit and thus sacrifice of some internal effectiveness (dividend). Thus, for each level of the contingency variable, there is always a clear-cut, overall optimal fit, that is, a meta-fit. It is either the contingency or the institutional fit. (In a minority of cases, the contingency fit and the institutional fit are identical.) In the majority of cases, where the contingency and institutional fits conflict, there is a best organizational design that can be recommended to the company. This result holds regardless of whether the institutional fit is at a structural level that is high, middle or low. The exception is where the contingency and institutional fits have the same monetary effects, so that both are optimal designs, which can create a range of equally beneficial structures, rather than a clear-cut preferred structure; however, this is an unusual circumstance that is unlikely to apply to most real organizations.

REFERENCES

Burns, T., and Stalker, G. M., 1961, *The Management of Innovation*, Tavistock, London.

Burton, R. M., DeSanctis, G. and Obel, B., 2006, *Organizational Design: A Step by Step Approach*, Cambridge University Press.

Burton, R. M. and Obel, B., 2004, *Strategic Organizational Diagnosis and Design: The Dynamics of Fit*, Third Edition, Springer/Kluwer Academic Publishers.

Chandler, A.D. Jr., 1962, *Strategy and Structure: chapters in the history of the American industrial enterprise*, M.I.T. Press, Cambridge.

Child, J., 1975, Managerial and organizational factors associated with company performance, Part 2: A contingency analysis. *Journal of Management Studies*, **12**: 12-27.

DiMaggio, P.J., and Powell, W.W., 1983, The iron cage revisited: institutional isomorphism and collective rationality in organization fields, *American Sociological Review*, **48**: 147-60.

Donaldson, L., 1987, Strategy and structural adjustment to regain fit and performance: In defence of contingency theory, *Journal of Management Studies,* **24 (1)**: 1-24.

Donaldson, L., 2001, *The Contingency Theory of Organizations*, Sage, Thousand Oaks.

Fligstein, N., 1985, The spread of the multidivisional form among large firms, 1919-1979, *American Sociological Review*, **50**: 377-91.

Hamilton, R.T., and Shergill, G.S., 1992, The relationship between strategy-structure fit and financial performance in New Zealand: Evidence of generality and validity with enhanced controls, *Journal of Management Studies*, **29**: 95-113.

Keller, R.T., 1994, Technology-information processing fit and the performance of R&D project groups: A test of contingency theory, *Academy of Management Journal*, **37**: 167-79.

Kesner, I. F. and Dalton, D. R. 1986, Boards of Directors and the Checks and (Im)Balances of Corporate Governance, *Business Horizons*, September-October, 17-23.

Khandwalla, 1977, *The Design of Organizations*. New York: Harcourt Brace Janovich.

Meyer, J. W. and Rowan, B. 1977, Institutionalized Organizations: Formal Structure as Myth and Ceremony, *American Journal of Sociology* **83**: 340-63.

Meyer, J. W. and Scott, W. R., with the assistance of Rowan, B. and Deal, T.E., 1983. *Organizational Environments: Ritual and Rationality*. Beverly Hills, CA: Sage.

Parsons, T., 1961, Suggestions for a sociological approach to the theory of organizations, in: *Complex Organizations: A Sociological Reader*, Holt, Rinehart, and Winston, Amitai Etzioni, New York, 32-47.

Pfeffer, J., 1982, *Organizations and Organization Theory*, Pitman, Marshfield.

Rogers, M., 2005, *Contingent Corporate Governance: A Challenge to the Theories of Universal Board Structure*. PhD Thesis, Australian Graduate School of Management, Universities of New South Wales and Sydney, Sydney.

Scott, W. R., 1995, *Institutions and Organizations*, Sage, Thousand Oaks.

Van de Ven, A.H., and Drazin, R., 1985, The concept of fit in contingency theory, *Research in Organizational Behavior*, 7, Edited by B.M. Staw and L. L. Cummings, JAI Press, Greenwich, 333-65.

Chapter 3

COMPARING EVOLUTIONARY AND CONTINGENCY THEORY APPROACHES TO ORGANIZATIONAL STRUCTURE

Charles Williams
Assistant Professor of Strategy, Duke University, Fuqua School of Business Box 90120, Durham NC 27708

Abstract: Evolutionary research is beginning to fulfill the promise of the behavioral theory of the firm and explore the impact of administrative structure on adaptation and change in firms. This chapter compares the evolutionary approach to structure with contingency theory, the most prominent stream of organizational research focused on administrative structure. In comparing evolutionary and contingency approaches to organizations, I find that both build from the foundations of information-processing and behavioral theories of the firm, and that adaptation plays an important role in both theories. More recent evolutionary work differs from contingency theory in its approach to the selection environment and the efficiency of managerial decision-making in organizations. These differences lead to radically different predictions concerning the causal relationship of structure and strategic choices: administrative structure shapes the information environment in firms, which in turn affects strategic decisions such as market entry and exit. The chapter concludes by examining the theoretical and empirical challenges faced by evolutionary studies of structure and strategic change, as well as considering the new theoretical questions that arise from this approach.

Key words: Structure, evolution, adaptation, and contingency theory.

1. INTRODUCTION

Evolutionary research on organizations has begun to examine the impact of structure on the adaptation of organizations over time. Recent work has

R.M. Burton et al. (eds.), *Designing Organizations*, doi: 10.1007/978-0-387-77776-4_3,

examined how aspects of structure such as business unit structure, changes in units, movement of managers between units, and central or decentralized control affect innovation, market entry, and growth. Much of this work explains the influence of structure on adaptation builds from behavioral and information processing approaches to firms in an evolutionary framework.

One might characterize this work as applying contingency theory, which was similarly grounded in the logic of information processing, to studies of firms over time. Yet the predictions of the evolutionary approach are often opposed to the fundamental proposition associated with contingency theory – that strategy shapes appropriate structural decisions for firms. In this growing evolutionary tradition, studies have predicted, and found, the opposite – over time different structural configurations are associated with different strategic outcomes.

I was introduced to contingency theory through journal articles, which typically measured the association between different aspects of environmental uncertainty and the structures adopted by firms. In this version, the theory is cross-sectional, and largely static. Schoonhoven (1981) laid out a withering critique of this tradition for its lack of attention to the precise cross-sectional relationship that the logic suggests between environment, structure, and performance. So my initial interpretation was that contingency theory lacked a theory of adaptation, which evolutionary economics could add to the study of structure and strategy.

Reaching deeper into the contingency literature, however, reading the rich studies and theories published as full books, shows that adaptation, as a concept and a causal mechanism, plays an important role in most contingency theories. Examination of several touchstone contingency texts makes clear the richness of the dynamic portrait that these theorists drew of organizations. But this realization makes all the more important coming to understand what is truly different about an evolutionary approach to structure, and why (as well as when) it leads us to different predictions.

I attempt to address that question in this paper. In the first section of the paper, I look at adaptation in contingency theory – what role did adaptation play in some of the touchstones of the theoretical tradition. In the following section, I move to the evolutionary research program and structure – its foundations and central mechanisms. I look specifically at the core elements of an evolutionary treatment of structure. In the conclusion, I consider what new questions this approach inspires and discuss some of the challenges for an evolutionary approach to structure.

2. WHAT ROLE DID ADAPTATION PLAY IN CONTINGENCY THEORY?

Most contingent theories include adaptation as a causal link for how organizations arrive at the optimal structure given their environment, and sometimes strategy. The theories vary, however, in the extent to which it is an explicit or implicit link between situation and structural choices. The most managerial theories tend to treat the link more implicitly, viewing the theory itself as playing a role in helping managers choose optimal structures that will increase their performance. Other approaches make the role of adaptation more explicit, most notably Miles and Snow (Miles and Snow 1978) who put the adaptive cycle between three managerial problems at the center of their theory. The underlying assumption for all of these theories is that managers are pursuing organizational goals with presumptive, if not perfect, rationality. Mistakes tend to fall into the error term – the theory describes optimal outcomes and at its most practical predicts that these will be observed in predictable patterns in empirical samples. Thus adaptation of managers and selection by competition play the role of justifying predictions of largely rational outcomes across organizations.

Table 1 summarizes the treatment of adaptation across several works of contingency. The table separates the triggers for adaptation, the actual mechanism by which adaptation is accomplished, and the outcomes of adaptation in each work. These touchstones are most uniform in their treatment of the outcome of adaptation. Each theorist treats structural choices of the firm as the outcome of adaptation. The aspects of structure may vary – product divisions in Chandler or linking mechanisms in Galbraith – but the focus on structural choices as the outcome of adaptation is common to each work.

The choices that managers make across these works – their reaction to information and to the information processing demands of their situation – are the mechanism by which adaptation occurs. Chandler (1962) details the innovative reactions of managers across GM, Dupont, Sears, and other firms that led to the emergence of the multidivisional firm. The other theories distill these varied tales of innovation to a stronger prediction that managerial problem-solving will, on average, lead to the efficient solutions proposed by the authors. Miles and Snow (1978) state directly, "Management's strategic choices shape the organization's structure and processes." When managerial adaptation is treated more implicitly, such as in Galbraith (1973) and Burns and Stalker (1961), the work comes closer to the philosophy of operations management, in which ideal solutions are derived that should direct manager's decisions once they understand the solutions.

Table 1. Adaptation in Contingency Literature.

1.	1. Adaptation Trigger	1. Adaptation Mechanism	1. Adaptation 2. Outcome
1. Chandler, 1962	2. Coordination Failures	2. Extended description of managerial innovation & restructuring	3. Product divisions with corporate coordination through budgeting.
1. Burns and Stalker, 1961	3. The rate of technical change, or 'the appearance of novelties'	3. Implicit assumption of managerial adjustment to environmental conditions.	4. Mechanistic or organic organizational forms.
1. Lawrence and Lorsch, 1967	4. • Rate and nature of information to be processed from environment 5. • Inter-group conflict	4. • Managerial adaptation to environmental demands 5. • Integration mechanisms to resolve inter-group conflict	5. Differentiation and integration of groups within the organization.
1. Galbraith, 1973	6. Mismatch between information demands of task and organization.	6. Implicit assumption of managerial adjustment to task demands.	6. Organizational choices to reduce need or increase capacity for info processing.
1. Miles and Snow, 1976	7. Three inter-related problems that arise in organizations: 8. • domain 9. • technology & process 10.• rationalizing and stabilizing activities	7. "Management's strategic choices shape the organization's structure and processes."	7. Coherent organizational types with alignment between their approaches to the three problems.

In two of these works, elements of organizational structure also play a role in adaptation. In Lawrence and Lorsch's work, *Organization and Environment* (1967), the integration mechanisms in the organization that help resolve inter-group conflict also shape the ultimate structural choices of the firm – the extent to which the organization enables differentiation between groups within the firm and creates the necessary coordination mechanisms for integrating the actions and output of these groups. Miles and Snow, on the other hand, acknowledge that the structural choices made in resolving the administrative problems at one point in time will influence the nature of entrepreneurial problems and solutions addressed later, but this is the least developed area of their theory.

Finally, the trigger for adaptation among these works is generally some flow of information from the environment to the organization. The specific instances of triggers for adaptation, however, vary widely. In Galbraith, a mismatch between the demands of the environment and the capacity of the organization leads to adaptive changes either to reduce the information processing demands of the task or increase the information processing capacity of the structure. In Lawrence and Lorsch (1967), coordination failures within the organization lead to conflict between groups, and the process for resolving that conflict establishes the extent of both specialization within groups and cooperation between groups. Similarly in Chandler's history, coordination failures lead managers to create a new set of structures and systems that comprise the multidivisional firm. In several of the works it is not the specific nature of the information that triggers adaptation, but the rate of flow of that information (Burns and Stalker 1961; Lawrence and Lorsch 1967; Galbraith 1973; Miles and Snow 1978).

It's clear, then, that adaptation plays a central role in most contingent theories of organization that focus on structuring firms. And in most of these theories, adaptation is carried out by rational, albeit boundedly-rational, agents with the goal of efficiently arranging the operations of the firm. With much in common between contingency theory and evolutionary approaches to organizations, why do they lead to divergent predictions for the relationship between structure and strategy?

3. EVOLUTIONARY APPROACHES TO ORGANIZATIONS AND STRUCTURE

At its heart, evolution is the study of change in populations over time. That change can come from entry and exit of different types of organizations, or through change of individual organizations. The new structural research in evolution is emerging in the area of evolutionary economics, founded by Nelson and Winter (1982). This approach has a particular concern with how large firms – those that dominate our economy

– change over time. Evolutionary economics is just one part of a broader program of evolutionary interpretation of organizations.

The evolutionary program is a broad initiative. As Aldrich and Ruef (2006) explain, it is more of an algorithmic theory than a causal theory. That is, many other organizational theories can be couched within the evolutionary framework. Evolution categorizes causal mechanisms for organizations as sources of *variation* – how differences arise across a group of organizations – *retention* – how particular characteristics are preserved in organizations, and *selection* – how organizations with certain characteristics are more likely to survive in a population. At its highest level, evolution does not specify particular mechanisms for these categories. Aldrich groups six other organizational theories – ranging from population ecology to institutional theory – by the particular mechanisms they propose for variation, retention, and selection.

Evolutionary economics falls largely in what Aldrich characterizes as theories of organizational learning. In this approach, the primary source of variation is search over local information spaces for alternatives when performance falls below aspirations. The practices adopted by firms are retained through automatic behaviors by organization members, labeled routines or programs. And selection occurs through the mechanism of managerial choice between alternatives discovered through local search.

Clearly this approach arises from a very similar theoretical tradition as contingency theory. Many of the foundational works for both traditions include the Carnegie School classics by March and Simon (1958) and Cyert and March (1963). This tradition begins with an information processing framework (Simon 1947) and builds to the behavioral theory of the firm, which focuses on the imperfect decision frameworks that arise because of bounded rationality and shifting coalitions within organizations (Cyert and March 1963).

The behavioral theory of the firm contained the foundational statement of local search as the fundamental mechanism of learning and change in organizations (Cyert and March 1963). The theory proposes that firms will search the local environment for solutions when problems arise. For many decisions, "The set of alternatives considered depends on some features of organizational structure and the locus of search responsibility in the organization." (p. 83, Cyert and March 1963) It is clear from this perspective that the structure of the firm will affect the choices and the behaviors of the firm, and a primary goal for the research program is "to study the effects of organizational structure and conventional practice on the development of goals, the formation of expectations, and the execution of choices"

(p. 1, Cyert and March 1963). But these goals had little influence on the subsequent development of organizational studies.

Contingency theory, in fact, adopted the information processing framework while focusing on managers' search for effective administrative structures once the organization's strategic direction was set. The evolutionary tradition emphasizes the role the administrative structure plays in shaping subsequent strategic decisions, such as market entry and exit. This difference in emphasis leads to very different predictions for evolutionary approaches to structure.

In Organizations in Action, Thompson (1967) proposes that firms face a series of fundamental problems in relating to the environment, and the solutions that firms arrive at for these problems becomes the structure of the firm. An evolutionary approach poses the relationship in the opposite fashion. The problems that a firm perceives will be shaped by the structure of the firm. For instance, Will Mitchell and I (Williams and Mitchell 2004) describe the structure of the firm as a lens, which shapes the information that flows into the firm from the environment and amplifies some information through sharing. As a result, the business units into which a firm groups its activities will influence the product markets that the firm enters. Similarly, the structure will shape the potential solutions that a firm will perceive and act upon. The most extreme version of this might be considered the anarchic organizations described by the garbage can model of choice (Cohen, March et al. 1972) (they propose universities as a common example of these), which are composed of solutions in search of a problem.

The evolutionary approach to organizations has become increasingly popular as new empirical methods for panel data (longitudinal) and event history (survival) analysis have become more sophisticated and more accessible. These statistical techniques open the potential to study events over time rather than in cross-section if we take the time to gather longitudinal data sets. Most empirical work in the evolutionary tradition, however, has remained firmly focused on the inertia hypothesis. The inertia hypothesis is probably the baseline of evolutionary theory – that firms will tend to remain the same over time. Population ecology studies have documented in great detail the costs of certain types of changes – to core technology and structure – and the importance of newly founded firms as a source of variation in fields of organizations (Carroll and Hannan 2000). Even empirical studies in the evolutionary economics tradition, however, have tended to emphasize that firms will stay close to prior choices (Helfat 1994).

This emphasis on inertia, however, runs counter to the theoretical interest within evolutionary economics in adaptation in changing environments. The theoretical interest in how firms manage changing situations through adaptation and innovation dates at least back to Burns and Stalker's work on innovation, since dynamic environments demand regular and constant innovation (Burns and Stalker 1961). In the evolutionary view of organizational systems, change is fundamental to most organizations. As Chester Barnard proposed, one fundamental rationale for hierarchical organizations is to adapt to changing environmental conditions (Barnard 1938).

The constant adaptation in organizations arises because coordination by its very nature implies unforeseen contingencies. If all contingencies in the environment could be predicted, then all coordination could occur through automatic routines. While contingency theory emphasized that firms would do everything in their power to fit unexpected events into their repertoire of programmatic behavior, a greater emphasis on adaptive search allows that coordination will regularly require innovation within the firm. So even if we treat firms as simple systems for coordinating economic behavior, change is baked into the cake. Similarly, contingency theory tended to treat adaptation as occurring in predictable cycles – managers act, observe, react, and repeat. The evolutionary approach focuses on the adaptations between feedback loops, and how they lead to gradual drift in firms.

As a result, it is not only the case that evolutionary theory offers new insights for structure. Structure is an observable characteristic of organizations that is likely to affect their adaptation, and so it becomes possible to study how characteristics that influence information processing in firms influence the adaptive choices that the firms make. This opens new avenues for studying organizations as ongoing adaptive entities, and broadens the field beyond the simple inertia hypothesis. Evolutionary studies of structure and adaptation enable empirical studies to inform a richer theoretical picture of adaptation in organizations.

Table 2 contrasts the driving questions, theoretical mechanisms, and empirical focus of contingency and evolutionary approaches to structure. As I have outlined, while the two share a common theoretical tradition and foundation, the prism through which they view structure is quite different. Contingency theory treats structure as the outcome of problem solving within the firm, while evolutionary theory treats structure as the landscape over which problem solving occurs in firms.

Table 2. Contingent and Evolutionary Approaches to Structure.

1.	1. Contingency Theory	1. Evolutionary Theory
1. Core question	2. Which sets of organizational features are appropriate in different settings?	2. How do firms change over time?
1. Central Mechanism	3. Managerial reaction to environmental opportunities and coordination pressures in the firm.	3. *Retention* - Organizational routines. 4. *Variation* – Problem driven search and historical inheritance. 5. *Selection* – Social and economic forces inside and outside firms.
1. Empirical Focus	4. What organizational forms are associated with high performance in different environments?	6. How does organizational structure influence the adaptation of firms?
1. Assumptions / 2. Taken for Granted	5. Unbiased internal and external selection pressures that leave organizations close to the efficient choice.	7. Change is good. Firms must adapt continuously for changing markets to deliver products and services that customers value.

Table 3 lists several aspects of structure that are likely to affect the evolution of firms through their effect on retention, variation, and selection within the organization. Theoretically, the summation above suggests that the properties of interest should be structural features that are relatively stable and which affect the organization's perception of problems or the solution landscape over which it searches. I have explored several aspects of structure in my empirical work that I believe have these characteristics. The first is the top level business units in the firm, or the grouping principle used. Grouping leads to pooling of knowledge and rich sharing of information about a common set of information from the environment. When looked at in detail, grouping rarely follows the simplistic choice of functional or product divisions suggested in the literature. Firms often group different units long different dimensions – product, function, location, and geography – and they frequently mix those dimensions within a single unit, such as a business data services unit at a telephone company, which combines customer and product dimensions. Naturally, these units need to be linked to coordinate the interdependent resources in each unit. I have found that the movement of top managers between divisions – creating rich information links between the units as well as diverse skill bases among top executives – has a significant impact on the dynamism of the firm. Next, authority and coordination mechanisms shape the use and transmission of information in the firm, and enshrine some interdependencies, which can constrain adaptation if those interdependencies change.

Table 3. Evolutionary Impact of Administrative Structure.

1. Aspect of Structure	1. Evolutionary Impact	1. Explanation
1. Business Units 2. (divisions)	2. Retention	2. Between group activities more automatic/routinized and difficult to change (Henderson and Clark 1990)
1. Business Units 2. (divisions)	3. Variation	3. Primary units focus information processing, lead towards some opportunities and away from others (Williams and Mitchell 2004)
1. Linking 2. Mechanisms	4. Variation	4. Information and people transferred between units increase variety of perspectives and lead new activities and innovations (Williams and Mitchell 2004; Williams and Karim 2007)
1. Decentralization	5. Variation	5. Strengthen or weaken incentives for experimentation and change (Rumelt 1995; Williams 2005)
1. Business Unit 2. Reconfiguration	6. Variation	6. Innovation arises from established and combined units, not from acquired units. (Karim 2006)
1. Centralization	7. Selection	7. Movement of executives into and out of corporate office increases focus on selection criteria for new and existing activities (Williams and Mitchell 2004; Williams and Karim 2007)

In the end, studying the evolutionary impact of these structural elements of organizations is likely to reduce our emphasis on straightforward contingencies between the environment and firm choices, since the adaptations encouraged by different structures can lead firms to evolve in significantly different fashion in the same environment.

4. CONCLUSION: NEW QUESTIONS AND NEW CHALLENGES FROM AN EVOLUTIONARY APPROACH TO STRUCTURE

One of the notable challenges of a longitudinal approach to structure is developing a theoretical picture of structure that describes the implications of its two-way relationship with strategy. The two theories of structure imply two different dynamics for the evolution of organizations, call them the efficiency dynamic – in which organizations modify their structure to meet the coordination challenges of the set of markets they serve – and the adaptation dynamic – in which organizations innovate and change the set of markets they serve as a result of the information landscape created by their structure. Organization studies and strategy are fields where many different theories coexist because they explain different aspects of firms. If we take this notion seriously, then we need to acknowledge that the efficiency and adaptive dynamics imply an endogenous relationship between the structural characteristics of a firm and its strategic choices.

Endogeneity is a particular challenge for empirical studies, because the correlation established by regression can be the result of multiple causal relationships. A panel data gives some headway on this problem by establishing the temporal precedence of either structure or strategy. For instance, in looking at the classic issue of diversification and the multidivisional form, Amburgey and Dacin (1994) find that increased diversification precedes the adoption of the multidivisional form, but that adoption of this form also leads to subsequent increases in diversification. This temporal precedence can establish Granger causality, the notion that one event must precede another in time.

However, this temporal aspect of causality is only interesting to the extent that managers are quite constrained in the extent to which they make decisions with foresight. If managers select structures with an expectation of future strategic decisions, then simple temporal precedence may not establish that a choice of structure causes the strategic choices that follow. One cannot rule out that the two choices were determined simultaneously, even though the structural change preceded the strategic change. There are a number of additional techniques for establishing causal relationships in panel data, most notably instrumental variables analysis, but these are only useful to the extent that we understand the nature of the endogenous relationship between our variables of interest – structural and strategic choices. Unfortunately, our theory still is best at addressing the relationship in one direction or the other, not at exploring the interaction of the two dynamics.

How can we, then, develop our theoretical understanding of the interaction between the dynamic of structural efficiency and strategic adaptation? Computational modeling is one of the most powerful theoretical tools we possess for exploring dynamic relationships in theoretical models. One interesting potential starting point for modeling is the Cohen and March's garbage can model (1972), which specifies a causal relationship quite similar to the evolutionary approach to structure. In the garbage can model, the social structure of agents within the firm determines which solutions get considered as problems present themselves to the organization. If we add a feedback effect in which the past solutions to organizational problems, say the choice of markets to serve, affects the social structure of agents, then we could explore the patterns of evolution that emerge when the two dynamics interact. Theoretical progress in understanding the potential interactions between the two dynamics is an important first step in untangling the complex, two-way relationship between strategy and structure.

4.1 Implications for theory

Ultimately, the success of the evolutionary approach to structure in strengthening our understanding of organizations will be the new questions that it inspires us to ask and the potential insights that they can generate. Thus, I conclude the paper with a consideration of the new questions inspired by the approach and the potential insights that they offer for evolutionary approaches to organizations, strategy, and our understanding of the role of structure in managing organizations.

From the perspective of evolutionary theory, a focus on structure enriches the field by allowing us to move beyond the inertia hypothesis. Theoretical interest in evolutionary economics has more recently focused on the ongoing adaptation of organizations. The study of structure and adaptation creates the potential for a much more fruitful interaction between our theory and empirical studies. In this paper and elsewhere, I have advanced the proposition that structure acts as a lens, shaping the flow of information through the organization and to key decision makers. Structure can influence which problems are tackled by an organization and which solutions are considered in search efforts. Evolutionary studies of structure have recently examined how grouping, linking, and ownership structures influence future adaptations, but there is considerable room to explore how additional aspects of formal and informal structure influence adaptive outcomes in organizations.

In addition, evolutionary theory inspires two additional areas of inquiry that have not yet been addressed by research into structure. The first is whether and how structure shapes the selection environment within firms. That is, in what ways do structures provide or shape metrics by which potential solutions to problems will be measured. One of the peculiarities of organizations that has been overlooked by learning theories is the relative paucity of information that organizations face when choosing between potential alternatives. Because actual experiments in organizations are costly and rare, and the relationships between specific activities and organizational outcomes are frequently ambiguous, the choice between alternative courses of action frequently occurs in a selection environment dominated by rhetorical and political considerations. Organizational structures are likely to influence this selection process through the metrics chosen and the coalitions within the firm which shape the set of alternatives considered.

The second area of inquiry opened by evolutionary study of structure is how structure influences adaptive outcomes by enabling some decisions while ruling out others. In essence, this posits a relationship between structural aspects of the firm and the retention of specific activities or routines. For instance, the extent of buffering of core technological routines may constrain the adaptive choices open to firms. Since the firm's core is protected from outside influences, it is also prevented from adapting to meet new conditions. In particular, we might ask when the cost of this buffering outweighs the benefits elaborated in earlier organizational theories (Thompson 1967).

From a strategic perspective, as we explore the ongoing adaptation of organizations through the study of structure and strategy, we might ask whether there are common adaptive paths for firms to follow? In essence, this would be the longitudinal equivalent of the coherent clusters that contingency theory searched for in cross-sectional samples. The question in a dynamic setting is are there patterns of adaptive choices that firms make, and on which environmental or organizational characteristics do these depend? In particular, we might come to understand more of the ways in which technical and productive capabilities tend to emerge in firms. Do some choices in organizations naturally generate rich information to define the next problem and solution that a firm will address. In other words, what are the conditions necessary for common learning models, in which production naturally leads to efficiency gains, to emerge? Since the resource-based view of strategy currently emphasizes the potential value of organizationally-embedded capabilities, evolutionary approaches to structure might help us understand the mechanisms by which some firms develop more effective or more valuable sets of routines and practices. From a strategic perspective, then, firm-level decision-makers operating in fast-moving, ambiguous environments often do not shape technical and operational routines directly. Structural choices are the levers by which firms shape the emergence of capabilities, thus structure is an important influence on the paths by which firms develop key competitive resources.

4.2 Implications for practice

From a more managerial perspective on structure, the evolutionary approach naturally suggests the question of whether we should structure firms differently when we consider the future evolution of the organization. From a longitudinal perspective, interdependent structures can constrain action by enshrining dependencies between parts of the organization. For instance, a matrix structure may be quite well adapted to the particular interdependencies required for a firm's current production and coordination problem, but when technology or competition shifts and introduces a different set of potential relationships, structures with greater bilateral interdependence between parts of the organization may be slower to adapt to the new conditions. This raises the question of the adaptive costs and benefits of common coordination mechanisms, such as hierarchy or inter-group linking. Similarly, complementarities between parts of the organization – the fit commonly prescribed by contingency theory – may create inertia since change requires more simultaneous changes negotiated between parties than in a situation with lower interdependence. Finally, I have found that transferring business unit leaders between units leads to much more dynamic patterns of market entry and exit (Williams and Mitchell 2004; Williams and Karim 2007). This suggests that HR practices can also influence the adaptive and innovative path of organizations.

Hopefully this discussion makes clear that a program of research into the evolutionary impact of structure, or the adaptive dynamic of structure, offers quite a number of new questions we can ask about how organizations evolve and adapt over time. The research addresses important limitations of the evolutionary research program, sheds light into new areas of organizations, and may lead to very different prescriptions for managers. This paper compares this evolutionary approach to structure to an older tradition, contingency theory approach. I find that there is more overlap than a cursory examination might suggest. Both theories emphasize the role of adaptive mechanisms in shaping the relationship between structures and strategic choices. Despite a common theoretical foundation and use of adaptation as a causal mechanism, however, the approaches have fundamentally different approaches to the nature of problem identification and problem-solving in firms. Contingency theory lies in a tradition that puts more emphasis on finding efficient solutions to coordination problems in firms (an efficiency dynamic), while the evolutionary perspective focuses on the ways that structure shapes the very nature of defining and solving problems in firms (an adaptive dynamic). The theoretical challenge going forward is to understand when the efficiency dynamic or the adaptive dynamic will dominate, and how the two will interact when they exist simultaneously in evolving organizations.

REFERENCES

Aldrich, H. E. and Ruef, M., 2006, *Organizations Evolving,* 2nd edition. Thousand Oaks, CA, Sage Publications, Inc.

Amburgey, T. L. and Dacin, T., 1994, As the left foot follows the right? The dynamics of strategic and structural change. *Academy of Management Journal,* **37**: 1427-1452.

Barnard, C. I., *1938, The functions of the executiv,* Cambridge, Harvard University Press.

Burns, T. and Stalker, G. M., 1961, *The Management of Innovation*, London, Tavistock Publications.

Carroll, G. R. and Hannan, M. T., 2000, *The demography of corporations and industries*, Princeton, NJ, Princeton University Press.

Chandler, A., 1962, Strategy and Structure: Chapters in the *History of the Industrial Enterprise,* Cambridge, MA, MIT Press.

Cohen, M. D., March, J. G., et al., 1972, A garbage can model of organizational choice, *Administrative Science Quarterly,* **17**(1): 1-25.

Cyert, R. M. and March, J. G., 1963, *A behavioral theory of the firm,* Englewood Cliffs, NJ, Prentice-Hall, Inc.

Galbraith, J. R., 1973, *Designing complex organizations*, Reading, MA, Addison Wesley Publishing.

Helfat, C. E., 1994, Evolutionary trajectories in petroleum firm R&D, *Management Science,* **40**(12): 1720-1747.

Henderson, R. M. and Clark, K. B., 1990, Architectural innovation: the reconfiguration of existing product technologies and the failure of established firms. *Administrative Science Quarterly,* **35**: 9-30.

Karim, S., 2006, Modularity in organizational structure: the reconfiguration of internally developed and acquired business units, *Strategic Management Journal,* **27**(9): 799-823.

Lawrence, P. R. and Lorsch, J. W., 1967, *Organization and Environment: Managing Differentiation and Integration,* Boston, Division of Research, Harvard Business School.

March, J. G. and Simon, H. A., 1958, *Organizations,* New York, John Wiley and Sons.

Miles, R. E. and Snow, C. C., 1978, *Organizational Strategy, Structure, and Process,* New York, McGraw-Hill Book Co.

Nelson, R. R. and Winter, S. G., 1982, *An Evolutionary Theory of Economic Chang,.* Cambridge, MA, Belknap Press.

Rumelt, R. P., 1995, *Inertia and transformation. Resource-Based and Evolutionary Theories of the Firm: Towards a Synthesis,* C. A. Montgomery. Boston, Kluwer Academic Publishers, 101-132.

Schoonhoven, C. B., 1981, Problems with contingency theory: Testing assumptions hidden within the language of contingency theory, *Administrative Science Quarterly,* **26**: 349-377.

Simon, H. A., 1947, *Administrative behavior: a study of decision-making processes in administrative organizations,* (fourth edition), New York, The Free Press.

Thompson, J. D., 1967, *Organizations in action,* New York, McGraw-Hill Publishing Co.

Williams, C., 2005, The influence of ownership structures on firm expansion in the global cellular industry, *Working paper*.

Williams, C. and Karim, S., 2007, Parallel paths: How top executive movement shapes the market evolution of firms, Duke University, *Working paper.*

Williams, C. and Mitchell, W., 2004, Focusing firm evolution: The impact of information infrastructure on market entry by U.S. telecommunications companies, 1984-1998, *Management Science,* **50**(11): 1561-1575.

PART II: THE DESIGN OF ORGANIZATIONAL PROCESSES

Chapter 4

RATIONAL EMOTIONALITY: INTEGRATING EMOTIONS INTO PSYCHOLOGICAL CLIMATE

Dorthe Døjbak Håkonsson[1], Børge Obel[2], Richard M. Burton[3]
[1]*Centre for Organizational Renewal and Evolution, Aarhus School of Business, Aarhus University;* [2]*Aarhus School of Business, Aarhus University;* [3]*Duke University, The Fuqua School of Business*

Abstract: This chapter discusses the notions of affective events and employee emotions, and integrates these concepts into previous work on psychological climate, as represented in the multicontingency model (Burton et al., 2006; Burton and Obel, 2004). Furthermore, this chapter discusses the effect of organizational emotions on organizational information processing and decision making, which helps to explain the role of organizational climate in the multicontingency model. In the first part of the chapter, we define the concept of psychological climate and its apparent lack of association with employee behavior. Building on recent research findings on the role of emotions in organizational behavior, we propose psychological climate as affective events, which influence employee emotions. Emotions, in turn, represent a conditional state of mind, which influences employee information processing and consequent behaviors. Thus, psychological climate, conceptualized as affective events, is an important concept within the multicontingency model of organizational design. The final part of the paper provides a first step towards integrating emotions, through their relationship with psychological climate, into the multicontingency model. Here, we discuss the concept of rational emotionality, which captures how emotions influence peoples' abilities to make rational decisions.

Key words: Rational emotionality, employee emotions, psychological climate, information processing, multicontingency model, organization design.

R.M. Burton et al. (eds.), *Designing Organizations*, doi: 10.1007/978-0-387-77776-4_4,

1. INTRODUCTION

Psychological climate has been defined differently by various authors (Koys & DeCotiis, 1991; James & Jones, 1974; Zammuto & Krakower, 1991). Despite the differences, there is a clear consensual agreement amongst the authors that psychological climate relates to an experiential-based and enduring perceptual phenomenon, which is widely shared by the members of a given organizational unit, and which influences members' behaviors (Denison, 1996; Woodman & King, 1978; James & Jones, 1974). Yet, two basic questions remain largely unanswered; *how* and *why* does the psychological climate influence behavior?

By integrating psychological climate into their multicontingency model, Burton and Obel (2004) provide one possible explanation of *how* - arguing that climate influences employees' information processing behaviors. Yet, the reasoning remains somewhat diffuse. The multicontingency model relies on assumptions of bounded rationality (Simon, 1956, Conlisk, 1996), as well as task uncertainty (Galbraith, 1974), which may not fully explain the information processing as determined by psychological climate.

However, recent neuroscientific findings (Bechera and Damasio, 2005; Adophs & Damasio, 2001; Damasio et al., 1996; Lazarus, 1993) have proven that emotions can influence cognitive processes. Building on emotion research and Affective Events Theory (AET) (Weiss & Cropanzano, 1996), we integrate this knowledge into Burton and Obel's (2004) multicontingency model by arguing that psychological climate essentially captures affective events, which in turn, influence employee emotions. Because emotions have been found to function as directors of attention, memory, and sensation, they are very much part of what is commonly described in psychology literature as rational decision making (McDermott, 2004; Kaufman, 1999). In this manner, climate constitutes what could be referred to as an "emotional rationality" aspect of human behaviors, and consequently, should be treated in addition to the bounded rationality aspect of employees' behaviors, since climate, similar to bounded rationality, influences employees' information processing behaviors.

2. PSYCHOLOGICAL CLIMATE AND ITS IMPACT ON BEHAVIOR

In earlier psychology literature, James and Jones (1974) argued that psychological climate is a set of global perceptions held by individuals about their internal organizational environment. It is a summarized feeling made up of actual events and based upon the interaction between actual events and the perception of those events. Later on, Koys and DeCotiis (1991) defined psychological climate as an "experiential-based, multidimensional, and enduring perceptual phenomenon which is widely shared by the members of a given organizational unit". The common notion for most psychological climate research is that it is based on employees' perceptions of organizational events, and that these perceptions in turn, form employees' behaviors in particular ways.

However, despite many excellent reviews (Patterson et al., 2005; Denison, 1996, Glick, 1985; Schneider, 1990, 1975; Woodman & King, 1978, James & Jones, 1974) of climate research, the concept remains somewhat diffuse. Some of the problems often raised in psychological climate research relate to measurement, meaning how to capture an essentially individual process (perception) at the organizational level. A complementary problem is measuring an objective concept as individual perceptions. Furthermore, the *how* and *why of* climate influences on employees' behaviors are open questions.

To this end, Burton and Obel's conceptualization of climate provides one step along the way in answering the *how*. Burton and Obel (2004) integrate psychological climate into their multicontingency model by arguing that climate influences employees' information processing abilities. Building upon notions of bounded rationality (Simon, 1956, Conlisk, 1996) and task uncertainty (Galbraith, 1974), the researchers hypothesize how different climate types are likely to influence particular information processing behaviors. They have gained support for these hypotheses through empirical studies, which show that misfits between climate and strategy (Burton, Lauridsen, Obel, 2004) and climate and leadership (Haakonsson et al., 2007) have negative implications for performance.

An even more perplexing question, which has yet to be fully understood is *why* climate influences information processing. We believe that the answer can be found in the assumptions underlying the information processing perspective (Galbraith, 1974. Simon, 1956, Arrow, 1974), which are not sufficiently rich to explain the influence of psychological climate on employee information processing.

Information processing theories rest largely on the assumption of bounded rationality, as developed by Simon (1956), and later on by Conlisk (1996). While this concept has clearly been a major contribution towards understanding the limits of human decision making, it is also clear that it relates only to humans' limited computational abilities and selective memory and perception, in other words, limitations that prevent us from making decisions that maximize gains in relation to specific goals.

Earlier, Commons (1934) observed that human behavior is goal oriented and purposive, but behaviour is also influenced by "stupidity, ignorance, and passion" (1934:874). However, the Simon concept of bounded rationality, in its representation of cognitive processes as characterized by calculation, omits passion to a large degree (Kaufman, 1999).

Yet passion today, usually referred to as emotions, has previously been regarded as a distracter of the important processes (i.e. the rational, and cognitive processes). However, recent neuroscientific advances have begun to integrate notions of emotions and their influence on information processing. We believe these new findings on emotions and their impact of information processing may help explain *why* psychological climate influences behavior.

3. HOW EMOTIONS ARE NECESSARY FOR RATIONAL DECISION MAKING

The term, emotions, has various definitions. We use Forgas' (1995) definition, which is consistent with other influential authors (Lazarus, 1993, 1982; Fisher & Ashkanasy, 2000, Fischer, 2000). Following Forgas, emotions are discrete, affective states, which are perceived by the individual to have an identifiable cause, object, and/or referent. In contrast, mood is a diffuse affective state, in other words, moods have no clear referent, object, or cause. Affect is a generic label, comprising of both mood and emotion.

Because emotions relate to affections, there has been a tendency within literature, to separate emotions completely from rationality and cognition (Hilgaard, 1980). Theories of decision making have focused on rational cognitive processes, and emotions have at best, been recognized to function either as shortcuts to complex judgements (Klaaren et al., 1994) or as unconscious moderators of cognitive judgement making processes (Forgas, 1995). Now, neurological findings highlight emotions as an important part of rational decision making processes. (Bechera & Damasio, 2005; Adophs & Damasio, 2001; Damasio, 1995; Lazarus, 1993; Oatley, 1992).

Following neuroscience, (LeDoux, 1995; Lazarus, 1993, 1991), whenever humans meet external stimuli, the information passes through a two-stage cognitive appraisal process (Lazarus, 1996; Huy, 2002). These appraisal stages occur primarily in the brain's limbic system (including the thalamus and the amygdala – both emotional centres of the brain). In the first stage, evaluation of information is made in respect to peoples' own goals and concerns. If the information is evaluated as beneficial to these goals and concerns, pleasant emotions are aroused. If not, unpleasant emotions are aroused (Lazarus, 1996; Huy, 2002). In the second stage, the focus is on dimensions, such as potential for coping and consequences of the event. If based on the evaluation of information, people believe they have the adequate resources for dealing with the information, they will be likely to respond actively and arouse active emotions. If people do not believe they have adequate resources, they will be more passive, and avoidance emotions will be aroused (Lazarus, 1996). Throughout the appraisal process, information that has once been received through physical senses is stored as learning based on experiences in an "emotional memory". This serves as heuristics for future decisions, by providing a sense of what is good and bad, causing pleasure or pain etc. (Damasio et al., 1996).

As part of the human survival system, information is only passed on for higher level abstract rational processing (in the prefrontal cortex) when there are no signs of immediate emotional emergency (Lazarus,1982, McDermott, 2004). If there *are* signs of immediate emotional emergency, the emotional brain will react to the threats (McDermott, 2004). This processing hierarchy evolved originally to help humans survive fight-or-flight situations (McDermott, 2004), but it is still very important for rational decision making. For example, a person needs to hit the brake on his/her car at the red traffic light before reflecting on whether or not the traffic light is light orange rather than pale red, and also, whether or not the person's foot would have better contact with the break if they wore sneakers rather than pumps, etc.

There is continuous debate amongst psychologists (Charland, 1997) as to whether or not emotions are post cognitive (Lazarus, 1982), meaning that they presuppose certain judgements and as a result, are evaluative, or whether or not emotions are precognitive (Zajonc, 1980). New neuroscientific findings have demonstrated that emotions are clearly interlinked with higher level cognitive processes, and therefore, they are essential to what can be referred to as rational decision making.

Studies by Damasio in particular (Damasio et al. 1994, 1996; Adophs and Damasio, 2001) have documented that emotions are essential for human information processing, and important for rational decision making. And two studies in particular have been used as examples of the consequences of not having intact emotional brains: One study (Damasio et al., 1994) explains how a patient, in the wake of surgery for a brain tumor, suffered damage to his ventromedial prefrontal cortex - a part of the brain that remains critical for emotional processing. Because this patient was not able to reference emotion-memory, he was unable to negotiate his social world properly, despite an intact intelligence. Consequently, the patient could take half an hour to choose one of two dates for making an appointment, using sophisticated "rational" strategies involving cost-benefit calculations, a process that might be optimal, but not effective in everyday life.

In another study, Damasio et al. (1996) compared patients with brain lesions in the ventromedial cortex, with patients who did not have brain lesions, using a game of cards for the experiment. Subjects were presented with a loan of USD 2000 play money and four decks of playing cards. Each card represents an amount of money that the player wins or loses. Subjects were given two "bad" decks of playing cards, which gave the subjects many early rewards in the game, but then later on in the game, it caused them to pay large penalties. Two "good" decks paid lower rewards, but also took less money away from them. Unimpaired subjects quickly learned to make correct decisions about which cards to play, even before they could say why they were doing so. After a few trials, they made decisions based on a "right feeling." Skin conductance tests demonstrated that the unimpaired subjects received physiological feedback as they played, while the impaired patients lacked the bodily signals that stimulate the formation of appropriate emotional memories. Thus, because their emotion processing centers in the brain were not properly connected with their decision making centers in the cortex, the impaired subjects were not able to rely on the apparent "hunches" that the non-impaired subjects used.

Studies also exist which document how affections influence specific information processing behaviors. In particular, moods have been shown to influence the *process* of thinking (Forgas & George, 2001). Positive moods promote internally driven and flexible styles which at the same time, rely much on pre-existing schematic knowledge as opposed to new, situational information. Negative moods promote externally oriented and systemic thinking styles, and more use of new information. (Forgas & George, 2001, Bless, 2000, Fiedler, 2000, Forgas, 1995). Moods have also been shown to influence the *type* of information that people recall, attend to, select, and interpret, where it has been shown that affect can act to prime judgments through selective influence of cognitive stages (Forgas, 1995).

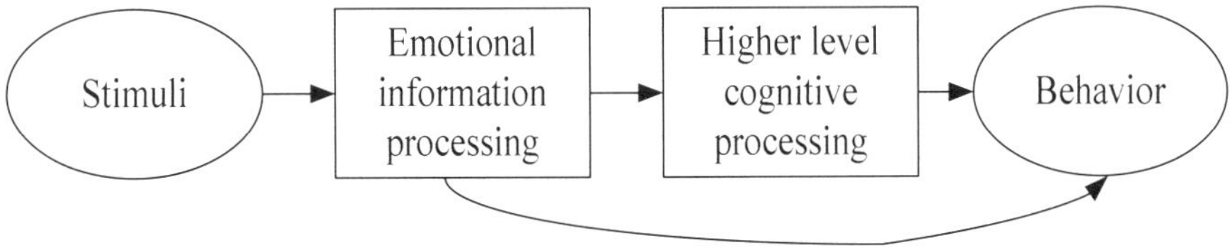

Figure 1. Illustration of human information processing

Source: Authors

Figure 1 illustrates the process of human decision making described above. When humans meet with stimuli, it passes through the brain's limbic system, a relatively primitive part of the brain which references to our emotions and our emotional memory. When the information indicates a threat for survival, higher-level processes are shut down, and immediate action (such as flight, or hitting the brake) results. In the case of no danger, information passes on for higher level processing.

Thus, emotional information exerts an influence before, and sometimes instead of (in terms of bypassing) higher-level cognitive functioning. Emotions, in this way, do not interfere with rational processes; they support rational processes (McDermott, 2002, Lazarus, 1982), whereas, emotions influence humans' abilities to process information rationally.

As demonstrated, emotions function as directors of attention, memory and selection, and in this manner, they are highly rational. We believe this has substantial relevance to the multicontingency model and its conceptualization of climate. Rather than relying only on notions of task uncertainty (Galbraith, 1974) and bounded rationality (Simon, 1956, 1982) to explain climate and its influence on employee behavior, we feel it is essential to incorporate emotions as well, and their influence on employee information processing. Simon's notion of bounded rationality rests on assumptions that cognitive constraints relate to limited computational ability, selective memory, and perception. To fully understand climates' influence on information processing behavior, we find it worthwhile to incorporate a notion of what could be termed rational emotionality as well, in order to capture how emotions influence peoples' abilities to make fully rational decisions. This notion is similar to Kaufman's (1999) idea that emotional arousal may serve as a source of bounded rationality and yet, different in the sense that it relates to how employees' shared emotions serve as a filter for their information processing behaviors. We believe that this understanding would enable us to go from a black box understanding of how different climates tend to influence employees' information processing behaviors, towards an understanding of why this is so.

4. AFFECTIVE EVENTS, EMOTIONS AND BEHAVIOR

The affective events model (AET) describes how work place conditions influence moods and emotions, and subsequent behaviors. According to AET, individuals have endogenous patterns of affect, such as personality-based predispositions towards certain emotions. However, work life is punctuated by events that interfere with these endogenous patterns and act as exogenous influences on affect (Weiss & Cropanzano, 1996). Such events comprise stable features of the workplace conditions (e.g. job design, job scope), which determine the occurrence of discrete "affective events" (e.g. daily hassles and/or uplifts in interactions with superiors, peers, or subordinates). These affective events in turn, lead to affective responses such as moods and emotions. As a result, these moods and emotions influence individuals' attitudes and behaviors. AET also describes how emotions may lead to impulsive behaviors or, in the long term, may accumulate to influence more stable work attitudes, such as job satisfaction. Attitudes, such as job satisfaction, may influence on higher cognitively driven behaviors such as the decision to quit.

Thus, the central tenet of the AET model is that affective states, such as moods and emotions, determine much of the way employees think and behave at work (Fisher & Ashkanasy, 2000).

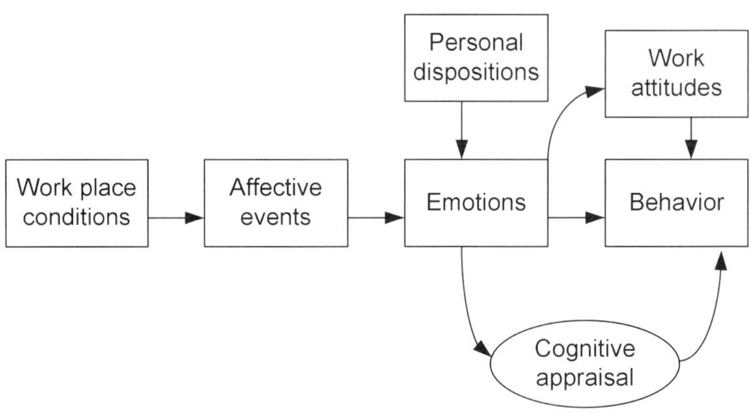

Figure 2. Illustration of the AET model

Source: Based on Weiss and Cropanzano, 1996, and Fischer and Ashkanasy, 2000

Figure 3 displays the AET, which proposes that workplace conditions (stimuli) determine the occurrence of discrete affective events, which in turn, lead to affective responses (emotions). These emotions influence behaviors either directly or by accumulating to influence work attitudes that then influence behaviors.

What is particularly relevant for our purposes is that the AET model allows us to open up the black box between the work environment and subsequent employee emotions and behavior.

4.1 Conceptualizing psychological climate as shared emotions

In comparing emotion theory and the AET theory to psychological climate, there seems to be many reasonable arguments for proposing psychological climate essentially as capturing affective events.

Relating first, to how affective events are defined, Weiss and Cropanzano (1996) defined affective events as "A happening, especially an important happening". The notion's later definitions (Basch & Fischer, 2000) have turned to cognitive appraisal theory and define affective events as "An incident that stimulates appraisal of and emotional reaction to a transitory or ongoing job-related agent, object, or event" (Basch & Fischer, 2000:37). This definition makes it clear that peoples' constructs about situations are what matters, as opposed to the objective situation itself. The fact that events are appraised and perceived by the employee, as opposed to the objective event, matches well with definitions of psychological climate, which refer to "a set of summary of global perceptions held by individuals about their organizational environment". Therefore, it is not the actual organizational context, but the perception of it that counts. Similarly, the notion that the psychological climate is a summary feeling about actual events, based upon the interaction between actual events and the perception of those events, is also very consistent with definitions of affective events.

By integrating AET, we also seem to gain conceptual clarity on one of the classic debates within climate research. Because climate research relies on perceptual measures, it has been argued that it is difficult to know whether it implies an attribute of the organization or an attribute of the perceiving individual. James and Jones (1974) propose the notion of psychological climate to capture climate as an individual attribute, as opposed to an organizational attribute. Yet, the differentiation between the objective and the subjective is very clear when relying on AET, because affective events relate clearly to the situation as it is actually perceived – not how it necessarily is, objectively. All told, AET fundamentally describes the objective and the subjective as distinct variables in the model.

One further argument for proposing climate as essentially capturing affective events can be found in the fact that affective events have a cumulative nature, wherefore it is not the intensity of events, but rather their frequency that matter for employees' affective states (Fisher, 2000). Thus, according to AET theory, it is the accumulation of positive or negative events, which determine employees' thoughts and feelings at work (Fischer, 2000). Therefore, emotions as well as feelings are transient and short term (Fischer, 2000). However, because psychological climate conceptualizes as affective events, which have an accumulative nature and are stored in an emotional memory (Damasio et al., 1996), and therefore slow to change, our conceptualization of climate fits well with the idea that climates are not transient, though more subject to change than organizational cultures (Denison, 1996).

Finally, previous work has referred to the influence of affect on team climate (Pirola-Merlo et al., 2002), and emotional climates (Brown & Brooks, 2002). Our definition of climate is based on this work, in that it captures climates as affective events and explains its influence on shared emotions and follows employee information. Yet, out view builds on and elaborates on previous work, and it is not contradictory to it.

Overall, we find it reasonable to relate to psychological climate as capturing those organizational events that produce affects. Thereby, climate essentially captures those events that produce particular emotions. Climate in this way, refers only to the objectivity of events when appraised emotionally, i.e. it "captures" and relates to employees' emotional reactions to organizational events. This conceptualizing makes it possible to differentiate climate distinctly from culture research (Denison, 1996), because culture includes the organization itself, whereas climate is clearly created by organizational variables which, as a result, influence or create a particular climate.

By integrating AET theory, we have gained a process description of how workplace conditions actually determine affective events, leading to affective responses. While climate is commonly described as feelings that are influenced and which emerge because of the particular workplace conditions, with AET theory, we are able to be more explicit to the extent that it describes how emotions arise, as responses to the work environment. This process of understanding has long been missing in climate research.

4.2 Individual versus shared emotions

When relating to climate as affective events, which subsequently determine emotions, it is essential that we relate to shared organizational emotions, and not individual emotions. This relates to similar issues in climate research on how to capture notions of shared perceptions, as opposed to individual perceptions.

There are several arguments supporting the fact that affective events are shared. As argued by Lazarus (1996), people will only feel the same emotions if their appraisal of events is the same. Within climate research, it has been argued that since climate is reality based, it is capable of being shared; it is the "communality of experiences" (Woodman & King, 1978:818) which enables a climate to influence employees' behaviors. Affective events, by their very definition, also relate to discrete, objective events, and are capable of being shared. The AET model recognizes that personal dispositions, e.g. in the form of trait affectivity, also contribute to the formation of emotions. Yet, according to AET, these endogenous patterns of affect are punctuated by exogenous events that interfere and act as exogenous influences on affect. At the same time, cognitive appraisal will be biased by emotional memories (Damasio, 1996), which are influenced by experiences with cumulative affective events, and therefore, are very likely to be shared amongst employees.

Other theories have also supported this view, for instance, George's (1990) notion of "group affective tone". George (1990, 1992) describes a group's shared sense of affect as "affective group tone", and argues this construct to be meaningful if group members experience similar kinds of affective states at work. Similarly, Barsade's work (Barsade, 2002, Barsade & Gibson, 1998; Kelly & Barsade, 2001) also describes how emotions are subject for being shared, e.g. through emotional contagion.

Altogether, we suggest that conceptualizing organizational climate as affective events, which in turn affect shared employee emotions, is a more descriptive way to conceptualize psychological climate in the multicontingency model. Moreover, it enables us to understand how and why a psychological climate influences employees' behaviors.

5. INTEGRATING AET AND EMPLOYEE EMOTIONS INTO THE MULTICONTINGENCY MODEL

While the AET model has gained increasing support, not many researchers have focused on exploring what specific events arouse affect at work. One study, which explores this, is Basch and Fischer's (2000) event-emotion matrix that shows the relationship between categories of job events and the corresponding emotions experienced by people. Examples of categories of job events that correspond to positive emotions are: receiving recognition; coping with a challenge; acts of work colleagues, as well as goal progress, and disconfirmation of negative expectations. Examples of categories of job events that correspond to negative emotions are: acts of management (i.e. when a very good employee is reprimanded), acts of colleagues (e.g. when others are not offering to help, when colleagues resent requests for assistance), task problems, making mistakes, lack of receiving recognition, and lack of goal achievement (Basch & Fischer, 2000).

5.1 The relationship between organizational variables, employee emotions, and behavioral outcomes

To integrate employee emotions into the multicontingency model, we need to explain the relationship between organizational variables, emotions, and behavioral outcomes. One candidate for establishing this relationship is the Multi Contingency Model, which represents an encompassing model of organizational design. Building on the information processing perspective (Galbraith, 1974, Simon, 1956), the model rests on the premise that in order for organizations to achieve coordination across and between its contingencies, they need to process information. Yet, information is costly, so organizations must balance their need to process information with their ability to do so (Ashby, 1948). Whenever this match is not present, meaning, whenever the organization processes too much information or too little information, the organization is misaligned; there is a misfit between its contingencies. Because misfits are costly (Donaldson, 2001; Burton, Lauridsen, & Obel, 2002), management needs to react to them. The Multi Contingency Model is illustrated in figure 3.

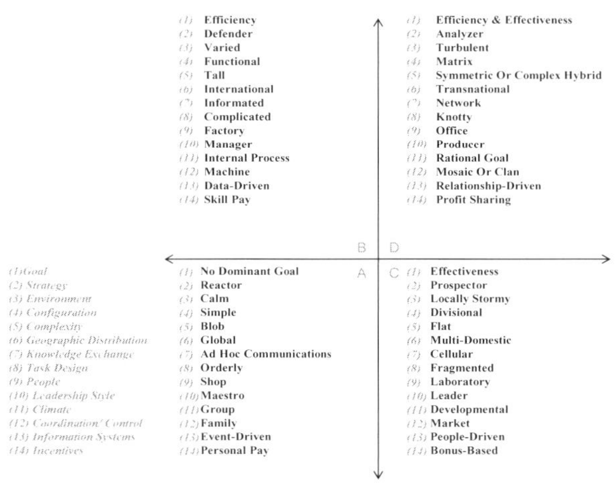

Figure 3. The Multi Contingency Model

Source: Burton et al., 2006

As figure 2 shows, there are 14 contingencies in the model (goal, strategy, environment, and configuration, etc.). All 14 contingencies are positioned on two by two dimensions. These dimensions represent the contingencies' information processing demands or capacities. For instance, firms that are pursuing a defender strategy (quadrant B) will usually have few products, little product innovation, but at the same time, high process innovation. This type of organization entails low task uncertainty (Galbraith, 1974), where decision making is usually more centralized (e.g. a manager leadership style, cf. quadrant B), as the information processing demands will not overload the information processing capacity of the executive, as defined by his bounded rationality (Simon, 1958). For an organization to be in a fit position, it is necessary to have all contingencies situated within the same quadrant.

In the multicontingency model, Burton and Obel (2004) build on Zammuto and Krakower (1991), who propose four climate types: the developmental, the rational goal, the internal process, and the group climate (cf. figures 2 and 4). Zammuto and Krakower (1991) define psychological climate by the dimensions of: leadership credibility, morale, equity in rewards, scapegoating, resistance to change, and conflict. Through confirmatory factor analyses, Burton, Lauridsen, and Obel (2002) found that these dimensions could be reduced to two dimensions: tension and resistance to change. Tension is high when morale, leadership credibility, and equity in rewards are low, and scapegoating is high. Resistance to change loads is based on one factor. Using these two dimensions, climate can be categorized into four climate types, as shown in figure 4.

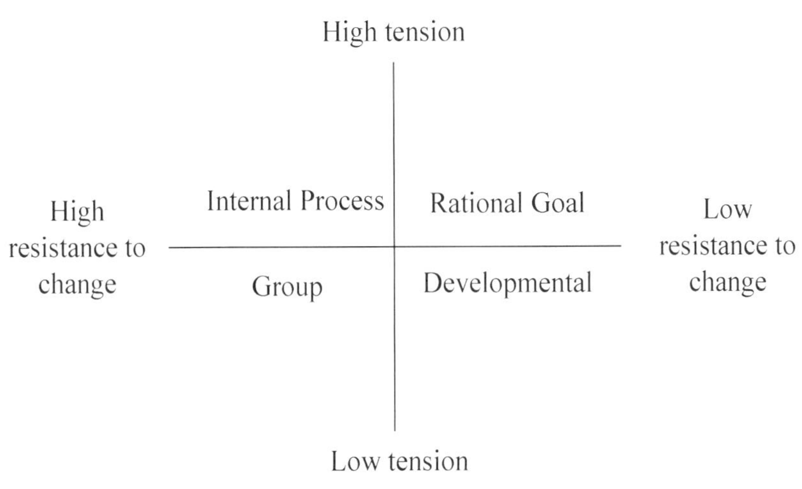

Figure 4. Mapping psychological climate on the competing values model

Source: Burton et al., 2006; Burton and Obel, 2004, 2002

We can gain further support for proposing psychological climate as affective events, by comparing the affective event categories by Basch and Fischer to those of Burton and Obel. For instance, Basch and Fischer's category of "receiving recognition" seems similar to Burton and Obel's notion of "equity in rewards". The categories of "discrimination of negative expectations" as well as "acts of colleagues" seem similar to Burton and Obel's "morale". Basch and Fischer's "making mistakes" category seems similar to "scapegoating". Finally, "acts of management" seem similar to Burton and Obel's "leadership credibility" dimension. As described above, these affective events will be subject to a cognitive attribution process, resulting in shared emotions.

Many typologies of "basic" emotions contain five to ten items, such as: fear, anger, sadness, disgust, joy, and love (Plutchik, 1994). Emotional lexica contain hundreds of items (Averill, 1975). Huy (2002), in one of the few empirical managerial studies, adapts the Larsen and Diener (1992) circumplex model to encompass a variety of emotions, and overall, dimensions of emotions. Huy (2002:35) categorizes emotions along two dimensions: The hedonic valence (pleasant – unpleasant); and the intensity of arousal, or action readiness (high vs. low activation). Whether employees associate events with pleasant versus unpleasant emotions will depend on whether or not they perceive the event as a threat to their own goals and concerns. Whether high or low activation emotions are aroused depends on whether employees believe they have the ability to cope with change. If they believe they have the adequate resources to deal with change, they are more likely to respond actively. Otherwise, they may adopt a more passive/avoidance approach.

Now, the following part of this section will compare Burton and Obel's climate typology with the Circumplex Model of Emotions.

Tension is defined as: a state of strained relations; uneasiness due to mutual hostility; stress: a balancing of forces or elements in opposition (Webster's New World Dictionary). Tension comprises the factors of: leadership credibility, morale, equity in rewards, conflict, and scapegoating. In the Huy model, tension seems most likely to relate to the pleasant-unpleasant dimension in the sense that affective events of high tension are very likely to be followed by feelings of unpleasantness and vice versa, for events of low tension.

Resistance to change was originally defined by Lewin (1951) as a system's tendency to return to status quo. Comparing this dimension to Huy's dimensions, we see that the notion of high vs. low activation relates to whether employees, given previous experiences, believe that they have the adequate resources for dealing with changes. If they do, they are likely to respond actively. Otherwise, they may adopt a more passive/avoidance approach. This avoidance approach can be interpreted as a form of resistance to change (Lazarus, 1993; Huy, 2002). In that sense, emotional activation seems clearly related to resistance to change. Now, by integrating the Huy (2002), Burton and Obel (2004) models, the figure illustrates what emotions are likely to emerge from particular climate types. Figure 5 illustrates this idea.

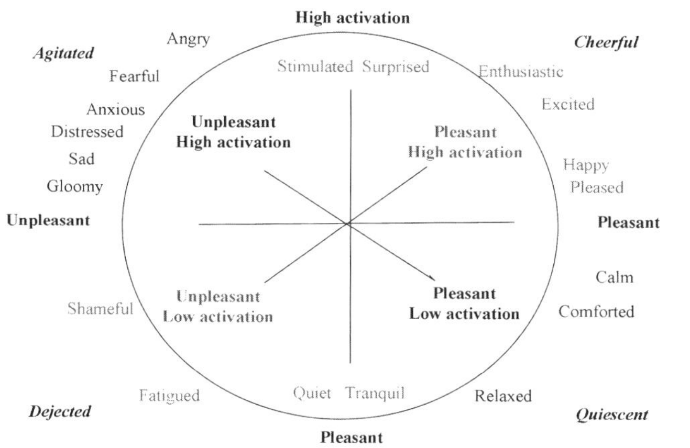

Figure 5. The Huy (2002) Circumplex Model of Emotions

Source: Huy's (2002) adaptation of the Larsen and Diener (1992) model

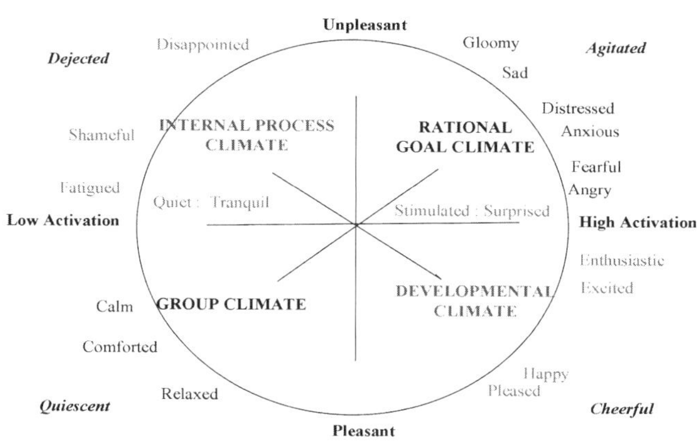

Figure 6. Huy's emotions associated with Burton and Obel's climate types

Source: Authors' integration of Huy (2002) and Burton and Obel (2004).[1]

[1] The axes for the Huy circumplex model representation are rotated 90 degrees for easy comparison

5.1.1 Internal Process Climate

The internal process climate is characterized by high resistance to change and high tension, and it is a climate in which there are many conflicts. Rewards are perceived to be given in an inequitable way, while change is perceived as something bad. Following the Huy model, such affective events are likely to lead to emotions such as shame, fatigue, and disappointment. Regardless of the actual stimuli employees receive, such organizations are affected by their cumulative experiences of previous affective events. Previous affective events are likely to have resulted in emotional memories, making employees relate to change as something, which they do not believe they have the adequate resources to cope with. Regardless of the actual events they are exposed to, employees are most likely to first perceive emotional memories as unpleasant, because previous experiences tell them that this is most likely. Comparing such emotions to findings, demonstrating how emotions influence information processing (Forgas, 1995), information processing in the internal process climate can not be expected to be very proactive, with respect to assuming responsibility of making decisions and on sharing information. Information is likely to be ignored, just as people are not likely to share information willingly.

5.1.2 Rational Goal Climate

The rational goal climate is characterized by low resistance to change and high tension. Emotional reactions to such climates are anger, anxiousness, distress, and fear. This is a climate in which employees believe they have the adequate resources to deal with change, because employees will be open towards change in their information processing. This openness towards change is also based on distress and fear, with respect to the current situation and at the same time, it is also a climate characterized by unpleasant emotions. One example could be a competitive climate where employees are not likely to have experienced positive emotions, like admitting mistakes, or getting rewards. Relating this to theories of the impact of emotions on information processing (Forgas, 1995, Forgas & George, 2001), we can expect that employees are not willingly open towards admitting mistakes, just as they are not likely to share information willingly. But, they may be proactive in initiating and assuming responsibility.

5.1.3 Developmental Climate

The developmental climate is a climate in which there are few events relating to conflict; the morale is high, and change resistant events are few. Since they are the typical events employees are experiencing, they are likely to prevail a feeling of having the adequate resources to deal with change, (high activation) as well as having the feeling that new events are generally pleasant. Subsequent emotions are therefore: enthusiasm, excitement, and happiness. Relating these emotions to likely behavioral actions, one would expect information to flow willingly in such organizations. Plus, the willingness to assume decision making responsibility and be proactive is supported.

5.1.4 Group Climate

The group climate is characterized by high resistance to change and few events of high tension. Based on cumulative experiences with such events, prevailing emotions are calmness, comfort, and relaxation. In terms of information processing, it seems reasonable to assume that climates of this type focus on information relating to the internal organization, and disregard external information. Simultaneously, interpersonal relations are positive, because people are likely to share information willingly. But, they do not recognize the urgency to be proactive in decision making.

6. IMPLICATIONS OF EMOTIONAL BOUNDEDNESS FOR THE MULTICONTINGENCY MODEL

The multicontingency model builds largely upon Galbraith's (1974) notion of task uncertainty, as the underlying reason organizations need for processing information for coordination and cooperation. Simon's (1956) notion of bounded rationality puts limits on the organization and explains *how* organizations proceed.

Yet, in terms of conceptualizing climate in the multicontingency model, we have argued that this it is not sufficient for describing how and why climates influence organizational behavior. The notions of task uncertainty and bounded rationality enable us to predict the "how", meaning how the four different climate types are likely to lead to different information processing typologies. This "how" can be derived from the underlying task uncertainty that is associated with each climate type and how this, due to limits on decision maker's bounded rationality, will affect information processing. However, the notions of task uncertainty do not allow us to open up the black box connecting organizational variables with climate and consequent behavior. Therefore, they do not provide a process understanding of *why* this is so – i.e. why particular climates influence employees' information processing behaviors in particular ways. Instead, we argue that conceptualizing climate as affective events enables us to achieve this understanding. Climate in this way, constitutes the emotional rationality aspect of human behaviors, and consequently, should be treated in addition to the bounded rationality aspects of employees' behaviors. Based on this, we suggest that conceptualizing climates as affective events is a contribution to climate research, because we are now able to provide an explanation of why climates influence employee behavior.

We also believe that conceptualizing climate as effective events is a contribution to the multicontingency model. By conceptualizing climate as employees' emotional boundedness, it is important for organizations to reduce this "boundedness" of employees' information processing. This can only be achieved by matching or "fitting" climate with other organizational contingencies, because this is how the emotional boundedness of employees' information processing behaviors can be complemented. Thus, what matters is to support the information processing capacity of employees with the information processing demands the organization is creating and facing. This is consistent with Ashby's law of requisite variety, and it is an interaction and fit argument, that is very relevant for the multicontingency model.

One remaining question is whether the notion that emotions influence humans' information processing should be integrated with other elements of the multicontingency model. The multi contingency model includes system factors (e.g. technology, strategy, and environment), and human factors (e.g. size, leadership style, and climate).

Relating first to the system factors, it seems unrealistic to posit that system factors are influenced by human elements, at least in the short run. Therefore, the information processing demands, as represented by technology, strategy, and the environment, would seem unaffected by emotions.

In terms of relating to human factors, we could discuss its relevance for size. Size, as defined by Burton and Obel (2004), combines the number of people and their educational level. The assumption is that the more educated the individual, the larger their information processing capacity. This is a cognitive rationality in the sense that it assumes that the more experienced the mental maps, the more complex the mental maps, and thereby, the more information they can process. Still, integrating emotions would be difficult in that we do not know anything about these people. Moreover, in the multicontingency model, while size does integrate notions of bounded rationality, the way size is integrated in the model, it is mostly used to prescribe notions of span of control, wherefore the bounded rationality assumptions seem sufficient.

In terms of relating rational emotionality to leadership style, leadership style rests again on the idea of bounded rationality. This notion is integrated by acknowledging that different persons are bounded in different ways, and consequently, they have different preferences characterizing their information processing behaviors. To that extent, it would seem relevant to integrate notions of emotions in leaders, in order to describe their information processing preferences. This would be different from organizational emotions, which we argue, is an organizational level phenomenon. As argued above, organizational emotions are also influenced by individual's perceptions, and this would then be the focus of this conceptual distinction. Another aspect of emotion research, which would seem relevant to integrate into leadership, is the idea of emotional intelligence. Emotional intelligence relates to being able to identify, understand, process, and influence one's own emotions and those of others, in order to guide feeling, thinking, and action (Mayer & Salovay, 1997).

7. INFORMING THE THEORY OF ORGANIZATIONAL DESIGN

Conceptualizing psychological climate as affective events, which influence emotions and thereby, employees' information processing behaviors, provides an explanation for understanding information processing in an organizational context. Psychological climate constitutes the emotional boundedness of human behavior, a particular type of boundedness, which has previously been known to influence human information processing and which, therefore, should be examined in addition to the bounded rationality aspects of employee behavior. Our framework enables a more integrated understanding of the human processes, underlying much organizational behavior. This integrated understanding bridges, simultaneously, individual and organizational levels of analysis.

Not only does this theoretical framework contribute to our overall understanding of how organizations function, it is also a contribution to climate research. In particular, this contribution is an increased understanding of how organizational variables (climate) influence human processes (information processing and decision making). By integrating our model into the multicontingency model of organization design, we make a preliminary link between individual employee behavior and overall organization design.

8. INFORMING PRACTICE

We believe that our view of psychological climate enables us to provide concrete advice on how climate can be managed, because it provides a more explicit understanding of how climates affect individual behavior.

Specifically, we believe that the main role of a leader is to support and complement the psychological climate of the organization. This leader-role is different than what is commonly assumed in climate research, where the leader is often portrayed as mainly responsible for formulating and/or influencing the climate towards a particular "one best" type. In our view, there is no "one best" type of climate. Different climates will lead to different types of emotional boundedness in employees' information processing. The way in which the leader can support or complement the climate is through his or her leadership style, particularly as it relates to information processing and decision making. For instance, the leader may decide that it is necessary to "buffer" employees who are not able to deal with large amounts of new information, through a reduced focus on the long term, and/or in terms of taking on more decision making responsibility himself or herself. To manage this job well requires that the leader accurately perceives the climate. A leader's perception of the climate is dependent not only on his or her understanding of how the current climate is. Yet, because the climate is reflective of affective events, which include organizational variables such as strategy and technology, it is also important that the leader is aware of how his or her actions relating to the overall organization are likely to indirectly influence the climate..

Finally, to complement the climate well requires that the manager is aware of his or her own leadership style and his/her consequent information processing and decision making biases.

9. CONCLUSION

We have developed the notions of affective events and organizational emotions and integrated these concepts into previous work on psychological climate, as represented in the multicontingency model of organization design.

In particular, we have argued that individual emotions function as a mediator of information processing and decision making behaviors. Thus, emotions constitute a rational emotionality, which is highly relevant for employees' information processing behaviors. Integrating notions of affective events and emotions into the multicontingency model has enabled us to understand more so, what is in the black box that we have thought of, as connecting psychological climate with employee behaviors. This understanding has enabled us to demonstrate with more rigor, how and why climate influences employees' information processing behaviors.

We believe this new understanding of the notion of psychological climate has wide theoretical, as well as managerial implications, and we believe that future research should study the relationship between climate and organization design in more detail. As a first step in this regard, we are currently studying the assumption that the leader's role in managing psychological climate is to complement employee emotions, through his or her own leadership style (Hakonsson et al., 2007). To test the model further will require that we gather data systematically related to emotions. We believe that the four-quadrant model provides an excellent framework for such data gathering and empirical analysis.

REFERENCES

Adophs, R. and Damasio, A., 2001, The interaction of affect and cognition: A neurobiological perspective, In Forgas (Ed.) *The handbook of affect and social cognition*, Mahwah, NJ, Lawrence Erlbaum Associates, Inc., 27-49.

Arrow, K., 1974, *The Limit of Organization*, New York: W. W. Boston.

Ashby, W. R., 1956, *Introduction to Cybernetics,* London, Methuen.

Averill, JR., 1975, A semantic atlas of emotional concepts, JSAS, *Catalog of Selected Documents in Psychology*, **5** (421): 330.

Barsade, S. G., 2002, The ripple effect: Emotional contagion in groups, *Administrative Science Quarterly,* **47**.

Barsade, S. G., & Gibson, D., 1998, Group emotion: A view from top and bottom, In D. Gruenfeld, B. Mannix, And M. Neale (eds.) *Research in managing groups and teams*, Stamford, CT, JAI Press, 81-102.

Basch, J. and Fischer, C. D., 2000, Affective events-emotions matrix: A classification of work events and associated emotions, *Emotions in the Workplace, Research, Theory, and Practice*, Ashkanasy, Härtel and Zerbe (Eds.)Quorum Books, Westport, 36-48.

Bechera, A, Damasio, A. R. (2005): The somatic marker hypothesis: A neural theory of economic decision. *Games and Economic Behavior,*. **52** (2): 336-372

Bless, H., 2000, The interplay of affect and cognition: The mediating role of general knowledge structures, In J. P. Forgas (Ed.), *Feeling and thinking: The role of affect in social cognition*, New York, Cambridge University Press, 201-222.

Brown, R. B. and Brooks, I. (2002): Emotion at work. Identifying the emotional climate of night nursing. *Journal of Management in Medicine*, **16**,(5): 327-344

Burton, R., DeSanctis, G., Obel, B., 2006, *Organizational Design: A Step by Step Approach.* Cambridge University Press.

Burton, R. and Obel, B., 2004, *Strategic Organizational Diagnosis and Design*: The Dynamics of Fit. Dordrecht: Kluwer Academic Publishers.

Charland, L. C., 1997, Reconciling cognitive and perceptual theories of Emotion: A representational proposal, *Philosophy of Science,* **64**(4): 555-579.

Commons, J. R., 1934, *Institutional Economics: Its Place in Political Economy*, Mac Millan, New York.

Conlisk, J., 1996, Why Bounded Rationality? *Journal of Economic Literature,* **31**: 669-700.

Damasio, A., Everitt, B.J., and Bishop, D., 1996, The Somatic Marker Hypothesis and the Possible functions of the Prefrontal Cortex. Philosophical Transactions: *Biological Sciences,* **351** (1346): 1413-1420.

Damasio, H., Grabowski, T. Frank, Galaburda, A. M., Damasio, A. R., 1994, The Return of Phineas Gage: Clues About the Brain from The Skull of a Famous Patient. *Science, New Series,* **264** (5162): 1102-1105.

Denison, D. R., 1996, What is the difference between organizational culture and organizational climate? A Native's point of view on a Decade of Paradigm Wars. *Academy of Management Review,* **21**(3): 619-65.

Donaldson, L., 2001, *The Contingency Theory of Organizations*, Thousand Oaks, CA: Sage Publications.

Fiedler, K., 2000, Towards an integrative account of affect and cognition phenomena using BIAS computer algorithm. In J. P. Forgas (Ed.) *Feeling and thinking: The role of affect in social cognition*, New York: Cambridge University Press, 223-252.

Fischer, C. D., 2000, Mood and emotions while working: missing pieces of job satisfaction. *Journal of Organizational Behavior,* **21**: 185-202.

Fischer, C. D. and Ashkanasy, N. M., 2000, The Emerging Role of Emotions in Work Life: An Introduction, *Journal of Organizational Behavior,* Special Issue: *Emotions in Organization,* **21**(2): 123-129.

Forgas, J. P., 1995, Mood and judgment: the Affect Infusion Model. *Psychological Bulletin,* **117**: 39-66.

Forgas, J. P., and George, J. M., 2001, *Organizational Behavior and Human Decision Processes,* **86** (1): 3-34.

Galbraith, J., 1974, *Organization Design*, An Information Processing View. Interfaces, **4** (3).

George, J. M., 1990, Personality, affect, and behaviour in groups. *Journal of Applied Psychology*, **75**(2): 107-116.

George, J. M., 1992, The role of personality in organizational life: Issues and evidence. *Journal of Management,* **18**: 185-210.

Glick, W. H., 1985, Conceptualizing and Measuring Organizational and Psychological Climate: Pitfalls in Multilevel Research. Academy of Management Review, **10** (3): 601-616

Haakonsson, D. D., Burton, R. M.; Obel, B. and Lauridsen, J., 2007, How misfits between Climate and Leadership Style affect Performance, *Working Paper.*

Hilgaard, E., 1980, The trilogy of mind: Cognition, Affection, and Conation. *Journal of the History of the Behavioral Sciences*, **16** (2): 107-117.

Huy, Q. N., 2002, Emotion Management to Facilitate Strategic Change and Innovation: How Emotional Balancing and Emotional Capability Work Together, *Emotions in Organizational behaviour*, Härtel, Zerbe and Ashkanasy (eds.), Lawrence Erlbaum Associates, Mahwah, New Jersey, 295-316.

James, L. R., and Jones, A. P., 1974, *Organizational Climate:* A Review of Theory and Research, Psychological Bulletin, **81**(12): 1096-1112.

Kaufmann, B. E., 1999, Emotional arousal as a source of bounded rationality, *Journal of Economic Behavior & Organization.* **38** (2): 135-144.

Kelly, J. & Barsade, S., 2001, Moods and emotions in small groups and work teams, *Organizational Behavior and Human Decision Processes*, **86**: 99-130.

Klaaren, K. J,. Hodges, S. D. and Wilson, T. D., 1994, The role of affective expectations in subjective experience and decision-making, *Social Cognition,* **12** (2): 77-101.

Koys, D. J. and DeCotiis, A., 1991, Inductive Measures of Psychological Climate. *Human Relations*, **44** (3): 265-285.

Larsen, R. J. and Diener, E., 1992, Promises and problems with the circumplex model of emotions, *Review of Personality and Social Psychology,* Clark, M. S., **13**: 25-59.

Lazarus, R. S., 1993, *Emotion and Adaptation.* New York: Oxford U-Press

Lazarus, R. S., 1982, Thoughts on the Relations Between Emotion an Cognition, *American Psychologist*, **37** (9): 1019-1024.

Lazarus, R. S., 1991, Emotion and adaptation. New York: Oxford University Press.

LeDoux, J. E., 1995, Emotion: Clues from the brain, *Annual review of psychology*, **46**: 209-30.

Lewin, K., 1951, Field Theory in Social Sciences. New York: Harper & Row.

Mayer, J. D. and Salovey, P., 1997, What is emotional intelligence? In P. Salovay & D. J. Sluyter, *Emotional development and emotional intelligence: Educational implications*, New York: Basic Books, 3-34.

McDermott, 2004, The Feeling of Rationality: The Meaning of Neuroscientific Advances for Political Science, *Perspectives on Politics,* **2** (4): 691-706.

Oatley, K., 1992, Human emotions: function and dysfunction. *Annual Review of Psychology*, **43**: 55-85.

Patterson, M. G., West, M. A., Shackleton, V. J., Dawson, J. F., Lawthom, R., Maitlis, S., Robinson, D. L., Wallace, A. M., 2005, Validating the organizational climate measure: Links to managerial practices, productivity and innovation, *Journal of Organizational Behavior*, **26**: 379-408.

Pirola-Merlo, Härtel, A., Mann, C., Hirst, G., 2002, How Affective Events and Affective Climate relate to Work-Related Satisfaction in R&D Teams. *Leadership Quarterly*, **13**: 561-581.

Plutchik, R., 1994, The psychology and Biology of Emotions. Harper-Collins, New York.

Schneider, B. (Ed.), 1990, Organizational Climate and Culture. Jossey-Bass, San Francisco.

Schneider, B. 1975, Organizational Climates: an essay. *Personnel Psychology*, **36**: 19-36.

Simon, H. A., 1956, *Administrative Behavior,* New York: Free Press.

Simon, H. A., 1982, Models of bounded rationality, MIT Press, Cambridge, MA, **2**.

Weiss, H. M. and Cropanzano, R., 1996, Affective Events Theory: A theoretical discussion of the structure, causes and consequences of affective experiences at work, *Organizational Behavior*, **18**: 1-74.

Woodman, R. W. and King, D. C., 1978, Organizational Climate: Science or Folklore? *Academy of Management Review.*

Zajonc, R.B., 1980, Feeling and thinking: Preferences need no inferences, *American Psychologist*, **35**:151-175.

Zammuto, R. F. and Krakower, J. Y., 1991, Quantitative and Qualitative Studies in Organizational Culture, Research in *Organizational Change and Development,* **5**: 83-11.

Chapter 5

ORGANIZING FOR ASYMMETRIC COLLABORATION

Jørn Flohr Nielsen[1] and Henrik Bendixen Sørensen[2]
[1]*University of Aarhus, Denmark, School of Economics and Management, University of Aarhus, Building 322, 8000 Aarhus C, Denmark;* [2]*University of Aarhus, Denmark, Department of Management;* [3]*University of Aarhus, Building 322, 8000 Aarhus C, Denmark*

Abstract: The vision of new organizational forms consists of less-organized networks and alliances between organizations, in which collaborative capabilities are assumed to be crucial (Miles et al., 2005). The path to such new forms may go through fragile cooperative efforts. Despite the good will of many participants and optimistic plans for cooperation between equals there are still poorly understood barriers, and attempts at interorganizational cooperation may lead to frustration. It is too often assumed that the parties are equally eager, trusting, and dependent or at least have some symmetry in how they meet each other. On the contrary, we assume that asymmetry is both important and normal; moreover, asymmetry should be considered to be more complex than economists indicate with their concept of asymmetric information. Thus, the aim of the paper is to explore how asymmetries related to partners' different motives and different situational factors appear in an interorganizational setting. We classify interfaces according to the symmetry/asymmetry in the respective parent organizations' resources, commitment, and control of representatives and indicate how classification schemes can be used to support better diagnosis and as a starting point for more detailed analysis, including interpersonal and processual perspectives, Furthermore, we propose how different situations need different kinds of change interventions. Although including asymmetries in interorganizational analysis does add more complexity to already complex models, we claim that our approach has practical implications: it offers rather simple diagnostic cues to change agents that are coping with the barriers to management and collaboration among loosely coupled units.

Key words: Alliance, asymmetry, collaboration, interface, inter-organizational relationships, network.

R.M. Burton et al. (eds.), *Designing Organizations*, doi: 10.1007/978-0-387-77776-4_5,

1. INTRODUCTION

Understanding cooperative interorganizational relationships (IORs) has become a major research area and item on the business agenda. Common to all interorganizational relationships is that much effort, both in terms of research and on the part of involved companies, has been devoted to analyzing the conditions for company participation in them. Researchers have identified various theoretical approaches to understanding IORs, various coordination mechanisms used to sustain interfirm cooperation, and various discrete network forms (Nohira, 1992; Powell and Smith-Doerr, 1994; Grandori and Soda, 1995; Oliver and Ebers, 1998)

Other researchers stress that both the initial conditions for and learning processes of such alliances are important in determining that the alliances evolve positively over time (cf. Doz, 1996). Underlying this point of view is the belief of many researchers and companies that a symmetrical alliance, in which the companies balance each other as equally as possible, best ensures progress. Ring and Van de Ven (1994) have focused extensively on how IORs emerge, grow, and evolve over time, while still others have developed frameworks describing how companies establish their interorganizational relationships (cf. Lorange and Roos, 1993; Sørensen, 1993).

Many of these efforts are aimed at finding the best conditions for the establishment of and cooperation in interorganizational relationships; a main argument is that as collaboration evolves, symmetries form between the cooperating companies and that this is in the best interests of the cooperation. Contrary to that point of view, this paper argues that asymmetries are at least as important to the evolving alliance as symmetries are. Some degree of complementarity is the raison d'être of collaboration and is closely related to some dimensions of asymmetry. But unlike symmetries, asymmetries may both help an alliance evolve, and block its evolution as they are connected to the fragility of relationships. Our focus is on different perspectives on asymmetries, such as independent asymmetries of resources and horizons, and concurrent asymmetries of both resources and horizons. These different types of asymmetries lead to different problems and may call for different organizational interventions. The aim of the paper is to explore how asymmetries related to partners' different motives and different situational factors appear in an interorganizational setting.

Thus, this paper analyzes the organizing of the linkage between collaborating organizations with asymmetric characteristics. It is a theoretical paper built on the idea that micro-level analyses are essential for 'unbundling' the building blocks of interface design and understanding organization design.

First, we briefly review central parts of the literature on interorganizational relationships, paying special attention to the treatment of asymmetries. Second, we introduce our conceptual framework, focusing on a taxonomy of the interorganizational linkages and interfaces, and based on four propositions concerning the parties' asymmetric incentives and situations. This is a starting point for discussing processes: how interorganizational linkages emerge, evolve, and dissolve. Third, we discuss the implications of our approach, stressing practical planned change perspectives on coping with the barriers to the management of and collaboration among loosely coupled units. In conclusion, we suggest that future empirical research could use our micro-level concepts as a bridge to the analysis of interorganizational dynamics and planned change.

2. PERSPECTIVES ON ASYMMETRIC ORGANIZATIONAL RELATIONSHIPS

A vision of new organizational forms that rely on collaborative efforts has recently been articulated by Miles et al. (2005). However, the authors are themselves aware of the barriers that may hinder the development of collaborative capabilities, as over the years several research streams have contributed by fragments to the building of a complex picture of interorganizational relationships.

Institutional economists have analyzed the issue in terms of a comparison between alternative transactions and governance structures (i.e., markets, hierarchies, and hybrids). If neither the market nor the organizational hierarchy is feasible and if transactions are frequent and well understood, some degree of collaboration is an efficient governance structure (Williamson, 1979). Some management researchers have further analyzed the relationships from an organizational economics viewpoint (Barney and Ouchi, 1986), while lawyers have focused on the contract that should regulate the relationship (Macneil, 1980). Organizational sociologists have attempted to explain how contingency factors are associated with the formation and structure of cooperative relationships (cf. Oliver, 1990).

Most researchers in these streams have ignored process (Ring and Van de Ven, 1994) and it is often implicitly assumed that there will inevitably be some symmetry in how the parties meet each other. However, asymmetries have not been totally neglected. Asymmetric information as a concept is perceived by economists as playing a crucial role in the analysis of adverse selection problems in interfirm collaboration (Reuer and Koza, 2000). Asymmetries involved in collaboration between large and small organizations have been related to fragile relationships (Doz, 1988; Khanna,

Gulati, and Nohria, 1998). Research that pays more attention to the dynamics of interfirm collaboration seems to focus more on issues of asymmetry as well. Regarding the processes of negotiation, commitment, and implementation involved in cooperation towards the development of interorganizational relationships, Ring and Van de Ven (1994) stress the importance and difficulty of "fair dealing." Furthermore, it is difficult to perceive convergent interests if the organizations involved are under different competitive pressures to learn (Khanna, Gulati, and Nohria, 1998; Ring et al., 2005).

Asymmetries are in this paper used to label inequalities and differences in several aspects of inter-organizational relationships. Basically, it is an extension of the economists' notion of asymmetric information of agents in the market. Alliance partners – or potential alliance partners - have different information, but asymmetries are also related to different motives and incentives which in turn can be traced back to different resources and company size, where larger companies may have greater bargaining power than smaller firms. The asymmetries are expected to be reflected in asymmetric needs for control of the interface. The organizing of the interface and in turn the behavior of its participants is constrained by these specific contextual factors.

ome guidelines for the design of interorganizational relationships can be found in the literature. A visible and formal point of departure in interorganizational relationships is the contract. In establishing partnerships between large and small organizations in a business context, both parties have interests in formalized contracts. However, a contract governs only a small part of an organization's activities. In a vertical relationship, contracts are restricted to clarifying the conditions of transactions, and there will be few formal guidelines regarding organization *per se* (Grandori and Soda, 1995). In a horizontal relationship concerning R&D and technological cooperation, there will also be a low degree of bureaucratization, in accordance with traditional design theory (Kreiner and Schultz, 1993; Grandori and Soda, 1995).

Fewer guidelines can be found concerning the interventions involved in the processes of forming and changing alliances and networks. From an organizational development perspective, there are few references to how to handle the fragility inherent in collaborative relationships as underorganized systems or to how to facilitate organizational learning (Cummings and Worley, 2005). More specific guidelines apparently require that distinctions be made between different situations.

3. CONCEPTUAL FRAMEWORK: TOWARDS A TAXONOMY

To focus on the interface is to focus on the linkage between parties (Brown, 1983). We regard *cooperation* as any joint effort of some duration in which two or more parties deliver some resources, tangible or intangible, while an *interface* can be described as (1) a number of people (at least one from each parent organization) who (2) work together over a period of time, and accordingly (3) develop a set of cooperative norms and/or rules that can be considered to comprise a social system or organization in its own right. Even an entire network can be considered as a single organization (Thorelli, 1986). However, the interface concept stresses a particular important focus; a schematic of our point of view is depicted in Figure 1.

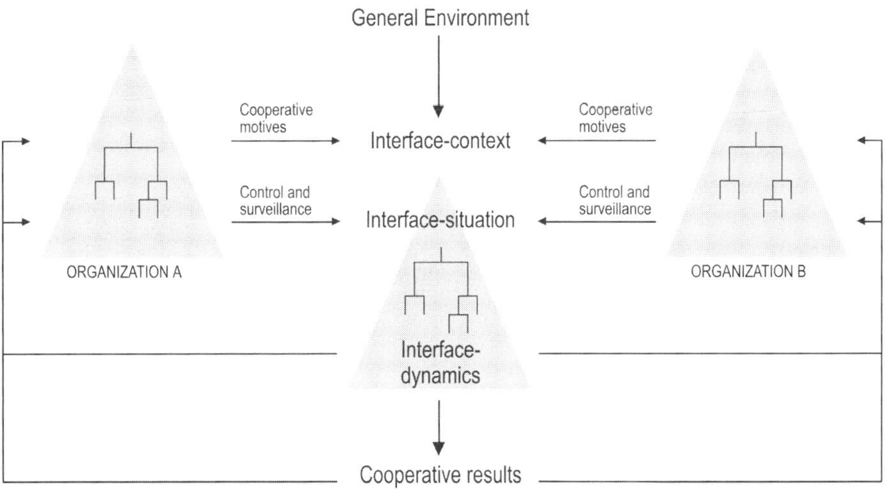

Figure 1. Connections between interface and parent organizations

As with all other organizations, the interface is dependent on its context, which consists of the general environmental conditions and the two parent organizations. The motives underlying the parent organizations' wish to cooperate are accordingly an integral part of the *interface context*. Given the context, the parent organizations will employ mechanisms for controlling and monitoring the decisions and developments in the interface. These mechanisms, together with the interface context, constitute the *interface situation*: the conditions that already confront the representatives before the cooperative work begins. This is our overall structural perspective. When the "real work" begins, the representatives interpret the situation and respond to the perceived conditions when cooperating. It is the interface behavior, the *interface dynamics*, that completes the interface organization, leading to the cooperative results and the evolution or dissolution of the relationship. Experience gained from this development process may modify the parent organizations' initial motives and control mechanisms. Thus, the perspective gradually shifts from a focus on impersonal structure to a focus on process and persons. We claim that this way of looking at interfaces not only applies to cooperation between organizations, but with minor modifications, also to situations in which one or both parties are individuals or groups inside a bigger organization. In fact, the concept of organizational interfaces may lead to useful intra–interorganizational analogies when conflict management and intergroup techniques are considered (Brown, 1983).

Our focus on the interface provides an approach that are intended to take advantage of the theories of organization and organization change. Thus, parent organizations are mainly treated as parts of the context although we recognize the importance of an inside-out-look on organizational boundaries and how promising developments in these theories include the boundary conceptions of efficiency, power, competence, and identity (Santos & Eisenhardt, 2005).

Motives and incentives of parent organizations

Reviewing the literature on interorganizational relationships and new organizational forms reveals several criteria for developing a taxonomy. In our close-up of asymmetries at the interface we emphasize asymmetric incentives, which are derived from the different resources, sizes, and strategies of the parent organizations. The organization of an interface is of course dependent on its context, and successful organizing may follow rules similar to those of general contingency theory. We assume that uncertainty, interdependence, and outside control are important factors that constitute the near environment with which the interface has to cope.

It has to be stressed, however, that this view is only a snapshot of initial factors that may have some determining influence. As soon as contacts are established, these factors may have a decreasing unidirectional impact on the organization of the interface. Influential actors in the interface will try to reduce uncertainty, modify interdependencies, and even struggle for autonomy.

It is our claim that asymmetries of the parent organizations' motives for joining an interface are generally central to any understanding of interorganizational relationships. These asymmetries are often derived from differences in size and resources; firms thus have asymmetric incentives to invest in partnerships, a fact that may become even clearer as an alliance evolves (Khanna, Gulati, and Nohria, 1998).

Thus, to distinguish between different interface arrangements, we first consider the motives of the parties—their need for cooperation and their commitment to cooperation—and make simple dichotomizations in both dimensions. The first class, *need for cooperation*, consists of one partner choosing to make a voluntary approach to the other: the organization has no problems, but sees a possible advantage in some kind of combined effort with another organization. The other class consists of situations in which the organization is destitute and its survival depends on a cooperative arrangement. The need for resources is "the most important factor that stimulates interorganizational coordination" (Van de Ven and Walker, 1984, p. 617).

The *commitment to cooperation* reflects the intended time span of the arrangement, a source of asymmetry also thought to be important by Khanna, Gulati, and Nohria (1998). We differentiate between the short term and the long term in this regard. This dichotomy cannot only be developed around a calendar or timetable, but must rather be seen as distinguishing a wish for cooperation on a single known project from a wish to cooperate intimately on many (and possibly unknown) future projects.

Combining the two dichotomies gives four situations that can be illustrated as follows: (1) Strong organizations seeking short-term encounters with a prospective partner can be characterized as *seeking a venture*. There are—at least at the beginning—no intentions of giving up autonomy. (2) Strong organizations seeking a long-term partnership can best be described as *seeking marriage*. (3) Destitute organizations seeking short-term encounters but that have faith in their own long-term abilities accordingly seek a partner that can act as "booster" and supply some badly needed energy. These organizations can be characterized as *seeking revival*. (4) Destitute organizations seeking long-term partnerships are *seeking shelter* from a world in which they are unable to cope. They look for a partner that can put the firm's assets to better use.

When there are two parties and each party is faced with any of the four identified motives, we find 16 possibilities of paired motives of which six are asymmetric. The possible combinations are presented in Figure 2. These asymmetries are assumed to have obvious implications.

Asymmetric horizons entail a need for negotiation. Ring and Van de Ven (1994) refer to the central (initiating) stage in the development of interorganizational relationships as a negotiating stage. If the prospects of the cooperative effort are promising, the partners will probably agree to accept the briefest commitment as an experiment. However, the asymmetry is not necessarily recognized (Khanna, Gulati, and Nohria, 1998) and more clarification may be needed. If both parties are unaware of the differences, they are in for a surprise that can endanger the project. If only one of them is aware of the differences, there is also latitude for opportunistic behavior.

B's MOTIVES: seeking ... **A's MOTIVES:** seeking ...	**VENTURE** (voluntary, short term)	**MARRIAGE** (voluntary, long term)	**REVIVAL** (necessary, short term)	**SHELTER** (necessary, long term)
VENTURE (voluntary, short term)				
MARRIAGE (voluntary, long term)	Asymmetric time horizon			
REVIVAL (necessary, short term)	Asymmetric needs	Asymmetric time horizon AND needs		
SHELTER (necessary, long term)	Asymmetric time horizon AND needs	Asymmetric needs	Asymmetric time horizon	

Figure 2. Asymmetric interface contexts

Asymmetric horizons can be illustrated by considering the *aim* of interfirm development activities. If one of two parent organizations forming an interorganizational relationship is concerned with developing new technology while the other is concerned with developing markets for an existing technology, asymmetric time horizons will arise. These may also arise if one of the partners is entering into the relationship with the aim of doing basic research while the other wants applied research. According to Gupta and Singh (1990), asymmetric horizons can also arise if one company in a collaboration is engaged in upstream activities (e.g., research) while the other is engaged in downstream ones (e.g., marketing and distribution). This situation likely occurs frequently, because upstream activities are often associated with small flexible companies and downstream activities with large bureaucratic companies, and in cooperation between them an organizational barrier will arise (Miles et al., 2005)

With *asymmetric resource bases* the partner with the most resources will tend to acquire some dominance in the cooperative arrangement. In line with Pfeffer and Salancik (1978), we would expect resource dependence to lead to centralization, and probably with the resource-strong party's representative occupying the central position. *Double asymmetry* will involve both of the aforementioned consequences: the commitment will have to be negotiated, and a dominant partner may well decide the terms. Eventually, dominance problems have to be resolved. Underlying these organizational problems is the problem of resource supply: obviously, an interface between two resource-rich partners will have better possibilities of acquiring needed external resources.

To summarize, we put forward the following two propositions regarding the influence of contextual factors:

Proposition 1:

Asymmetric resources in parent organizations lead to pressure favoring dominance by the resource-rich party's representatives in the interface.

Proposition 2:

Asymmetric time horizons in parent organizations lead to conflicts regarding the commitments and time frames of the interface.

Control and surveillance

In the literature on interorganizational relationships, the parent organizations are normally treated as wholes. Notions such as "strategic intent" indicate that even a large organization is treated as an individual and (possibly) rational actor; one consequence of this is a partial view of the interaction across organizational boundaries.

In this section we will stress the relationship between the parent organizations and their representatives in the interface. These "boundary spanners" are often powerful employees conferred with considerable discretion, due to their important information-processing functions (Thompson, 1967; Aldrich and Herker, 1977). For example, an R&D manager in a large firm stresses the role of the representatives and demands systematic and effective personalities (Sørensen, 1993).

In the general struggle for autonomy, however, any parent organization inevitably possesses some resources that are considered critical. If a private firm has vulnerable resources, strategic alliances are not easily formed and core competencies may to some degree be excluded from any cooperation that does arise. Similarly, public organizations may want to protect their legitimacy or funds. This means that such a parent organization may want to limit the boundary spanner's discretion, and the traditional means to this end is a set of formalized rules. The coupling between parent organization and interface then becomes tight, and boundary spanners are only allowed to act within narrow limits. For example, in R&D consortia each interface may comprise a steering committee containing members drawn from various management levels of all interacting parent organizations; in this way, a tight coupling will be secured between the parent organizations and the interface (Sørensen, 1993).

This, of course, will have a pronounced effect on the boundary spanner's behavior in the interface, and hence on the development of the cooperative effort between the two parent organizations. In abstract terms, part–whole considerations and the concepts of tight versus loose coupling combine to form a general picture (Astley and Van de Ven, 1981; Weick, 1979), for example, by indicating that tight coupling inside an interface might very well be connected to loose parent organization–interface coupling.

In seeking a pattern in the parent organizations' needs for control over the interface, we start by distinguishing between the tightness of the coupling and the methods employed in the actual coupling.

As the *felt need for protection* grows, tightness of coupling is assumed to be more and more conspicuous. The need for protection stems from a range of sources, and we may assume that the felt need for protection will grow as (1) dependence on the other party increases, (2) the extent of the commitment increases, and (3) the contribution made is increasingly regarded as a core resource.

The more *well-defined and tangible* the exchanged contributions, the more obvious is the use of formalized control systems. The coupling methods are apt to vary between quantitative and qualitative methods as the exchange of contributions becomes more intangible. As long as the contributions are material and well defined, it is easy to develop quantitative plans and programs for the work in the interface. But if the transaction is a service (by definition intangible) and thus difficult to standardize, concepts in the service management literature become useful in analyzing the interface, i.e., stressing the frontline functions, socializing, decentralizing, and developing performance measures such as service quality assessment and "balanced scorecards." To manage intangible services, traditional budgeting and accounting should be supplemented with other more qualitative performance controls based on such measures.

These points of view are summarized in Figure 3, which shows how control and surveillance are supposed to change with changes in protection need and contribution type.

FELT NEED FOR PROTECTION	TYPE OF INTERCHANGED RESOURCES	
	TANGIBLE	INTANGIBLE
LOW FELT NEED	Rudimentary plans and programs	Goals supplemented by time- and cost-limits
HIGH FELT NEED	Much planning, programming and policies	Goals and limits Organizational values Highly socialized Boundary-spanners

Figure 3. Types of control between parent organization and interface

The most tangible resources are materials while the most intangible one is knowledge, and the felt need for protection is either low or high as the resources at stake are either common to many or are core resources of the organization. The types of control presented in Figure 3 are referred to according to this understanding.

The aforementioned four types of control are obviously connected to only one party in a given interface. If the other party is taken into account there are 16 combinations, i.e., 16 different interface situations, but again we are paying special attention to the asymmetric situations. In asymmetric cases the interface is bound to begin with cooperative work that faces a latent initial conflict, i.e., conflict as to the extent of control and/or degree of formality.

Take, for example, a case in which the management of parent organization A feels that it is sharing some core competence with parent organization B, which regards the exchange as trivial. Then it is to be expected that A will exert quite a lot of control to protect itself from exploitation, while B will rely on only a few controls to keep things running. If B does not recognize A's need, then there will be plenty of opportunities for alienation and distrust.

Or if A delivers tangible, easily measured resources to the interface while B delivers "brain work," this can easily result in a cultural confrontation. A's representatives are accustomed to a concrete, formalized, quantitative planning approach, while B's representatives normally work in surroundings characterized by abstract thinking and informal behavior control. These differences in terms of abstraction level are conducive to misunderstandings and communication problems.

To summarize, we put forward the following two propositions:

Proposition 3:

Different needs for protection may lead to distrust and conflict between the representatives.

Proposition 4:

Different abstraction levels may lead to communication problems between representatives.

The four propositions articulated thus far supplement more traditional contingency views. Considering the interface as an organization in its own right means that it should be organized in a way that is consistent at least with its size, technology, "crew," and environment. The tasks required for such organizing are poorly understood if they are regarded as simply the autonomous choices of rational actors (Astley and Van de Ven, 1981). Thus, interdependency can be both the result of choice and, as Thompson (1967) saw it, a constraint on practical organizing. This becomes clear when we consider different ways to organize interfaces and intervene in planned change. The options range from joint ventures and formalized networks to rather informal contacts. Many of these design options involve problems of information processing, differentiation, and conflict resolution that contingency theorists treated long ago (Thompson, 1967; Lawrence and Lorsch, 1967; Galbraith, 1977). Without further commenting on the usefulness of contingency theory, suffice it to say that the only major difference between interfaces and independent organizations is that the interface has direct access to an important "environmental" factor: the parent organizations. However, even this perspective had already been recognized in ordinary organizational theory in Pfeffer and Salancik's (1978) views on resource dependency.

4. INTERFACE DYNAMICS IN DIFFERENT SITUATIONS

We are now able to construct a more comprehensive table based on all four propositions (Figure 4); this is the point of departure for a more dynamic perspective. The 16 cells in the table present the combined consequences of asymmetry, in terms of both context and control, from the parent organization. It appears that all asymmetrical situations are prone to meeting with some kind of initial conflict. This, in turn, will call for managerial remedies, which will differ according to the situational factors.

If the two parent organizations are honest in articulating their desire to cooperate, it is reasonable to expect that asymmetrical time horizons may limit the development of further collaboration or even lead to a breakdown, unless one of the parties changes its commitment. It may also be expected that the partner with the shortest time horizon will "win"—unless there is a strong dependence, which will increase the probability that the stronger partner's view will come out as the winner. The managerial consequence is that both early diagnosis and the involvement of people who can commit/uncommit the parent organizations are important.

The managerial remedy in situations where one partner is prone to dominate the other is somewhat like the one mentioned above: to give up (part of) the organization's autonomy is a matter for the high-level management to decide. Often, parent organizations need to have high-level managers as negotiators in order to give up even a small part of their autonomy (Sørensen, 1993).

Generally speaking, asymmetrical context can thus only be expected to develop into a productive cooperative effort if diagnosis of asymmetry is made early on, conflict does not develop into a dysfunctional level, and upper management is able to settle for a common (but maybe temporary) motivation.

CONTROL AND SURVEILLANCE: CONTEXT:	SYMMETRICAL CONTROL	ASYMMETRICAL EXTENT OF CONTROL *proposition 3*	ASYMMETRICAL FORMALIZATION OF CONTROL *proposition 4*	ASYMMETRICAL EXTENT AND FORMALIZATION OF CONTROL *propositions 3 & 4*
SYMMETRICAL CONTEXT	No situational problems	Distrust	Communication problems	Distrust Communication problems
ASSYMMETRICAL RESOURCES *proposition 1*	Dominance problems	Distrust Dominance problems	Communication problems Dominance problems	Distrust Communication problems Dominance problems
ASSYMMETRICAL HORIZONS *proposition 2*	Commitment problems	Distrust Commitment problems	Communication problems Commitment problems	Distrust Communication problems Commitment problems
ASSYMMETRICAL RESOURCES AND HORIZONS *propositions 1 & 2*	Dominance problems Commitment problems	Distrust Dominance problems Commitment problems	Communication problems Dominance problems Commitment problems	Distrust Communication problems Dominance problems Commitment problems

Figure 4. Situational consequences of different interface contexts

Proposition 5:

When asymmetric contexts do exist, the path to the next stages of collaboration depends on more clarifying/structuring organizational interventions.

Further development into less organized, deliberate forms of collaboration may be difficult because of the organizational, institutional, social, philosophical, and conceptual barriers identified by Miles et al. (2005). Asymmetries make it more difficult to overcome these barriers.

Asymmetrical motives or context reflect asymmetrical stakes *outside* the interface, which implies that such conflicts ought to be resolved outside the interface as well (i.e., by upper management). Asymmetrical needs for control, on the other hand, partly reflect different stakes *inside* the interface, in which case these conflicts ought to be resolved within the interface.

Different extents of control call for a proactive agenda, in which the parties exhibit their vulnerable spots (assuming honest intentions) in order to make their desires for control understandable.

Asymmetric formalization reflects different degrees of contribution tangibility, and possibly therefore different abstraction levels and communication problems. These may be solved by involving a heterogeneous body of representatives, including people from both parties, representing both high abstraction levels and concrete, action-based experience. To overcome these problems it is probably necessary that those involved in the interface display great interpersonal understanding and responsiveness.

Proposition 6:

When asymmetric formalization occurs, the path to the next stages of collaboration depends on more human process interventions.

It is tempting but too easy to predict that situations with many latent conflict areas will automatically give rise to hostility, and therefore to the eventual collapse of the cooperative arrangement. Although this may be the case, it is necessary to acknowledge that our perspective so far adds up to a rather deterministic prediction. The interface, however, is only partly structured by impersonal factors; other factors reflect the view of upper management, who may well change. Even if interorganizational relationships are more dependent on roles than on persons (Ring and Van de Ven, 1994), all changes will be initiated by the actions and perceptions of the representatives in the interface. People act and interact; organizations do not. Thus, attitudinal barriers to collaboration are very important (Miles et al., 2005), and this is not only a matter of upper managers or boundary spanners. All employees involved in interface contact should often be reminded that collaboration is a good idea (Sørensen, 1993).

Personal factors, then, can at least reinforce or moderate the aforementioned tendencies to conflict.

We expect reinforcement to occur if there is asymmetry and incongruent cognitive maps, for example, if the representatives are molded into a form too close to that of the parent organizations. If the management of one organization feels a great need for control and accordingly elects representatives of "the bookkeeping type," while the other organization stresses flexibility and chooses representatives with disrespect for plans and schemes, the interface is bound to be heading for trouble in terms of communication difficulties and distrust.

On the other hand, we would expect moderation if the personal characteristics of the representatives are such that hidden conflicts are faced early in the process. This may happen if the representatives are adequately socialized in their parent organizations.

Generally speaking, symmetry at the personal level in an interface can greatly help in overcoming barriers. This has been indicated in several recent studies, which stress that cooperation evolves because personal relationships help develop communication, trust, and confidence between the interacting partners (Håkansson, 1989; Thorelli, 1986; Turnbulla and Valla, 1985; Sørensen, 1993; Ring et al., 2005). At the same time, interacting persons may be seduced by their partners (Doz, 1988) into loosening ties to their parent organizations. Asymmetry, on the other hand, may raise or reinforce barriers, and boundary spanners may reinforce cooperative doubts in parent organizations, for example, when they are uncertain of their partner's motives and "hold their cards close to their body" (Sørensen, 1993).

Our perspective implies that an early assessment of the compatibility of the two parent organizations' motives is an important start. If compatibility is found to exist, or can be arrived at, it is time to "organize" the interface. During this phase consistency with important environmental and technological forces could be obtained. In this regard, it is certainly not important that some government-designed standard scheme be followed, for example, as is the case in the Danish Network Programme (Nielsen, 1993).

The fate of an interface organization may be dependent on its abilities both to achieve consistency of motives and to "organize" consistently in cooperation with important impersonal and personal forces. If an interface lacks one or both of these abilities, it is prone to get into difficulties.

If inconsistency of motives is not recognized immediately and the cooperative idea abandoned, the interface is certainly bound for trouble. If its organizing ability is great, it will undergo a series of organizational changes—one for every time an inconsistency crops up. Possible managerial remedies in such situations are what organizational change researchers refer to as "diagnostic arrangements." Some of the driving forces of processes with asymmetric incentives have been described by Khanna, Gulati, and Nohria (1998), who identify three different types of learning processes. First, what is called the "three-legged fallacy" occurs when the partners fail to recognize that they are in a race-to-learn situation at all, and act as if their fates are inextricably tied. Thus both partners maintain their original resource commitments at each stage of the relationship, neither stepping up nor reducing their resource allocation in response to the evolving asymmetries. Second, in the "reluctant looser" scenario the lagging partner fails to reduce its allocation, even though the leading partner has increased its allocation and seems likely to secure its own benefits. Third, in the "hesitant winner" situation, the leading partner fails to capitalize on its learning advantage, even though the lagging partner has reduced its resource commitment to the interorganizational relationship. All three examples represent asymmetries according to ongoing processes in the interorganizational relationship. They stand in contrast to a symmetrical situation in which, for example, the partner that has completed a first stage has to increase its resource allocation while the other partner has to reduce its resource allocation.

As long as motives are consistent, *organizational inability* will only mean that the organizational arrangement is inefficient. Possible remedies for such a situation will be action-planning arrangements. If, however, *both motives and organizing ability are inconsistent*, the interface may develop into a battleground or graveyard, according to the fighting spirit imbedded in the representatives (Brown, 1983).

Proposition 7:

With more asymmetries, more problems will be found and the path to the next stages of collaboration will come to depend on more complex organizational interventions.

It is important to note, however, that our analysis leaves the later stages of cooperation to further research. If cooperation is developed beyond the initial stages, simple contingency views need to be supplemented; at the very least, one must take into account the possibility that situations may change radically during the process.

Processual views not only stress personal factors; they also stress that actions and interactions are highly dependent on earlier experiences in the interface. Any encounter is an event that involves an assessment of the other party: Are transactions efficient and are "fair dealings" possible? Has learning reduced the degree of dependence, and has pressure towards autonomy reasserted itself? Is it becoming desirable to cut bonds? When these questions must be answered and interventions made at later stages, a closer look at the substance—the idea and output of cooperation—is needed.

In sum, the propositions 1, 2, 3, and 4 contains explicit formulation of the expectation of dominance, control, conflicts and communication problems related to the basic taxanomy of asymmetries of the interface contexts. Propostions 5, 6, and 7 add a dynamic view by formulating how asymmetries may become barriers to the development of relationships unless clarifying, human process and broader interventions are used

5. DISCUSSION AND IMPLICATIONS

The reasoning in this theoretical paper is partly based on Danish examples and on results of empirical research found in the international literature. The Danish examples range from R&D and technology collaboration (Sørensen, 1993; Kreiner and Schultz, 1993) and network organizing as part of the Danish Network Programme (Nielsen, 1993) to public available material on small supplier–manufacturer relationships. Our distinctions are not derived from quantitative analysis of empirical data as some organizational taxonomies. In these terms our classification schemes should rather be considered as traditional and conceptually derived typologies (Rich, 1992).

Although some conclusions regarding processes are based mainly on deduction from economic theory (Khanna et al., 1998) or an individual researcher's sense of reality, several problems seem to be substantiated in our sources. Some of the problems seem well documented, both in the sense that they are reported as structural phenomena and that they appear in the process of evolving or reducing collaboration.

Interorganizational cooperation is obviously difficult; furthermore, the problems encountered are different in different relationships and call for different solutions. Even when the conditions for forming a strategic alliance seem obvious, a contingency-based view of the choice of appropriate alliance form is recommended (Lorange and Roos, 1992).

Nevertheless, the management literature treating these issues is often very prescriptive and general, reluctance to give up autonomy being regarded as the enemy in such alliances. This is the point of departure for most prescriptions: success is achieving a more or less formalized interrelationship.

Our own prescriptions are more humble. Although our approach is characterized by a certain simplicity and a touch of mechanistic thinking, some managerial consequences—meant only as indications—have already been indicated. For example, problems related to asymmetrical motives may demand intervention at the top management level outside the interface, while problems related to the asymmetrical control of interfaces may be handled as conflicts inside the interface.

We find that the discussion of contingencies, such as asymmetries, and the focus on boundary spanners as persons are ways of tracing possibilities and diagnosing problems. Words like "obstacles" and "barriers" should be used with caution. A reluctance to give up autonomy is not necessarily dysfunctional: there can be very good reasons for maintaining autonomy, because in any organizational unit a striving for autonomy may be a vehicle for the improvement of goods and services.

To practitioners, whether managers or consultants, the consequence might be better diagnosing based on experience gained from initial encounters. The results of this diagnosing should be a better fit between relevant contingencies and the broad range of available organizational change interventions. How to intervene in the process may be more important than the content of a formal contract or temporary design.

We think that only by understanding the situation better can one hope to use the proper tool-box. If the situation is understood or problems are identified, the next steps may be easier. Perhaps the problem should be handled as an interpersonal conflict or as a communications problem. Perhaps the problem is a fundamental one that can only be solved by involving the top management of the parent organizations. Perhaps the problem is a bureaucratic matter that can be handled by drawing on inspiration from service management literature, or perhaps legal contracting could be the solution.

More specific implications may be evident from the dynamic and planned change perspectives.

The path to the unorganized Utopia goes through organizing. In the initial stages of such organizing, networks and multiorganization systems tend to be underorganized. Planned change interventions may support a process that involves clarifying leadership roles, structuring communication, and specifying responsibilities (Cummings and Worley, 2005). Contrary to other planned change interventions, third parties such as consultants may play a well-defined leadership role in reinforcing the practical organizing; they may even have a role in identifying the persons who can participate in organizing meetings.

In the next stages after relationships are established, it becomes more important to facilitate change. Change agents such as organizational development practitioners may help change the communication pattern among members. Sharing information may be important and third parties may help establish a balance between a well-informed, dominant part and a less-informed part.

Only through counterbalancing identified asymmetries is it likely to be possible to reach a stage at which authorities in parent organizations will rely on self-organizing. However, the refreezing of change efforts should not turn into a dysfunctional autonomy of the interface.

Thus, even when both parties have incentives to learn from a relationship, a learning interface organization does not emerge automatically. An ideal learning organizational structure emphasizing teamwork, lateral channels, and line-crossing work and facilitating the rapid sharing of rich information may be highly sensitive to symmetrical incentives. Asymmetric incentives for learning may not only foster distrust and disagreement as to deadlines; it will also make it difficult to adjust the parent organizations' different routines to suit the relationship. Consequently, there may be strong demands for organizational interventions, and change agents will have to consider using interventions from the organizational change and development toolbox, several of which are relevant to the learning organization (Cummings and Worley, 2005). To develop learning capabilities, techno–structural interventions, such as supporting process-based structure, self-managed teams, and reengineering could be supplemented by human resource management interventions and human process interventions such as team building. Human process interventions, notably third-party conflict resolution, may become especially important in the later stages of alliances.

6. CONCLUSION

The aim of the paper was to explore how asymmetries related to partners' different motives and different situational factors appear in an interorganizational setting.

We argue that asymmetries are at least as important to the evolving alliance as symmetries because some degree of complementarity is the raison d'être of collaboration and is closely related to some dimensions of asymmetry. But unlike symmetries, asymmetries may both help an alliance evolve and block its evolution as they are connected to the fragility of relationships.

We propose classification schemes that use the interface as a starting point for more detailed analysis. This can offer a way to bridge the gap between approaches in which relationships are regarded as individually unique and approaches in which relationships are regarded as all alike. So, our classifications intend to offer a general approach to the study of inter-organizational relationships. Ideally, we think that a sufficient understanding of the interface situation might lead to practical guidelines in the use of interventions, such as conflict management or intergroup techniques. However, a better understanding is our primary aim, not prescription.

The paper focuses on the taxonomy of interorganizational linkages and interfaces and takes as its point of departure that companies participating in interorganizational settings can have different motives, i.e. venture, marriage, revival and shelter.. Further, these asymmetries can emerge, evolve or dissolve the interorganizational setting. If asymmetries arise there is a need for negotiation and if this need is well known, understandable and accepted, the cooperative efforts are promising. If the asymmetries are poorly understood or even unknown, the collaborative setting is endangered. A practical perspective suggests that asymmetries may become barriers to the development of relationships unless clarifying, human process and broader interventions are used

Nevertheless, we find it dangerous to idealize certain forms of cooperation. Organizational costs and behavioral patterns are realities that should be taken into account, without losing the simplifying virtues of proper theory; this is where organizational researchers should be of more help.

REFERENCES

Aldrich, H. and Herker, D., 1977, Boundary Spanning Roles and Organizational Structure, *Academy of Management Review*, **2**: 217–230.

Astley, W. G. and Van de Ven, A. H., 1981, Mapping the Field to Create a Dynamic Perspective on Organization Design and Behavior, In Van de Ven and Joyce (Eds.): *Perspectives on Organization Design and Behavior*, New York: Wiley & Sons.

Barney, J. B. and Ouchi, W. G., 1986, *Organizational Economics*. San Francisco, Jossey-Bass.
Brown, L. D., 1983, *Managing Conflict at Organizational Interface*, Reading, Massachusetts: Addison-Wesley.
Cummings, T. G and Worley, C. G., 2005, *Organization Development and Change*, Mason Ohio, USA: Thomson-South Western.
Doz, Y. L., 1988, Technology Partnerships between Larger and Smaller Firms: Some Critical Issues, *International Studies of Management*, **18**: 31–57.
Doz, Y. L., 1996, The Evolution of Cooperation in Strategic Alliances: Initial conditions or Learning Processes?, *Strategic Management Journal*, **17**: 55–83.
Galbraith, J., 1977, *Organizational Design*, Addison-Wesley, Reading.
Grandori, A. and Soda, G., 1995, Interfirm Networks: Antecedents, Mechanisms and Forms, *Organization Studies*, **16**: 183–214.
Gupta, A. K. and Singh, H., 1990, Exploiting Synergies: External Alliances VS Inter-SBU Coordination, *Strategic Management Society*, Paper, 1-28.
Håkansson, H., 1989, *Corporate Technological Behaviour: Cooperation and Networks,* New York, Routledge.
Khanna, T., Gulati, R., and Nohira N., 1998, The Dynamics of Learning Alliances: Competition, Cooperation and Relative Scope, *Strategic Management Journal*, **19**: 193–210.
Kreiner, K. and Schultz, M., 1993, Informal Collaboration in Research-And-Development – the Formation of Networks Across Organizations, *Organization Studies*, **14**: 189–209.
Lawrence, P. R. and Lorsch, S. W., 1967, Organizations and Environment, Cambridge: Harvard Business School.
Lorange, P. and Roos, J., 1993, *Strategic Alliances—Formation, Implementation and Evolution*, Cambridge, USA, Blackwell.
Macneil, I. R., 1980, *The Social Contract. An inquiry Into Modern Contractual Relations,* New Haven, Yale University Press.
Miles, R. E., Miles, G., and Snow, C. C., 2005, *Collaborative Entrepreneurship: How Communities of Networked Firms Use Continuous Innovation to Create Economic Wealth.* Stanford, CA, Stanford University Press.
Nielsen, K., 1993, *Industrielle netværk*, Herning, Systime/Gad.
Oliver, C., 1990, Determinants of Interorganizational Relationships: Integration and Future Directions, *Academy of Management Review*, **15**: 241–265.
Oliver, A. L. and Ebers, M., 1998, Networking Network Studies: An Analysis of Conceptual Configurations in the Study of Inter-Organizational Relationships, *Organization Studies*, **19**: 549–583.
Nohira, N., 1992, Is a network Perspective a useful way of Studying Organizations?, In Nohira, N. and Eccles, R. G. (Eds.), *Networks and Organizations: Structure, form and action*, Boston MA, Harvard Business School Press, 1–22.
Pfeffer, J. and Salancik, G. R., 1978, *The External Control of Organizations: A Resource Dependence Perspective*, New York, Harper and Row.
Powell, W. W. and Smith-Doerr, L., 1994, Networks and Economic Life, In Smelser, N. J. and Swedberg, R. (Eds.), *Handbook of Economic Sociology*, Princeton, NJ. Princeton University Press, 368–402.
Reuer, J. J. and Koza, M. P, 2000, Asymmetric information and joint venture performance: Theory and evidence for domestic and international joint ventures, *Strategic Management Journal*, **21**: 81–88.
Rich, P., 1992, The Organizational Taxonomy: Definition and Design, *Academy of Management Review*, **17**: 758–782.
Ring, P. S., Doz, Y. L., and Olk, P. M., 2005, Managing formation processes in R&D consortia, *California Management Review*, **47**: 137–156.

Ring, P. S. and Van de Ven, A. H., 1994, Developmental Processes of Cooperative Interorganizational Relationships, *Academy of Management Review*, **19**: 90–118.

Santos, F.M. and Eisenhardt, K.M., 2005, Organizational boundaries and Theories of Organization, *Organization Science*, **16**: 491-508.

Sørensen, H. B., 1993, *Strategisk ledelse af interorganisatoriske relationer,* Dissertation, Aarhus School of Business.

Thompson, J. D., 1967, *Organizations in Action*, New York: McGraw-Hill.

Thorelli, H. B., 1986, Networks: Between Markets and Hierarkies, *Strategic Management Journal*, **7**: 37 – 51.

Turnbulla, P. W. and Valla, J.-P., 1985, *Strategies for International Industrial Marketing.* London, Croom Helm.

Van de Ven, A. H. and Walker, G., 1984, The Dynamics of Interorganizational Coordination, *Administrative Science Quarterly*, **29**, 598–621.

Weick, K. E., 1979, Educational Organizations as Loosely Coupled Systems, *Administrative Science Quarterly*, **21**: 1–19.

Williamson, O. E., 1975, *Markets and Hierarchies—Analysis and Antitrust Implications.* New York, Free Press.

Williamson, O. E., 1979, Transaction Cost Theories, The Governance of Contractual Relations, *The Journal of Law and Economics*, **22**: 233–263.

Chapter 6

ASYMMETRIC ADAPTABILITY OF TEAM DESIGNS: CHANGE AND BACK AGAIN

Frances Jørgensen[1] and Harry Boer[2]
[1] *Department of Management, Aarhus School of Business, Haslegaardsvej 10, 8210 Aarhus*
[2] *Center for Industrial Production, Aalborg University, Fibigerstraede 16, 9220 Aalborg*

Abstract: In this chapter, field observations from a longitudinal case study in an organization attempting to adapt its internal work processes to changes in its external context and strategy according to the basic prescriptions of contingency theory (e.g. Mintzberg, 1979; Burton *et al.*, 2006) are presented, analyzed and discussed. The paper highlights both the benefits and challenges that may arise as companies seek to obtain "fit" between their strategy, environment and internal structures. In particular, the experiences detailed here suggest that what has been referred to as asymmetric adaptability (Moon *et al.*, 2004), in which knowledge, skills, and abilities required to perform successfully in one environment may hinder performance in another environment, may occur when teams are reorganized and restructured. The issue of asymmetric adaptability emphasizes an important limitation to contingency theory, namely, the failure to address the ramifications of changing internal structure without considering the consequences of those changes on the people within the organization.

Key words: Contingency theory, team design, longitudinal action research study, adaptability.

1. INTRODUCTION

The introduction of contingency theory was quite revolutionary and liberating. No longer were management forced to follow the latest "one best way" of structuring and designing organizations that failed to allow for varying operating environments. They rather could, at least theoretically,

R.M. Burton et al. (eds.), *Designing Organizations*, doi: 10.1007/978-0-387-77776-4_6,

tailor decisions regarding organizational structure and design to the world in which the individual organization exists. However, critics of contingency theory, or certain aspects of the theory, cite a number of problems, including lack of sufficient empirical support for some of the proposed relationships between contingency and structural characteristics, lack of clarity in defining these characteristics and such concepts as "fit", "consistency", "alignment", and "match" as well as the precise nature of influence between relevant variables, and difficulties with implementing the approach in practice (Schoonhoven, 1981). Donaldson (1987) however suggests that fundamental (mis)perceptions may explain many of the cited issues and that contingency theory is in fact valid, albeit with some stipulations regarding how the contingency variables and structure are related. This type of discussion certainly highlights the importance of continued research on contingency theory, especially in terms of the intricacies involved in all of the potential relationships between an organization's internal and contextual characteristics.

2. THEORETICAL FOUNDATION

According to structural contingency theory, organizational effectiveness is dependent on congruence between, amongst others, characteristics of an organization's technology (Woodward, 1965; Thompson, 1967; Perrow, 1967), external context (Burns and Stalker, 1961; Lawrence & Lorsch, 1967), strategy (Chandler, 1962; Miles and Snow, 1978), size (Pugh et al., 1963) and characteristics of its organisational structure (see also Mintzberg, 1979; Donaldson, 1996). Much of the research on contingency theory has been targeted towards identifying ideal matches between these contingency factors and the ways an organization may choose to structure its work processes. One of the generally accepted outcomes of this line of research is related to departmentalization, or how work units are grouped to perform tasks, where it is suggested that the organization may realize greater effectiveness with functional departmentalization when environmental conditions are stable, while more turbulent environments warrant the increased flexibility gained from product/market departmentalization (Burns & Stalker, 1961; Lawrence and Lorsch, 1967). Similarly, organizations with simple and craftsman technologies (Woodward, 1965; Perrow, 1967) are better served with a relatively "organic" (Burns and Stalker, 1961), i.e. flexible, structure while more complex and routine technologies (Woodward, 1965; Perrow, 1967) are best supported by a more "mechanistic" (Burns and Stalker, 1961), i.e. bureaucratic, structure. The basis for this argument is that grouping work according to function creates a high degree of task and role specialization, which in turn reduces redundancy, and hence increases efficiency based on economies of scale. Alternatively, if the nature of the work changes frequently in response to environmental fluctuations, the focus has to shift from efficiency to flexibility and economies of scope, which is best supported using product/market departmentalization combined with simpler technologies and craftsmanship.

Thus, increased flexibility can be supported by transforming traditional work teams operating within functional departments to cross-functional, product/market-oriented teams (Townsend *et al.*, 1998). Reorganizing people into teams, moving from functional to product/market team structures, or vice versa, is however not something easily accomplished in practice. The knowledge, skills, and abilities required to complete necessary tasks in one environment will not necessarily be adequate to perform the tasks needed to meet the new setting demands. Moreover, some of the behaviors cultivated over extended periods of time in one situation (e.g. functional teams) may actually interfere with the team's effectiveness in the new situation. Moon *et al.* (2004) use the term *asymmetric adaptability* to describe how teams (fail to) acclimate to shifts from one type of departmentalization to another. According to their studies, teams shifting from a functional to a product/market departmentalization outperform teams moving in the opposite direction.

Although this research led to a number of hypotheses that could explain why adaptation in one direction is more effective, the studies are limited to experimental settings with university students. Due to the nature of work teams, including for example how group norms and organizational culture might enable or hinder adaptation, it is difficult to generalize these findings to an organizational setting. Clearly, there is a need for empirical studies that address how teams adapt to structural changes aimed at achieving a proper fit with the organization's external context.

The objective of this chapter is to contribute to the development of contingency theory by describing and analyzing the process by which an organization sought to align part of its work processes with changes in its strategy and external context, following the basic tenets of contingency theory. The analysis lends support to the premise that "fit" between an organization's strategy, environment and internal structure may enhance performance, but also to the suggestion that the adaptation process may be asymmetric (Moon *et al.*, 2004). Further, the chapter contributes to practice by highlighting both the opportunities and risks that may accompany structural adaptation.

3. EMPIRICAL BACKGROUND

The study presented in this chapter was conducted in one department of a production facility in a well-recognized and well-regarded company with headquarters in Denmark. At the time the research began in 2001, the company had over 3000 employees world-wide, approximately 1000 total in the Danish facility, and about 400 in the production facility. There were 62 shop floor operators and their 3 managers in the participating department.

Although the company had experienced considerable competitive pressures in the 1960-1970s and again in the 1990s, it had survived and prospered primarily due to the strength of its R&D and marketing and sales competencies. As most of the "crises" experienced by the company were resolved by changes in the R&D and marketing and sales strategy and only required relatively minor technological and organizational changes in the manufacturing processes, this facility had largely remained unaffected.

Approximately six years prior to the start of the study, in 1995, following the fashion of the day, the company decided to adopt a team-based structure throughout its organization. This involved the adoption of a functional team structure for all of the departments in the production facility. Furthermore, a middle management team was created comprising all the previous shift leaders. Finally, a production management team was formed involving all the production department heads and the production directors. In the year 2000, the HRM director was added to the latter team.

To support this transition, the middle managers received two weeks of rather general workshops and training on autonomous teams. The production teams received two weeks of "training" annually for the purpose of team development. All the courses were taught by an external training center. However, as these training activities were often unrelated to the day-to-day functioning of the teams and lacked attention for team skill development, the transition proved quite problematic. Other factors, such as a lack of an integrated strategy and numerous sudden changes in middle and upper management, exacerbated the difficulties the teams experienced.

In the year 2000 the company began to experience serious financial difficulties resulting largely from the general instability of the global economy and more stringent governmental and EU rules and regulations. Furthermore, rumors started to spread that the company would be sold. In response, several initiatives were undertaken to cut costs and reduce waste. Unfortunately, the success rate of these initiatives was moderate to low.

In Spring 2001, a Continuous Improvement (CI) project was started in which the present authors were involved as action researchers. According to the top management, the efforts (training, etc.) towards creating autonomous teams had not been successful. In the management's mind, poor leadership by middle management team was the main reason for this. Because the teams in each of the functional departments had already been experiencing difficulties in becoming semi-autonomous, the management hoped this project would strengthen the team competencies through education and participation in various CI activities. Further, as part of the project, the department managers were involved in educational, team-building, and coaching activities.

In 2002, the company sold its brands and the associated R&D and sales organization to a global leader in the beverages and food industry. The management perceived increased competition and customer demands, and adopted a business-to-business (B2B) strategy which, in turn, placed pressure on the production facility to provide better customer service (e.g. on-time delivery) and rapid product turnaround.

By late 2003, the CI project started to produce results. The shop floor teams and middle management team were working much more effectively and efficiently as judged by top management, which was attributed to the focus on CI and adequate training of the middle management. As, however, the management also perceived still higher instability in its market, competitive and legal environment, and a need, following from their B2B strategy, to become more flexible, customer driven and innovative, they decided to launch a pilot project aimed at implementing a product/market-oriented team.

Nearly two years later, in the course of 2005, the environment became more stable and less hostile in the management's perception, and it was therefore decided to abandon the pilot project and return to functionally aligned jobs and teams, with a focus on efficiency, as prior to 2003. The decision was primarily driven by economic considerations – functionally aligned teams were expected to work more efficiently, while it would also never be possible to undertake the major technological changes necessary to run product/market-oriented production throughout.

During spring 2006, the pilot team expressed its dissatisfaction after returning to functionally aligned jobs. This led to the decision to implement a "cross-functional" team design for the pilot team, with partial expansion to the remainder of the plant.

4. RESEARCH DESIGN

4.1 Research Problem

The focus of this study is on the teams' transition from functional to product/market departmentalization and then, at least partially, back to a functional alignment in which there was also a change from zero autonomy to a slightly higher level of autonomy via, however, an even higher level of autonomy. The objective of the study is to describe and analyze the process in which the teams adapted to the changes in their work processes in each of the settings and the challenges and opportunities the new states provided for the teams and the organization.

4.2 Methodology

The study started in 2001 with the involvement of the authors as part of an action research team, prior to and during the initial stages of the transition. The first author maintained contact with the case company in order to follow the teams' adaptation process and to support other ongoing change initiatives within the production facility.

4.2.1 Data Collection and Analysis

Data included in this chapter were obtained from notes from the authors' observations, which were entered into weekly journals, and from transcriptions of tape recordings of semi-structured and unstructured interviews with key actors in the participating department, including the operators/team members, the teams' managers, support personnel, and members of the production facility's management. For the purpose of validation, all data from the authors' notes and the transcribed sessions were reviewed by members of the organization present at the time the data were gathered.

In addition, data were derived from printed monthly performance reports with measurements of productivity, quality, delivery reliability, and safety. Data collection began mid 2001 and continued on a regular basis until spring 2003; periodic data collection has since taken place three-four times per year and is still ongoing as of spring 2006. The data are presented and analyzed according to a processual framework (Dawson, 1994) in order to highlight the contextual nature of the transition process as it occurred. The main events transpiring in the case company are depicted in Figure 1.

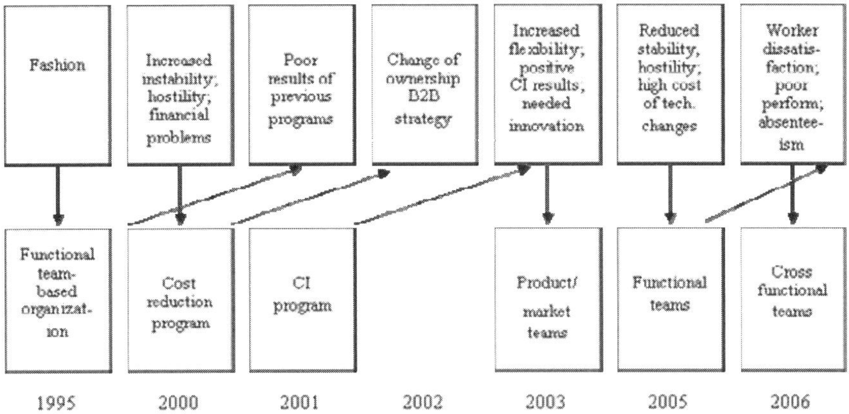

Figure 1. The Change Process and Change Drivers

5. TEAMS IN TRANSITION – AN ANALYSIS

5.1 Summer 2001: Initial Status

The operators employed in the participating department were responsible for various types of wrapping and packaging (e.g. individually wrapped, multi-packs, bulk packaging) of finished products; separate machines were used for each of these packaging options. As most of the wrapping is automated, the operators were expected to monitor the process for errors, remove defects from the line, and to fill materials into the machines at scheduled times. Once the finished products were packaged in cases or barrels, they were stacked on pallets before computer generated labels were affixed. From this point, the pallets were moved to the shipping department where they were sorted according to customer order. In addition to their primary responsibilities with overseeing the packaging process, the operators also completed relatively minor maintenance tasks on the machines, for example, cleaning and lubricating of external mechanisms. These tasks were recorded on standard forms. Further, the operators were responsible for packaging waste products and materials and completing waste check sheets.

Although efforts had been made to train all operators on all machines over the years – which are very similar in terms of operating procedure – there had been little actual job rotation within the department. Job rotation between departments, i.e. performing very different functions, was extremely rare throughout the company as a whole.

At the time the company made the transition to teams in 1996, the participating department consisting of 62 shop floor operators from three shifts was "reorganized" into six work teams – three day teams, two night teams, and one weekend team, with 6-11 members each. The operators were traditionally hired without educational or experience requirements and they received a minimum wage. The three department managers were each assigned teams according to the previous shifts (i.e. day, evening, weekend). As mentioned previously, the teams had received minimal education and training on autonomous teams. The team leaders were never provided with any training or education on team development or coaching but they had made efforts to "instill a team philosophy" (quote from team leader, August 2001). In the early years of this transition, the teams were encouraged to meet weekly to discuss production issues, but this practice was abandoned within a few months as it was considered a waste of resources by the facility's top management. According to the team leaders as well as the authors' observations, the teams were teams in name only; the employees functioned essentially as they always had, as individuals within day, evening, and weekend shifts.

5.2 Fall 2001-Fall 2002: Development of CI and Team skills

In connection with a research project involving the implementation of Continuous Improvement (CI) with shop floor teams, the authors designed and conducted weekly experiential learning activities that provided the teams the opportunity to learn basic skills related to problem-solving and process improvement, as well as team development skills (e.g. group communication and cooperation, time and meeting management). During the year in which these activities were facilitated, the teams became experienced at planning and implementing minor improvement projects involving the work processes in their own department. In addition, the team leaders, in a newly formed "middle management team" comprised of the twelve former department managers in the production facility, participated in weekly facilitated activities aimed at improving cross-functional/departmental cooperation and developing their team coaching skills.

Although many factors could and most certainly did affect the department's performance during the year in which these activities took place, performance measures indicated a reduction in costs, and particularly waste, of 14% and an overall productivity increase of 17% (adjusted for capacity and labor). Further, measures of employee satisfaction were markedly higher, rising from 24% very to extremely satisfied with their work environment to 54% falling into this category. The middle management team (i.e. the team leaders) was also functioning effectively at this point and had been formally recognized for several organization-wide improvement projects they had implemented.

5.3 Winter 2002-Fall 2003

The CI implementation was nearing its completion at the time the company sold a major part of its business to an international conglomerate in 2002. Although the operators were assured that the sale would not have a major impact on their employment conditions, it soon became apparent that the production facility as a whole would be under scrutiny for the first time. Initially, the teams were encouraged to increase efficiency and a number of improvement projects were initiated. However, with the announcement that a B2B strategy for the company would be adopted, the focus shifted again quickly to ways in which the company could improve its customer service. Analysis of the production processes suggested a need for increased flexibility to meet customer demands and the decision was made to reorganize the functionally aligned teams according to product type, which was in most cases consistent with product/market assignments. Due to their relative success with team development and CI, the six teams in the packaging department were selected as pilots in a study to determine the feasibility of the planned redesign.

One of the first challenges that arose even before the pilot study began involved the factory layout, as production was situated in three different buildings located between 300 and 800 meters from one another. One possible solution to the problem was to construct a temporary laboratory that would house one machine of each type necessary to complete one large customer's order; however, this solution was quickly dismissed as too expensive and time consuming. Therefore it was necessary to consider the pilot teams as "floaters" who would move from one building to another as required to manage the orders from start to finish. The operators' previous job responsibilities were assigned to temporary replacements.

The pilot study began with the operators visiting each of the functional departments for several days to gain an understanding of their work processes. Operators in those departments were encouraged to share knowledge regarding their work processes to facilitate the pilot teams' transition.

5.4 Winter 2003-Spring 2005

After approximately three months, the pilot teams, middle management/team leader team, sales and marketing representatives, production director, and planning engineers had developed a plan for the first "product teams" and the teams had demonstrated adequate knowledge of the processes to assume their new positions. Because it was understood that coordination of the work processes would be more complicated – not only due to the new design itself, but also because the teams would be expected to move in and out of the existing (functionally aligned) work processes, the teams were given the freedom to hold frequent meetings. In these meetings, scheduling and planning issues were discussed, often with participation of the functional team managers, schedulers, and planners. Further, the teams were encouraged to discuss any problems and frustrations they experienced in their new roles.

According to the teams, learning the technical aspects of their new positions was relatively easy. Within a few days, they felt comfortable operating the various machines and could produce the products without difficulty. Their greatest challenges involved the administration and coordination of the orders, as they had never been involved in this facet of the business. They felt that the recent team development and CI projects were extremely beneficial in easing this transition, as they had gained experience in inter- and intra-team communication, cooperation and problem-solving. The teams expressed a great deal of satisfaction over having developed skills in these areas and felt a strong sense of independence and autonomy because they could now make arrangements with the maintenance technicians, sales and marketing staff, suppliers and customers in order to better accomplish their work. They also expressed much deeper insight into the business as a whole.

5.5 Summer 2005-Fall 2005

By this time, changes in management as well as the time elapsed since the sale of the production facility had created a more stable environment for the company and it was time to evaluate the success of the pilot study to determine whether it should be continued, expanded, or abandoned. The pilot teams were very satisfied (employee satisfaction for these teams rose from 54% to 96% during this six month period) with their new roles and wished to continue. Certain performance indicators were also quite positive; for instance, the pilot teams had demonstrated their ability to quickly manage rapid shifts between product types to better accommodate customer demands and on-time delivery had improved from 89% to over 97% for the targeted market (i.e. one large customer). The operators had also registered a record number of improvement ideas pertaining to their own work processes and had been actively involved in the preliminary development of a new product concept they created.

Productivity measures were however substantially lower than previously, with an estimated fall of approximately 12%, and waste had risen approximately 6%. Start up and expected initial performance decline clearly accounted for some degree of this drop in efficiency, although most agreed that the new design was also responsible. Specifically, the increased degree of coordination necessary between sales and marketing, the planning engineers, and the operators was time consuming even after the operators gained experience. In addition, errors usually only associated with newly hired employees in the functional departments surfaced as the operators lost their expert status on any one particular machine. Finally, some errors were attributed to increased experimentation.

These measures, the more stable external context, and the anticipated costs of converting the production layout according to product/customer, led to the company's top management's decision to abandon the pilot project. The pilot teams were thus asked to return to their previous positions in the packaging department.

5.6 Winter 2005-Present

The first few months for the teams was filled with a great deal of frustration towards management for having involved them in a project that was (in retrospect) not realistic on a long term basis. They felt that their newly developed talents were wasted in their functionally aligned positions and they often complained of boredom and lack of meaningful contribution to the business. The operators began to submit complaints to their team leaders regarding performance in other departments that affected their on-time delivery and the "foolishness of some of the rules and procedures in the department" (quote from operator, January 2006). Several major altercations occurred with the maintenance department as well, as they had been forced to return to completing maintenance and repair request forms rather than calling the technicians directly when machines needed servicing. Absenteeism increased dramatically during this time, often being blamed on poor physical work conditions (e.g. standing at one machine for extended periods of time) and stress, and rumors of an employee strike began to circulate. Both operational performance (e.g. on-time delivery, quality, productivity) and people performance (e.g. number of improvements, employee satisfaction) for the packaging department fell dramatically during this time, to the lowest in the facility's history.

In an effort to address these issues, the first author conducted several workshops with the teams and their team leaders. Initially, the teams were given the opportunity to vent their frustrations openly and these were recognized by the team leaders as being understandable given the present situation. Thereafter, the teams were facilitated through problem-solving exercises in much the same as with the CI implementation, but this time with a focus on their specific complaints. For instance, the operators worked together to find solutions to the lack of autonomy and repetitiveness of their functionally aligned work processes. They were encouraged to consider how the skills they had developed in the pilot study could be used to improve their jobs. This process was repeated in small project groups until all the most important issues had been addressed.

The operators then presented an implementation plan to the production facility's top management that would involve increased cross-functional work processes within the existing production layout. As the teams presented this plan, they would be able to use their communication and planning skills and insight into the customers' wishes to improve the flow between the functional departments. In this way, they expected to be able to increase delivery reliability and the flexibility to shift operators more quickly between machines in a given department in order to get a particular order shipped more quickly. They acknowledged that this plan would potentially increase downtime for some machines when operators would abandon their posts at times to help complete rush orders. In addition, it would mean that all operators in a department would need to be trained on all machines as well as the order tracking system. Further, the operators wished to become more involved in the planning and scheduling of the orders, which would force active participation of the planning engineers and sales and marketing staff. Finally, the operators wished to take responsibility for scheduling of maintenance and serving of the machines in their departments.

The cross-functional team design was approved by the plant's top management and the teams from the packaging department were given additional resources to help facilitate rolling out the new work form to the remainder of the production facility. Although it is still too early to evaluate the consequences of the changes on operational performance, absenteeism has dropped substantially and the operators report general satisfaction with the new arrangements.

6. DISCUSSION

The field study observations presented in the chapter address important issues related to contingency theory. First, these observations highlighted the challenges that may arise when jobs are restructured and redesigned in ways that affect individuals and teams. In particular, these observations suggest that smoother adaptability occurs as teams move from functional to product/market departmentalization than when attempting to reverse their direction. In terms of operational performance, it appears that team effectiveness in the various settings is highly dependent on the particular measures in question. The department reported higher efficiency related performance (e.g. productivity and waste reduction) with the original functional team configuration, but increased process improvement, innovation, and customer service performance while configured along product/market-oriented lines. With this configuration, the teams were able to shift between orders much more quickly, and they were thus better equipped to satisfy short delivery times, experienced a significant increase in on-time delivery, and submitted far more improvement ideas and a highly promising new concept design. Further, the middle managers (i.e. team leaders) succeeded in implementing a number of organization-wide improvements during the time that their teams were aligned according to the product/market.

However, support was also gained for the research conducted by Moon *et al.* (2004) on asymmetric adaptability, which proposes that teams will adapt more easily and perform more effectively following a transition from functional to product/market departmentalization. The teams reported that they were able to use the knowledge and skills required to perform the functionally aligned jobs as a foundation for performing the tasks required under the new structure (i.e. product/market departmentalization). In this case, the transition was supported by the team training and development that occurred as a part of the CI implementation while the teams were still working in the functionally aligned structure. For example, the teams had received training in communication and problem-solving, which they found especially useful when working product/market-oriented. When forced back into a functional configuration, the teams experienced symptoms of role confusion, particularly in response to the increased standardization of their work processes, and to their frustration they were not able to use the skills they had recently developed. So, these findings support Moon *et al.'s* (2004) contention that the teams' past experience can serve as enablers but also as barriers to performance when the working arrangements are altered.

A very simple explanation for the findings presented here – and possibly even to some extent for those reported in Moon *et al.'s* (2004) study, is that the redesign of the jobs resulted in a more motivating environment for the operators, which in turn led to improved performance, according to at least some of the measures. The jobs within the product/market teams were inherently more appealing and motivating as they offered more varied use of skills, higher autonomy, and increased meaningfulness of the work. Increased motivation with the redesigned jobs would also be expected, according to Hackman and Oldman's (1980) job characteristics model. The operators became dissatisfied and de-motivated when they were forced to return to jobs they now considered boring and monotonous. The cross-functional design adopted in the end provided the employees with enough autonomy, meaningfulness, and skill variation to satisfy their individual needs. What this seems to suggest then, is that the efficiency gains assumed with functionally configured jobs may only be realized when the teams do not have prior experience with more satisfying job designs.

The second issue related to contingency theory raised in this paper pertains to the way in which an organization attempts to achieve fit between the characteristics of the external and internal environments. In this case, the company appeared to "do the right thing" with respect to making internal structural changes, based on their assessment of the external environment. However, both the based organization and cost reduction programs failed, which can be ascribed to poor implementation management. The CI program was meant to remedy this situation, worked quite well and, perhaps most importantly, provided the basis for the change towards product/market-oriented teams the management felt were needed for the organization to be able to cope with increased environmental instability (following their B2B strategy) and hostility (rules and regulations). When the situation settled, efficiency and productivity, rather than flexibility and innovation, were felt to have become more important again, and it also appeared impossible to make all the investments required to make the company's technology more flexible, the management decided to go back to a functional team-based design. This however invoked massive negative reactions in the form of worker dissatisfaction and de-motivation and, consequently poor worker as well as operational performance. In response to that, a cross-functional team design was adopted, which, so far, appears to work out quite well, both in terms of operational and worker performance.

7. IMPLICATIONS FOR THEORY

The findings from this study offer conditional support for a number of long-held assumptions regarding the fit between a range of contingency factors and the structure and design of a company's work processes. In particular, it was confirmed that functional departmentalization may result in increased efficiency in relatively stable conditions and that product/market departmentalization may increase flexibility in a more turbulent environment (Burns & Stalker, 1961; Daft, 1998; Townsend *et al.*, 1998).

However, the research also suggests that these general rules of thumb may be conditional on the previous experiences and expectations of the workforce, due to the potential effect of asymmetric adaptability. Moreover, asymmetric adaptability is perhaps only one indicator of an even larger issue with contingency theory, namely that this theory helps produce a picture of a given or future situation and the fit between the *structural* characteristics of the situation. The theory is not however quite helpful in addressing the impact of changing these variables on *social* characteristics, e.g. the motivation of or the social interaction between people. There is a rather mechanistic simplicity to contingency theory, which falls short of capturing the inherent complexity stemming from the social dynamics within organizations. Thus, one conclusion derived from this study is that contingency theory may usefully be developed so as to incorporate socio-dynamic effects on the actual functioning of organizations.

Since much of the research on the process by which an organization's structure and design are adapted to become more aligned to (changes in) its contingencies has primarily been limited to post hoc studies at a macro level, challenges related to the fit between, for example, structural changes and the human component, may not be recognized. By following the adaptation process at the team level, important insights are gained concerning the ramifications of initiating such a major change process. Of special note, this study emphasizes the need to consider fit with worker expectations, or lack thereof, as an enabler, or barrier for that matter, to changes in organization and job design. As mentioned above, the job characteristics model is helpful in explaining the relationship between job design, worker perceptions as expressed in, for example, job satisfaction and motivation, and effects on worker performance, but falls short in explaining the role of context and operational performance impact. Combining job design theory with organization design (contingency) theory may provide still more complex and meaningful explanations of these relationships.

Furthermore, the findings of this paper suggest a need to review the main drivers for the change processes. For this company, these drivers appeared to be:

- Fashion.
- Perceived environmental (in)stability and hostility/benevolence.
- (Change of) ownership.
- Strategy/strategic change.
- (Dis)satisfaction with operational and worker performance and the functioning of (different groups in) the organization, i.e. the job and work environment. (

The lack of technological adaptability – i.e. the company's inability to adapt the technology to accommodate the new work process, acted as a barrier to change. However, the company only became aware of that after the teams had been reorganized. Although the change of ownership in the company did not have any direct effects on the organization, it did lead to their adoption of a B2B strategy. While environment and strategy are "established" contingency factors, and also fashion and ownership have been reported in the literature (Mintzberg, 1979), employee (dis)satisfaction also appears to play an important, if not decisive role.

8. IMPLICATIONS FOR PRACTICE

The experiences in this company lend support to one of the primary concerns with contingency theory, namely the difficulties with implementing the model in practice. Switching from one type of organizational arrangement to another to ensure "fit" with changing conditions is easier to envision on paper than to implement in real life situations involving real people. The adaptation of the teams from a functional to a product/market departmentalization was relatively smooth and did indeed provide the company with the increased flexibility contingency theory recommends for an organization operating in an unstable environment. This transition was likely facilitated by the team members' recent and continued participation in Continuous Improvement (CI) activities. When the external context stabilized, the company once again attempted realignment according to the principles of contingency theory, reverting to functional departmentalization. Theoretically, greater effectiveness through efficiency should then follow. However, the employees' dissatisfaction with their return to their traditional (functionally aligned) jobs thwarted any potential benefits the company might have achieved from congruence between the organizational design, environment, strategy and technology of the company. Thus, it appears that designing jobs for efficiency – as was the case in the functional departments – may only be effective when the team members do not have prior experience with a more inherently satisfying job design or when they do not possess the knowledge, skills, and abilities that might foster expectations of a more fulfilling job design. In this case, a possible win-win solution was discovered in the form of cross-functional teams for companies seeking to attain congruence between their strategy, environment, technology, organization design and job design without necessarily sacrificing efficiency and productivity for flexibility, innovation and learning. This alternative to job design may be a viable option for companies wishing to the advantages of each type of configuration, and may actually present the best solution to satisfy worker expectations and thus avoid the impact of the asymmetric adaptability problem.

9. CONCLUSION

This chapter describes and analyzes the transitional processes of teams as they moved from a traditional functional departmentalization to a product/market departmentalization, and partially back again. The study provides a rich opportunity for an empirical analysis of how adaptation at the team level may occur. On a general level, the findings suggest that transition from one type of departmentalization to another is a major change process for the involved teams and their management. Further, the findings suggest that certain types of transitions may be less problematic from the team members' perspective, but that the opportunities realized for the organization may also be greater in these situations. Specifically, adapting from functional to product/market departmentalization appeared to be relatively easy while the move back was much more problematic. Flexibility, (contribution to) innovation and opportunities for knowledge sharing and organizational learning increased significantly when the teams moved from a functional to a product/market, and so did worker satisfaction and motivation, but this went at the expense of efficiency and productivity. The move back resulted in dissatisfied and de-motivated workers and did not consequently produce the expected operational performance results, i.e. higher efficiency and productivity. This finding confirms Moon *et al.*'s (2004) theory on asymmetric adaptability.

The analysis presented here suggests that management perceptions related to the "traditional" contingency factors, in particular environment, strategy, technology and also fashion and ownership (Mintzberg, 1979) *plus* perceived operational and worker performance are drivers of change. The "goodness" of fit between the contingency factors, organisation design, job design resulting from the change initiatives, *and* worker expectations, determines operational and worker performance. For this company, the "ideal" fit appears to be a team design falling somewhat between the two extremes offered by functional and product/market departmentalization. In essence, the company is exploiting the benefits, while minimizing the disadvantages, of both arrangements by adopting what they refer to as high performance cross-functional teams. Ostensibly, the structure and the design of the jobs should be functional *enough* to allow for greater efficiency, while still offering the advantages of flexibility, knowledge sharing, organizational learning, and higher employee satisfaction, regardless of the external market conditions. Further research is needed to determine whether this model in other types of environments.

Continued assessment of the teams' performance in the upcoming months and years is needed in order to determine whether the solution chosen by this company will be viable in the event of future changes in and around the company. More generally, research on how cross-functional teams can be structured to satisfy the needs of both stable/benevolent and unstable/hostile markets, competitive and legal environments, support different strategies, and allow making the best use of different technologies is certainly warranted.

REFERENCES

Burns, T. and Stalker, G., 1961, *The Management of Innovation*, London: Tavistock.

Burton, R., DeSantis, G. and Obel, B., 2006, *Organizational Design: A Step-By-Step Approach,* New York: Cambridge University Press.

Chandler Jr., A.D., 1962, *Strategy and structure. Chapters in the history of the American industrial enterprise*, Cambridge, Mass.: MIT Press.

Daft, R., 1998, *Organizational Theory and Design*, 6th ed., Mason, OH: Thomsen Southwestern.

Dawson, P., 1994, *Organizational Change: A Processual Approach,* London: Paul Chapman Publishing.

Donaldson, L., 1987, Strategy and structural adjustment to regain fit and performance: in defence of contingency theory, *Journal of Management Studies*, vol. **24**, no. 1, pp. 1-24.

Donaldson, L., 1996, *For positivist organization theory*, London: Sage.

Hackman, J.R. and Oldman, G.R., 1980, *Work Redesign*, Reading, MA: Addison Wesley.

Lawrence, P.R. and Lorsch, J.W., 1967, *Organization and Environment,* Boston: Harvard University Press.

Miles, R.E. and Snow, C.C., 1978, *Organizational strategy, structure, and process*, New York: McGraw-Hill.

Mintzberg, H., 1979, *The structuring of organizations*, Englewood Cliffs (NJ): Prentice-Hall.

Moon, H., Hollenback, J.R., Humphrey, S.E., Ilgen, D.R., West, B., Ellis, A.P.J. and Porter, C.O.L.H., 2004, Asymmetric adaptability: Dynamic team structures as one-way streets, *Academy of Management Journal*, Vol. **47**, No. 5, pp. 681-695.

Perrow, C., 1967, A framework for the comparative analysis of organizations, *American Sociological Review*, Vol. **32**, No. 2, pp. 194-208.

Pugh, D.S., Hickson, D.J., Hinings, C.R., Macdonald, K.M., Turner, C. and Lupton, T., 1963, A conceptual scheme for organizational analysis, *Administrative Science Quarterly*, Vol. **8**, pp. 289-315.

Schoonhoven, C.B., 1981, Problems with contingency theory: Testing assumptions hidden within the language of contingency theory, *Administrative Science Quarterly*, Vol. **26**, No. 3, pp.349-377.

Thompson, J.D., 1967, *Organizations in Action. Social science bases of administrative theory*, New York: McGraw-Hill.

Townsend, A., DeMarie, S.M., and Hendrickson, A.R., 1998, Virtual teams: Technology and the workplace of the future, *Academy of Management Executive*, Vol. **12**, No.3, pp. 17-29.

Woodward, J., 1965, *Industrial organization: theory and practice*, London: Oxford University Press.

Chapter 7

STRIVE FOR GREATER EFFICIENCY AND EFFECTIVENESS WITHIN A HUMAN RESOURCES DIVISION

Torben Andersen[1] and Per Krogager[2]

[1]Director, Ph.D., The Technical University of Denmark, Center for Technology, Economics and Management, Produktionstorvet, Building 421, 2800 Kgs. Lyngby, Denmark; [2]Executive vice president human resources, Tvillum-Scanbirk (part of Masco Corporation), Egon Kristiansens Allé 4, 8882 Fårvang, Denmark.

Abstract: HR divisions have traditionally had problems concerning their invisibility to the rest of their parent organization. They are now confronted with difficulties in measuring their exact contribution to the company's bottom line and many of them are not well prepared for the changes that would make them more professional, more profitable, and more visible. Danish medical company Radiometer has developed innovative strategies for addressing nearly universal efficiency and effectiveness problems within HR Divisions. In cooperation with each other, Radiometer's HR division and its top management team have used the tools they have developed to succeed in measuring profitability, efficiency, and effectiveness within their HR division.

Key words: Efficiency, effectiveness, HRM, ROI, HR Road Map, best practice.

1. INTRODUCTION

Over the last decade, the field of human resources (HR) has become more visible. Top management, especially in large companies, is paying increasing attention to human resources, giving HR divisions increased opportunities for gaining recognition and prestige. According to Larsen (1999 and 2001), this is opening up opportunities for HR managers to participate in their corporate top-management teams. And with divisional

R.M. Burton et al. (eds.), *Designing Organizations*, doi: 10.1007/978-0-387-77776-4_7,

representation on the board, HR divisions are enjoying increased effect on strategy formulation and consequent structural design. And this has been interpreted as an improved basis for HR divisions to contribute to the overall organizational effectiveness of a corporation.

But with increasing visibility comes increasing threats. HR divisions are under increasing pressure to provide evidence that they do "make a difference" and contribute to an organization's bottom-line [see e.g. Ulrich (ed.) (1998)]. This is not a new challenge; the demand for HR accountability was presented years ago [see Ulrich (1997), Phillips (1999); Fitz-Enz (1993) (2000) and Fitz-Enz and Davison (2001)]. However, with recent and increasing focus on out-sourcing, many HR-managers see an underlying threat of reducing, or simply closing down their HR departments. Ulrich and Smallwood (2003, p. 68) describe the pressures on HR as a consequence of companies increasingly focusing on operating efficiency and productivity, i.e. managing costs (mainly salaries). Therefore HR has to move from "welfare administration of people" to "contribution to profits" Tyson (1995, p. 229).

The management of costs and the following focus on effectiveness and productivity is by no means new in organizational theory – it has existed for decades (Child 1984, p. 143). Child, however, also claimed in the 1980's that management control should be directed towards more than one objective. Besides operational efficiency within a given individual manager's area of responsibility, there were also requirements for integration, development and flexibility. This argument is even more pronounced today: Child (2005, p. 379ff) mentions efficiency as the most *constant* need for corporations, however, all companies have their own combination of efficiency, adaptation and innovation. In other words, the modern company must address several bottom lines. From the individual divisional manager's point of view, this need accelerates with increasing internal as well as external competition.

Burton et al. (2006, p. 11) in their research condense these several requirements into dual demands: efficiency and effectiveness. Efficiency focuses on input: trying to reduce costs, where effectiveness focuses on output: revenue and innovation, for example. In more competitive environments, this dual demand gives the organization competing priorities, and the question becomes: when is each one dominant and how should the company try to strive for a balance (Burton et al. 2006, p. 13)? Tushman and Romanelli (1995, p. 175) argue that this balance is difficult to accomplish; it is often the case that *evolutionary* periods, where one of the two will dominate, will be succeeded by *revolutionary* period, where the other will take precedence. The balance is therefore reached over time, rather than simultaneously. Finally Huber (2004, p. 218) addresses conflicting goals in distinguishing between change and efficiency:

'Unfortunately, the impermanence associated with frequent change interferes with obtaining experience and with the associated efficiency that follows from experience. While changes directed specifically at increasing efficiency often increase in the long run, more generally, changes force learning but interfere with mastering. As a result, they frequently interfere with attaining high level of efficiency.'

Huber describes a dilemma: the attempt to pursue both efficiency and effectiveness, similar to March's exploration-exploitation challenge (1991). So how can HR divisions at the same time be more resource-accountable—pursuing efficiency within existing activities—and also successfully manage the highest level of effectiveness, which requires continuously changing activities in HR itself which meet the line organization needs? Gibson and Birkinshaw (2004) present empirical evidence that there are business units which are capable of pursuing both goals simultaneously. They emphasise the importance of not simply being innovative and proactive, but also effectively utilizing the value of the company's proprietary assets. Gibson and Birkinshaw refer to this practice as "ambidextrous" (2004, p. 47). This is a case study of how Danish pharmaceutical company Radiometer Medical Ltd. has worked practically to implement initiatives aimed at both pursuing efficiency and effectiveness within their HR Division.

2. A BRIEF HISTORY OF RADIOMETER MEDICAL, LTD

Radiometer Medical Ltd. (Radiometer) was founded in 1935 by Børge Aagaard Nielsen and Carl Schrøder. The two founders started modestly in the loft of Schrøder's residence in the city of Copenhagen. They developed and manufactured testing equipment for the field of radio - the so-called meter. Thus, the name Radiometer. The company grew quickly and it was during the polio epidemic of 1953-54 that paved the way for Radiometer today. By developing devices which would measure the acidity of blood via a pH measurement, and by using Equilibration technology - they made it possible to save polio patients who were suffering from respiratory paralysis. This type of measurement, which in the words of Radiometer's mission statement is the ability to deliver STAT information regarding the condition of critically ill patients (<u>S</u>hort <u>T</u>urn <u>A</u>round <u>T</u>ime), is the basis for Radiometer's future innovative activities.

With a focused strategy, Radiometer has constantly expanded its products, so that the company today manufactures a range of blood analysis instruments connected to information systems, as well as products and services all related to blood analysis. Radiometer's customers are primarily hospitals, where its products and services are used by doctors and nurses in emergency, operating, supervisory, intensive care, medicinal treatment units, and in maternity wards.

In 2002, Radiometer had a turnover of approximately $280 million (DKK 1.8 billion) and earnings that reach approximately $47 million (DKK 300 million) in its core business unit. The company has a global market share of 40% and is seen as the world's strongest producer of blood analysis devices with corresponding Information Systems and accessories. More than 95% of the company's share comes from markets outside of Denmark. The United States, Europe, and Japan make up the company's largest markets.

Radiometer employs approximately 1800 people, of which about half are employed outside of Denmark.

3. THE PHASES OF THE CHANGE PROCESS

In September 1999, Radiometer started to build an HR division which could provide professional support to the operation and progress of the organization - and to challenge its existing patterns of thought and action. The company's decision to establish a more efficient HR division was the result of two needs within the organization: one, the need for a somewhat bureaucratic and rules-oriented organization to compete in an increasingly turbulent and competitive market; and two, to meet the company's urgent needs for increasing managerial and employee competence.

Radiometer hired a new HR-manger to develop clear and communicative visions and objectives, so that employees, especially in the HR division itself, understood the company's strategic direction, and what the professional and personal implications of changes would mean to them. Finally, the job was to develop measurement and documentation tools, so that the HR-director and others in the HR division could continuously monitor the progress of the numerous activities at hand.

3.1 The road map

On the basis of research by Dave Ulrich (1997), the new HR manager's first endeavor was to develop an HR Road Map: an illustration of the different HR departments, their characteristics and inter-relations. The map was used to explain and illustrate development by comparing the future, desired HR division with the current HR division - including the existing personnel department. On the basis of the HR Road Map, the HR employees identified concrete measurement tools to map out the division's ability to support the operation and progress of the entire organization, and to determine the HR division's productivity itself. In addition, they also developed a model for estimating HR's profitability through the course of the changes underway.

In consultation with Radiometer's board of directors, HR could create a division capable of being both operational and strategic, and able to deal with the structural as well as the personnel relations in the company. At the same time, it was agreed that the division should *in no way* jeopardize already established administrative competence.

The overall expectations were twofold. The first was that the HR division's progress and expansion of its service platform could continue to support the organization's everyday operation and progress, but with fewer employees. It was certainly expected by top management that investment in a future HR division would be partly financed via rationalizing the existing administrative routines. On the practical level, preparations were made to eventually enable the HR division to manage administrative as well as development-oriented assignments with a pool of staff which would consist of somewhat less than the 18 employees working in the personnel department in August of 1999. These considerations resulted in a decision to implement a "matrix" organization in the HR division, geared towards four professional areas, and an equal number of "fluid" cross-organizational activities. The four professional areas (or departments) were to focus on running daily routine assignments in appropriate and effective ways and were labeled: 'Salaries & Wages', 'Recruiting', 'Competence Development' and 'Information & Communication'. The four "fluid" cross-organizational activities were labeled according to the roles the HR division here would be playing: 'Strategic Partner', 'Change Agent', 'Rationality Expert' and 'Employee Champion' (Ulrich, 1997). They were designed to have a more development-oriented perspective and a more proactive character, ensuring that HR strategies and Radiometer's strategic plans were actually realized.

By January 2000, a development plan was presented within Radiometer's HR department, dividing its past, present and future into four phases: An initial phase: the "Clarification Phase" was at the presentation of the plan in November of 1999 already near its completion. The purpose of this phase was to ensure that the goals and objectives the HR division would pursue were clearly defined. The second phase, "Reorganization and Establishment", which was anticipated to be completed in April of 2000, was meant to ensure that all employees in the HR division had knowledge and understanding of the new goals and challenges, and were mentally preparing for and slowly starting the necessary progress and reorganization process. In the third phase, "Consolidation and Progress", anticipated to be the longest-lasting and most burdensome phase in the development process, and not expected to be 'completed' until the middle of 2003, the focus would be placed on identifying and carrying out activities which would develop the division overall, but also the departments and employees individually. This phase was naturally seen as crucial and determining for the HR division - especially because the new HR director and the rest of the HR staff were very aware of the competence shortfalls in many areas of the division. A fourth and last phase, "The Excellent HR division", was the point where the division was close to reaching its goal. After approximately three and a half years of intensive work, Radiometer's HR division was well on its way into phase four, and it is both relevant and possible to assess the results.

The matrix structure was implemented and the different areas of responsibility were reshuffled, so that they were more appropriately located as mandated by the new structure. In terms of eliminating the non-value-based administrative tasks, it turned out that the line organization in many cases was surprisingly conservative, i.e. when it no longer received the staff reports and the administrative services it had previously received. To fulfill all of the ambitious goals the HR division had laid out for itself, the HR division took several simultaneous actions. It needed to acquire the desired efficiency through re-hiring, courses, training, and person-to-person teaching. At the same time, equal effort was put into professionalizing operations and service performances through a conceptualization of the different processes of the division. On the technological level the HR division was tormented by its numerous different and non-compatible IT systems. Consequently, a great deal of double work took place. Obviously, effort was put into changing this situation, and during the three and a half years quite a lot of time and resources have been spent on simplifying and rationalizing these systems.

In the spring of 2001, the desired rationalizations had been completed according to the original plan. In 2002, in close cooperation with the rest of the organization, the HR division identified additional administrative and supervisory tasks that without much consequence to the company could be eliminated and rationalized. In terms of employees, this meant laying off an additional two employees in May 2002. Nine administrative employees had either retired or had moved to other areas of the company, and three new employees had been hired. This meant a total staff reduction of slightly over 25% and an administrative rationalization of 50 %. Actually, despite the addition of many new types of service, the HR division's budget for 2003/04 had not increased since 1998/99. This happened simultaneously with - and this is a crucial point, perhaps the most crucial of all – a professional development within the HR division so that three and a half years after the commencement of the above-mentioned process, the HR division was capable of engaging in a number of consulting and business-support activities. And in the end, this was the ultimate purpose behind the initiative and efficiency development process.

3.2 The development of a more specific documentation and measurement tool

The dual demands of efficiency and effectiveness in the HR division was written in terms of the following two parameters:

1. The productivity of the HR division in itself
2. The ability of the HR division to positively influence the operation and progress of the larger organization

These two parameters became Radiometer's HR Road Map, outlining four distinct HR-divisions (Figure 1 below)

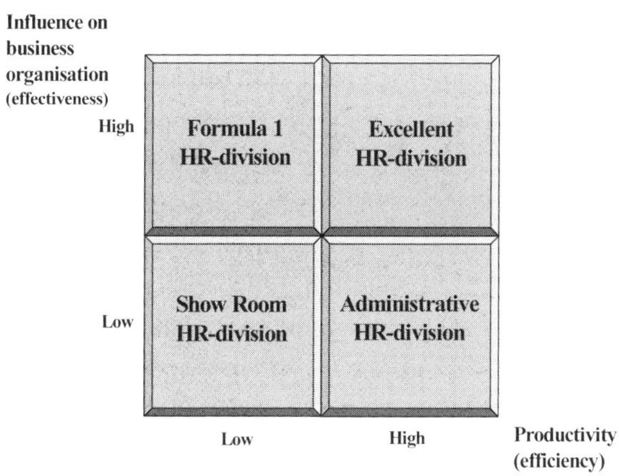

Figure 1. HR-divisions

The *Formula 1 HR Division* is characterized by an ability to add support to the decisions of the organization, but at a relatively high cost per activity. *The Show Room HR Division* is also characterized by its high level of cost per activity, but without as great a positive influence on business results as the *Formula 1 HR Division*. The *Administrative HR Division* has no particular influence on the decisions of the larger organization, but it does have a high productivity level. The *Excellent HR Division* is characterized both by having a large and positive influence on the decisions of the greater organization, and functioning efficiently and effectively as a division.

3.2.1 Measurement parameters

Top management determined that their demands required more specific measurement parameters—how to measure the HR division's ability to support the general operation and progress of the organization? They defined these parameters:

- to insure an alignment between business and HR-strategies
- to recognize the need for change in the organization and to provide support for the implementation of those changes.
- to initiate and support rationalizations and simplifications of business and administrative processes
- to secure manager and employee access to HR-information, -service and -support

In terms of measuring the HR division's ability to exert influence on the operation and progress of the organization, HR decided to use an entirely "subjective" method. It simply chose to ask the key clients of the HR division: top management.

In terms of measuring the HR division's productivity, they decided to measure it based on "Activity-Based Costing" principles, which, combined with "Best Practice", constituted the "relative productivity" of the HR division. In order to translate these measures into practice, they selected three traditional HR-processes. The three processes were by no means random: they are some of the most often used parameters for measurement, and they are the most relevant for Radiometer (and one might add: some of the most easily measured):

- The expense of processing payrolls
- The expense of recruiting
- The expense of one-day training courses

The plotting of these two sets of parameters determines an HR division's placement on the HR Road Map, and makes it possible to determine: 1. the HR division's starting point in terms of these parameters; 2: the path of action for a future HR division; 3. the speed with which a division has progressed.

3.2.2 Profitability estimation and measurement

Initially, HR did not consider these measurements to be contributions to any estimations of profitability. However, it soon became clear that the HR division wanted this measurement and documentation system to make a reasonably sound estimate of this. The profitability measures opens Return on Investment (ROI) for consideration (see e.g. Kearns, 1977); Figure 2 below. The model is slightly modified and illustrates what are considered to be likely cost-benefit correlations within HR divisions.

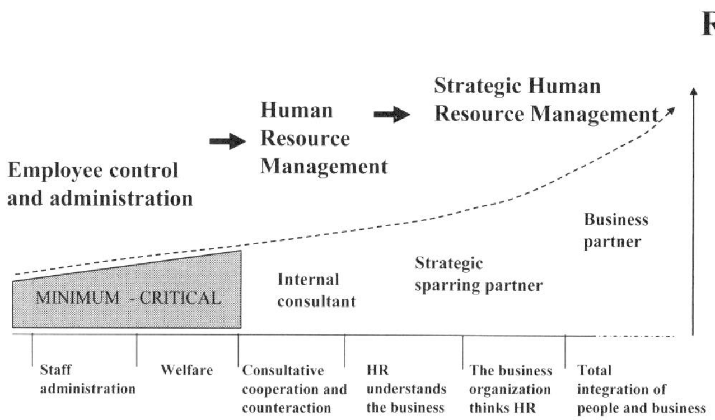

Figure 2. Kerns model of return on investment (ROI)

Typical personnel and administrative activities, such as time registration, salaries and payment of wages, etc., represent some of an HR division's most basic activities, but that they - as activities - have a poor Return on Investment value (ROI). This is based on their face value - and not taking any underlying, indirect effects into consideration. As the staff of the HR division begins to provide support and consulting, the HR division's ROI value rises (increases). But the highest value is found in HR divisions that are capable of working as a sparring and business partner and are able to provide strategic cooperation.

Of the four different HR divisions in the matrix (Figure 1), the *Show Room HR Division* is the one most likely to have the lowest (possibly even negative) profitability. It has a low productivity and it provides limited or no positive support or benefit to the operation. Nor does it contribute to the efficiency or effectiveness of the organization. The *Excellent HR Division* is expected to have the highest profitability. It is characterized by its high productivity and its considerable positive influence on the operation and progress of the larger organization.

Estimating profitability for the *Administrative HR Division* and for the *Formula 1 HR Division* appears, however, to be a more difficult task. Where the one type of HR division has advantages in terms of productivity, the other has an equally valuable ability to support the operation and progress of the organization. After a good deal of pondering, HR at Radiometer concluded that the answer was simple: The *Administrative HR Division* was more productive than the *Formula 1 HR Division*, and its production per activity actually less expensive. But the fact was that it had little positive influence on the operation and progress of the organization. With the *Formula 1 HR Division* it appeared to be different. Although it was not especially productive, it had a better profitability than either the *Administrative HR Division* or the *Show Room HR Division*, (because of its positive influence on the organization). Where the one type of HR division had advantages in terms of productivity, the other had an equally valuable ability to support the operation and progress of the organization. Again, when assessing profitability, as with everything else, it is more important to do the right things than to do things right.

After a number of interviews with CEOs, HR professionals and independent economists, where the exact relational profitability correlation between the Y- and X-axis of the road map was discussed and evaluated, HR created a very simple formula expressed as follows:

$$F(x,y) = y^2+x$$

The formula states that relative profitability (the F value) can be calculated as the value of influence raised to the second power and added to the value of productivity (the X-value). In other words, HR estimated that the profitability-related effects were considerably greater when enhancing an HR division's ability to support the organization in reaching its goals, rather than when merely streamlining and making the HR division more efficient. The effects are clearly greater when developing both of those parameters simultaneously.

A closer examination of the formula, including a number of simulations and concrete calculations, rendered it probable that they had developed a type of "mathematical gearbox" which enabled HR to transfer any given position in the two-dimensional HR Road Map to a one-dimensional scale within a model of estimating profitability. However, this same examination also revealed that the above-mentioned boxed function type of profitability estimations did not quite hold up. Profitability did not fall into boxed categories, as shown above, but rather, into parabola-like horizontal curves, as the illustration in Figure 2 shows. After performing additional simulations and calculations, and while waiting for the possibility of obtaining more exact empirical data, HR determined that those HR divisions that run through the center of the HR Road Map have a level of profitability that can be said to balance itself. The position, which is defined by the coordinates (2.5, 2.5) on the HR Road Map (see figure 5), is equivalent to a value of 8.75. HR divisions with similar values can for instance be found in the position (0.0, 2.96) and (5.0, 1.94). This means that HR divisions, which have calculated values lower than 8.75 (and are therefore situated below the middle horizontal line in the model above) have a negative level of profitability. HR divisions with calculated values higher than 8.75 (and therefore are positioned above the middle, horizontal line) have – according to the same hypothesis - a positive level of profitability.

This estimate implies that a *Show Room HR Division* can never have a positive profitability. It also implies that almost 15 % of *Administrative HR Divisions* have a positive profitability, and approximately 10 % of *Formula 1 HR Divisions* have a negative profitability.

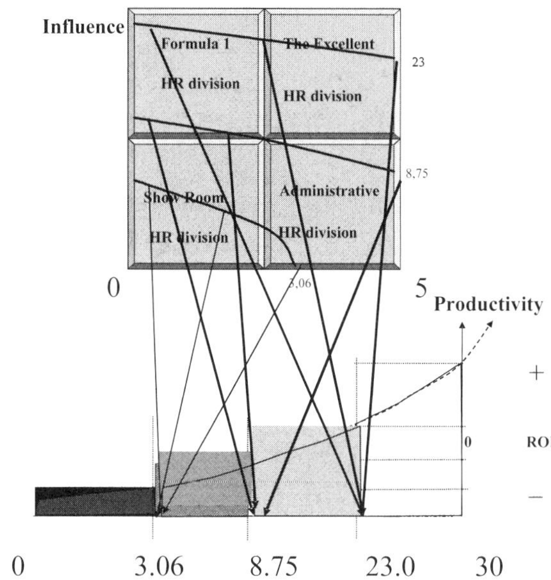

Figure 3. Linking the HR road map with Kearns' model

In other words, HR's work with the formula showed that because of the profitability value of the Y-axis, which is raised to the second power compared with the "normal" value of the X-axis, some of the administrative HR divisions which have high Y-values will have greater profitability than, for instance, a *Formula 1 HR Division*, which has a low Y-value.

The HR-division also initiated an examination of the exponential curve, which Kearns places in his ROI model to describe the connection between the services of an HR division and the division's ability to contribute to the company's bottom line. These analyses and considerations led them to conclude that it is more likely to find a connection between the movement on the ROI model's horizontal and vertical axes, which can be illustrated by an

S-curve rather than an exponential curve (Figure 4 below). This curve provides a more adequate description of a realistic and anticipated connection between different types of profitability and supply of HR divisions than Kearns' exponential ROI curve.

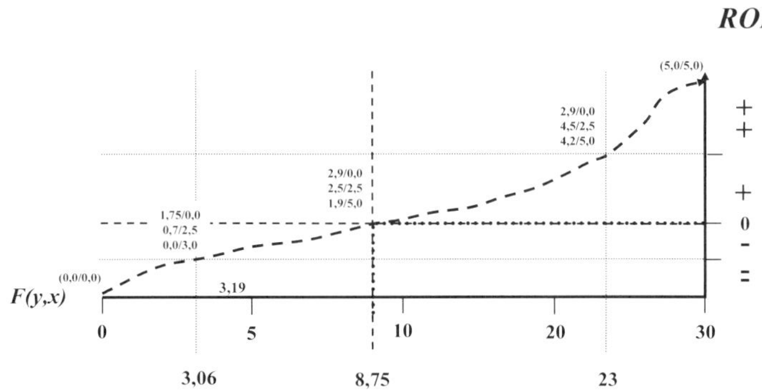

Figure 4. ROI estimation- A hypothesis

The model is based on a number of premises which are certainly up for debate. The premises are, however, exciting and thought-provoking considerations which offer HR division managers a number of different potential perspectives.

3.3 What do these measurements tell us?

What does the assessment, based on the above-described measurements and estimation tools, say about the actual development of an HR division from the personnel department's perspective? Radiometer's HR division developed three measures for monitoring its ability to support the operation and progress of the organization. In the first, which was completed in September of 2000, HR asked every director in Radiometer Medical A/S to assess the competence level of the HR division. The group of directors had experienced an increase in the value of the progress of the HR division's ability to support Radiometer's overall development. Calculations also illustrate a progress from 0.36 in 1999 to 3.16 in 2000 (see Figure 5 below). The corresponding calculation, completed in September of 2001, shows another slight increase to a value of 3.22. The calculation in September 2003 has a result of 3.19: a slight *decrease*.

Based on calculations on the basis of the productivity measures, one can conclude that a positive, although less radical, development has taken place. Where price/activity, as mentioned earlier, is compared with "Best Practice", there is a progress which translates into a movement on the X-axis from 3.38 in 1999 to 3.81 in 2000. In September of 2001, the productivity was measured at 3.74 and in September of 2002 at 3.64 (see figure 5 below).

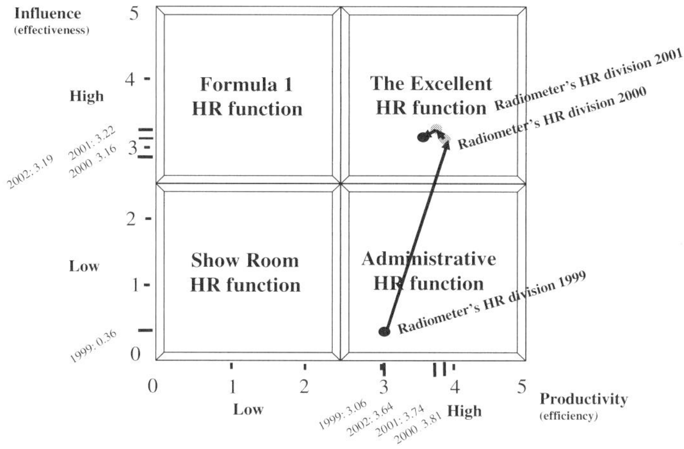

Figure 5. The development in Radiometer

If we plot the measured values of both influence and productivity on the HR Road Map we can see how the development of Radiometer's HR division from September of 1999 to September of 2001 went from a fairly efficient personnel division (but with an extremely miniscule influence) to an *Excellent HR Division*. Considering the short time interval here, this is a striking accomplishment.

If we plot the above-mentioned values into HR's estimated profit formula: $F(x,y) = y^2+x$, we register a development from a calculated value of 3.51 in September of 1999 to a calculated value of 14.08 in September of 2001. If we transfer these values to the generated profitability measurement model, we see progress. After having had a negative profitability in September of 1999, Radiometer's HR division had, according to the model, progressed to having a positive profitability in September of 2001 (see figure 6).

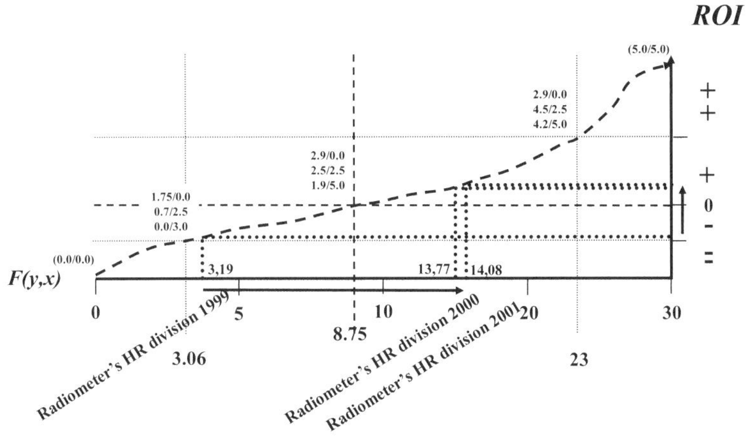

Figure 6. The development in Radiometer

4. IMPLICATIONS FOR THEORY

In order to meet new environmental demands, mainly (expectations of) increasing competition, the personnel department in Radiometer has changed to become a more modern HR-division. This process of re-designing a division, through the development of more performance oriented parameters, could prove to be one of the future elements in design approaches to organizational theory. Mohrman et al. have been arguing for the importance of this type of approach for a long time (see Mohrman, Galbraith and Lawler 1998).

We have mainly been treating the "vertical" fit, i.e. how local HR considerations and activities align themselves in relation to overall corporate strategy (Andersen et al. 2006). In the sense that we have not focused on "horizontal" fit aspects, both between the different elements within the HR-division, and between HR and other divisions, this is a very partial analysis. We have not addressed any total design solutions; and that begs the question whether divisional adaptations like this one will lead to overall design fit.

The dilemma confronting managers and organizations is, in the short-term perspective, to constantly maintaining efficiency, and in the long-term perspective, to secure effectiveness, which will provide viability. In this light it is perhaps most fruitful to follow Scott's approach (2003, p. 351). He mentions two important considerations: time horizon and level of measuring. Concerning the former, the question is whether the company, in the short–term, will concentrate on financial indicators (versus more enduring measures of performance). Concerning the latter, we can distinguish between individual participants, groups or departments. In this respect, measuring efficiency and effectiveness is a multiple-measures exercise, and the outcome is indeed highly dependent on the perspective of the organization. In other words, we cannot be sure that the "exercise" the HR-division has carried out will continue to be efficient and effective in the short-term future as well as in the long-term; and we do not know whether it will be efficient and effective for the whole of Radiometer Medical A/S. The HR division is quite convinced that it is, and will continue to be in the future. But it is still unknown as long as we have only limited knowledge of various causal links between the different organisational activities.

Radiometer's case is also an example of an attempt to carry out what several researchers have called difficult "ambidextrous activities", i.e. the pursuit of short term and long term goals simultaneously within the division. As Tushman and O'Reilly label it: to implement both incremental (improving efficiency) and revolutionary change (increasing effectiveness) (see Tushman and O'Reilly, 1996, p. 8). Many have distinguished between a structural and contextual ambidexterity, where the former links to the creation of separate structures for different types of activities, and the latter to individual employees making choices between alignment- and adaptation-oriented activities. One of the problems here is that structural separation can create isolation within the individual division, and HR is in this respect exposed. This could be why the HR-management emphasizes the simultaneous demand for pursuing efficiency and effectiveness. In other words, this case is not supporting any *structural* division as an answer to diverse environmental demands.

5. IMPLICATIONS FOR PRACTICE

The study here is an example of how an HR-division addresses accountability, and it is indeed an example of how management choices at the divisional level can make a difference. It is also an example of how a local initiative from a traditionally less strategic unit has managed to increase its influence through attracting top-management attention. In particular, Radiometer's new HR-manager and his new employees have worked actively with the implementation of new HR-measures and practices. "Real" implementation is often referred to as having accomplished effectiveness. In other words, HR has started to deliver tools and roadmaps to improve the implementation of its own activities, and even though some of theses measures are partly based on subjective data, top- and line-managers perceptions of the division, it still has quite important implications for the division itself.

The question is whether we will see continued change in HR-design and more focus on efficiency in the future. This change in design and focus is described by Tyson as: 'achieving greater outputs from the level of inputs made' and effectiveness as: 'achieving for a given input a better return on its output' (Tyson, 2005, p. 232). On the practical level, these two definitions have recently been translated into "productivity" and "added value" delivered by the HR-department. HR employees and activities are required to add value by increasing organizational competitiveness; add efficiency by focusing mainly on input and use of resources and costs, and to add effectiveness by focusing on output in products or services (and revenues).

Mainly because it has been considered to be extremely difficult to measure the output of many HR-activities, we see a long tradition in HR-divisions of focusing on measuring input and activities (e.g. like training days), rather than output (e.g. effects on performance in the line organization). By using Radiometer's example, HR practitioners can now learn from an HR-manager was able to convince top management that in a technician and engineering dominated organization, HR effectiveness and efficiency *can* be pursued at the same time.

6. CONCLUSION

Radiometer is a case-study of how the HR division of a larger corporation, without precedent, successfully managed to develop methods of pursuing greater effectiveness and efficiency simultaneously - an example of divisional ambidexterity. From rather simple measures of performance and competence, such as the monitoring of the division's capacity to support the operation and progress of the business, to development plans and measurement based dialogue with top-management, the HR-department acquired a central and visible position in the company. During this process, they developed three measurement tools for creating price/activity calculations to compare with "best practice".

Through the increase in competence of routine tasks such as pay/cost reduction and the aim at continuing to encourage process innovation, the HR-division has been able to pursue efficiency. Concerning effectiveness, the HR division has become much more visible and better at being a partner for the organization. Top- and line managers – the most visible end-users of HR – confirm this result. These subjective measures of effectiveness have been transformed into concrete changes in daily operations, and they are in addition documented through the developed measurement tools. The model and calculation tools tell the story that the HR division of today contributes to the overall organization by having a positive profitability, not merely a passive source of corporate expense. In this light, HR is now able to be held more accountable – similar to other divisional areas in companies. Finally, the increasing measurement of HR in business metrics enhances the status of HR work as evidenced by HR employees themselves. They perceive their division as a contributing member of the corporation, and that they have experienced a divisional professionalization.

REFERENCES

Andersen, T., Eriksen, B., Lemmergaard, J. and Povlsen, L., 2006, The many faces of fit, Burton, et al, *Organization design, The evolving state-of-the-art*, N.Y., Springer.

Becker, B.E., Huselid, M.A. and Ulrich, D., 2001, *Human Resource Scorecard. Linking people, strategy, and performance*, Boston, MA, Harvard Business School Press.

Brewster, C. and Larsen, H.H., eds., 2000, *Human Resource Management in Northern Europe. Trends, dilemmas and strategy,* Oxford, Blackwell Business.

Burton, R., DeSanctis, G. and Obel, G., 2006, *Organizational design. A step-by-step approach*, Cambridge, University Press.

Child, J., 1984, *Organization A guide to problems and practices*, London, Paul Chapman.

Child, J., 2005, *Organization. Contemporary principles and practices,* Oxford, Blackwell.

Fitz-enz, J. and Davison, B., 2002, *How to measure human resources management,* 3. ed., 1. ed., 1994, New York, McGraw-Hill.

Fitz-enz, J., 2000, *ROI of Human Capital: Measuring the Economic Value of Employee Performance,* AMACOM, New York.

Fitz-enz, J., 1993, *Benchmarking Staff Performance: How Staff Departments Can Enhance Their Value to the Customer,* Jossey Bass Business and Management Series, San Francisco.

Gibson, C.B. and Birkinshaw, J., 2004, The antecedents, consequences and mediating role of organizational ambidexterity, *Academy of Management Journal,* **47,** 2, 209-226.

Huber, G. P., 2003, *The necessary nature of future firm. Attributes of survivors in a changing world,* Thousands Oaks, Sage.

Kearns, P., 1997, Measuring Human Resources and the Impact on the Bottom Line, *Financial Times Management briefings*, Trans-Atlantic Publications, Inc.

Krogager, P., Schmidt, K., 2002, *Måling af HR-funktionen. Et bud på måling af HR-*funktionens indflydelse, produktivitet og lønsomhed, København, Dansk Industri.

Krogager, P., Schmidt, K., 2004, Fra administrativ personaleafdeling til forretningsorienteret HR-funktion, Andersen, T. and Hildebrandt, S., eds., *Human Resource Management,* Copenhagen, Børsen Forum.

Larsen, H.H., 1999, *Human resource management*, ti markante udviklingstræk, Rogaczewska, A.P., Larsen, H.H. and Skovbro, C., eds., Cranet-E undersøgelsen 1999. HRM in danske virksomheder, København: DMF og HHK.

Larsen, H.H., ed., 2001, *Human resource management, i modlys – spydspidser og dilemmaer,* København, DMF and HHK.

March, J.G., 1991, Exploration and exploitation in organizational learning, *Organization Science,* Vol. **2**, No. 1, 71-87.

Phillips, J.J., 1999, *Accountability in Human Resource Management*, Woburn, MA, Butterworth-Heinemann.

Rynes, S.L., Colbert, A.E. and Brown, K.G., 2002, HR professionals beliefs about effective human resource practices: correspondence between research and practice, *Human Resource Management,* Summer, 2002, Vol. **41**, No. 2, 149-174.

Scott, W.R., 2003, *Organizations. Rational, Natural and Open Systems,* New Jersey, Prentice Hall.

Tushman, M. L. and Romanelli, E., 1985, Organizational evolution: A metamorphosis model of convergence and reorientation, *Research in Organizational Behaviour,* vol. **7**, 171-222, JAI Press.

Tushman, M. L. and O'Reilly, C.A., 1996, Ambidextrous organizations: managing evolutionary and revolutionary change, *California Management Review*, Vol. **38**, No. 4, (summer), 8-30.

Tyson, S., ed., 1995, *Strategic prospects for HRM,* London, Institute for Personnel and Development.

Ulrich, D. 1997, *Human Resource Champions. The next agenda for adding value and delivering results,* Boston, Mass., Harvard Business School Press.

Ulrich, D., ed., 1998, *Delivering Results. A new Mandate for human resource professional,.* Boston, MA, Harvard Business School Press.

Ulrich, D., Losey, M. R., and Lake, G., 1997, *Tomorrow's HR management – 48 thought leaders call for change,* New York, John Wiley and Sons.

Ulrich, D. and Smallwood, N., 2003, *Why the bottom line isn't! How to build value through people and organization,* New Jersey, John Wiley and Sons, Inc.

Walker, G. and Macdonald, J.R., 2001, Designing and implementing and HR scorecard, *Human Resource Management,* Winter 2001, Vol. **40**, No. 4.

PART III: INNOVATION: OVERCOMING INERTIA AND CONFLICTS

Chapter 8

OPENING UP THE INNOVATION PROCESS

DIFFERENT ORGANIZATIONAL STRATEGIES

Sladjana Vujovic & John Parm Ulhøi
Aarhus School of Business, University of Aarhus, Dept. of Management, Centre for Organizational Renewal and Evolution (CORE), Haslegaardsvej 10, DK-8210 Aarhus V, Denmark, Tel.: +45 89486477, Fax.: +45 89486125

Abstract: An organization's ability to create, retrieve, and use knowledge to innovate is a critical strategic asset. Until recently, most textbooks on business and product development argued that managers should keep their new ideas to themselves and protect knowledge from getting into competitors' hands. Seeking, developing, and protecting knowledge is a costly endeavour. Moreover, apart from being expensive, the process of turning new knowledge into useful and well-protected innovations often slows the speed of development and increases costs. In this chapter, alternative strategies for innovation, in which sharing and co-operation play a critical part, are discussed. In particular, we address the involvement of users in opening up the innovation process which, in turn, offers participating actors some useful strategies for product development. Four archetypal strategies are identified and classified according to type of user involvement and the organizational level at which co-operation with external sources of knowledge takes place.

Key words: Innovation; product development; user-developer integration; open innovation; strategy design.

1. INTRODUCTION

The present state of competition and technological development puts increasing demands on the individual business actor to stay innovative and continuously develop new and improved products and services which, in turn, typically require access to external sources of state-of-the-art knowledge. Updated knowledge is a critical ingredient of the innovation process and as such is a necessary property of the learning environment in

R.M. Burton et al. (eds.), *Designing Organizations*, doi: 10.1007/978-0-387-77776-4_8,

which the organization operates (Cohen and Levinthal 2001). Bringing external sources of knowledge into an organization can have important implications, however. First, acquiring access to such critical and specialized knowledge is usually expensive. Furthermore, protecting a positive outcome in the form of a new invention, design, or patent is also likely to be costly. Second, acquiring external knowledge may affect organizational design, since it will involve social interactions external to the organization and thus introduce new social patterns of human interaction to replace and/or complement existing patterns. Depending on the magnitude of such changes, adjustments and/or changes of organizational design may therefore be required.

However, what if inventions and innovations were publicly available at no cost? What if access to critical knowledge providers were free? And what if the user became the innovator? While mainstream organization theory may not adequately explain such a scenario, it is far from being a theoretical vision, since there might be perfectly sound reasons for developing non-proprietary knowledge and/or turning proprietary knowledge into non-proprietary knowledge. This chapter considers open innovation as a strategic organizational decision and identifies different organizational design strategies for opening up the innovation process.

Innovative knowledge is developed within a continuum of private and collective agency (Ulhøi, 2004). While the former is based on the principle of closed source (i.e. proprietary and private), the latter is based on non-proprietary knowledge and collectivity (i.e. goods based on non-profit motives), where protective measures are used not to restrict the use of intellectual property but to ensure public access to it. Between the two pure modes of innovative agency, variations and combinations (hybrids) exist – and can be generally referred to as "open innovations" or the process of opening up the innovation process (OIP). Such hybrids, in turn, can be grouped according to differences in their strategic implications.

The purpose of this chapter is to identify and classify different archetypal strategies for opening up the innovation process. OIP is, among other things, characterized by user involvement and co-operation with external sources of knowledge (Chesbrough 2003). Involving users during the innovation process can be seen not only as an important part of exploring the environment for opportunities but also as a vital resource, a source of innovation which will enable organizations to respond to the market in an appropriate and effective way. By involving users in innovation and product development processes, organizations increase the usability of the outcome since the developers also represent future users. Such innovation processes represent an interesting social and/or organizational innovation in relation to new product or service development. Allowing the critical knowledge underlying an invention or innovation to be accessible to any interested third party is known from user-innovation networks, where users are mutually connected by means of information transfer via face-to-face, electronic, or other form of communication (von Hippel 2002).

In an open approach to innovation, organizational boundaries become blurred, thus enabling innovation to take place both within and outside the firm and/or in combinations thereof. In such a situation, organizations rely not only on internal ideas, but also on external ones, by exploiting both external and in-house pathways to the market (Chesbrough 2003). The remainder of the chapter is organized as follows. Section two addresses in more detail the role of users and co-operation during firms' innovative activities. In section three, non-conventional approaches to involving users in design and development activities are presented as cornerstones of an open-innovation design approach. Section four proposes four different archetypes of open-innovation strategy designs. The proposed framework is discussed in section five, including implications for research and practice. Section six is the conclusion.

2. THE ROLE OF USERS AND CO-OPERATION DURING INNOVATIVE ACTIVITIES

The term *user* refers to the end user of the product, and not the reseller. Users are individuals or organizations that "expect to benefit from *using* a product or a service" (p. 3, von Hippel 2005). By user participation is meant exploiting the environment for opportunities by making it possible for users to take part in product development processes. In the literature on management information systems (MIS), the terms user participation and user involvement have often been used interchangeably. However, Barki and Hartwick (1989) argue for maintaining a distinction between them. They refer to user involvement as "a subjective psychological state of the individual" and define it as "the importance and personal relevance that users attach either to a particular system or to IS in general". User participation, on the other hand, is used when "referring to the behaviors and activities that the target users or their representatives perform during the systems development process" (p. 59). Taking this definition a bit further, user participation can be seen as a set of behaviors and activities that end users carry out during the product development and innovation processes.

However, user participation can vary according to type (from direct to indirect) and degree of participation (from no influence to strong influence) (Ives and Olson 1984). What is important in this chapter are the different levels at which user participation takes place in a context characterized by open-source co-operation. Here, we focus not on the effect of contingency factors on user participation, but instead consider types of users, types of participation and organizational contexts when opening up the innovation process.

Before going any further, it is necessary to clarify what is meant by innovation in this context. By innovation in the context of open-source co-operation, this chapter refers to a change in technology (Christensen and Bower 2001). As used here, the term technology means "the processes by which an organization transforms labour, capital, materials, and information into products and services" (p. 429), which thus includes not only engineering and manufacturing functions but also a range of business processes (Christensen and Bower 2001). The chapter thus considers how innovation is approached through new ways of doing things and new patterns of human interaction, such as using non-traditional ways of involving users in design and development activities.

There are several examples of innovations which illustrate different aspects of opening up the innovation process. Some of the newer examples of open-source innovation include open-source software communities and sports communities such as windsurfing, snowboarding and skateboarding (Shah 2000; Franke and Shah 2003). However, a 'sharing approach' during the innovation process has a relatively long history. Earlier examples of opening up the innovation process (OIP) that have been noted in the literature include accounts from the nineteenth century, e.g. the U.S. steel industry, the steam pump engine in Cornwell (UK), the U.S. machine tool industry and the steel industry in Cleveland (UK) (Meyer 2003; Nuvolari 2003).

Other examples of commercial companies incorporating various parts of the co-operative and sharing philosophy of OIP activities into their business model are constantly emerging. Some organizations may choose to apply them on a more internal level, based on open-source-like co-operation principles – in such cases the "two-way communication" between users and company is not in balance (equal). The company thus seems to be more open to receiving input than to making its knowledge available to users. Put another way, the user is not as equal a partner as in open-source software projects or in cases where companies involve users by making some of their products non-proprietary. On the other hand, some companies have employed a more integrated strategy around open source which combines elements of both closed and open source. IBM, Sun Microsystems and Apple Computer, for example, divide software solutions into two parts, one of which is open source while the other stays in proprietary form (West 2003).

The underlying rationale behind OIP activities is to build co-operative organizations where value is created. OIP activities are found in rich, knowledge-intensive environments whose actors, artefacts, tools, practices, resources, meanings, etc., interact in loosely integrated structures (Lanzara and Morner 2003). Open-source projects thus use the principles of parallel and distributed development during the process of knowledge creation, whereby the speed and diversity of resources become critical factors of development and innovation. The dynamic interaction of multiple contributions and relationships in open-source projects leads to the creation of knowledge. New knowledge, it has been argued, comes more easily from diversity and surprise, which is only possible where there is room for controversy and multiple views (Lanzara and Morner 2003).

Different OIP approaches have demonstrated alternative forms of small- and large-scale co-operation as well as fundamentally changed knowledge-production processes (Weber 2004). In order to generate new perspectives on social co-operation, it is necessary to make a distinction between different types of open-source co-operation.

The varying degrees of interaction of OIP approaches redefine the boundaries between organizations, and between organizations and users. Moreover, the increased interaction between customers and organizations is perceived as a mobilization of organizational resources, and not as individual liabilities (Hirschhorn and Thomas 1992). However, open-source innovation is not only about bringing customers into the innovation process. It also includes sharing critical components of knowledge both intra-/inter-organizationally and between individuals. One of the keys of open-source innovation thus becomes the flow of resources between the involved parties.

3. USER-CENTERED INNOVATION PROCESSES

The transition from the economic growth and booming markets of the 1950s to the competitive and global marketplace of today is reflected in the way R&D has been managed (Nobelius 2004). The approaches to R&D and innovation have changed over time, from being seen as a primarily linear sequence of functional activities (Tidd et al. 1997) to seeing it as a process of matching and combining the interaction between both "push" and "pull" elements (von Hippel 1988; Tidd et al. 1997).

While there are many different types of innovation processes, the focus in this chapter is on those types where organizations use non-traditional ways of involving users in design and development activities, as is the case with open-source co-operation. Moreover, networks have long been seen as being driven by external factors, e.g. the distribution of technological resources or the social structure of resource dependence (Pfeffer and Salancik 1978). According to this view, organizations need to look outside the organizational boundaries and forge ties that help them obtain the resources they lack.

Choosing strategies which involve users in product development is generally assumed to result from a dynamic process driven by exogenous interdependencies. Organizations seek exchange, sharing and co-development with users for different reasons, e.g. blocking a competitor, extending networks, getting closer to users, commoditizing parts of competitors' businesses, etc. Increasingly, the ability to innovate requires access to new knowledge, which in turn emphasizes the importance of external networks. Allowing lead users to become actively involved in product development may be a strategic means to boost the speed of development and effectively reduce development costs (von Hippel 1988). This in turn promotes external learning from and with users.

Christensen and Bower (2001) argue, for example, that support for innovations within an organization depends on the role played by existing customers, i.e. their presence or absence, and also their ability to express the need for a certain innovation. The involvement of users in product development, and the opening up of organizational R&D and innovation processes, are important sources of knowledge. Recent empirical work has shown that large numbers of new industrial and consumer products are in fact developed by users (von Hippel 2005).

4. FOUR ARCHETYPES OF OIP APPROACHES

Von Hippel (2005) found from his analyses of user-led innovations that many users actually develop and modify products for their own use. OIP activities give users the opportunity to improve, modify and influence a product in such a way as to meet their needs and expectations. Weber's (2004) central proposition is that the open-source process is a new mode of organizing production which can be used in different settings:

"The notion of open-sourcing as a strategic organizational decision can be seen as an efficiency choice around distributed innovation (...) As information about what users want and need to do becomes more fine-grained, more individually differentiated, and harder to communicate, the incentives grow to shift the locus of innovation closer to them by empowering them with freely modifiable tools." (pp. 265–267).

Activities aimed at opening up the innovation process can be observed at different organizational levels and in different settings. But before attempting to arrive at a more comprehensive understanding of the conditions under which open-sourcing should be applied, it seems reasonable to make a distinction between the different ways in which it takes place.

Below, different modes of co-operation and knowledge production as a means of involving users in the innovation process are proposed. In practice, there are different variants of OIP approaches, all of which are inspired by the ideology behind open source. However, while not all of these variants are organized around the property regime specific to open source, they are all user-centred innovation processes that have similarities with open source. The following identifies and classifies these variants. Four archetypes of OIP strategies are proposed: (i) The unregulated collective invention strategy; (ii) The regulated open-source innovation strategy; (iii) The combined open/closed innovation strategy; and (iv) The boundedly open innovation strategy.

4.1 The unregulated collective invention strategy

While open-source development is not a recent phenomenon, it has received rapidly growing attention in the last couple of years. But there are also examples of this form of co-operation in the older literature on technological innovation, e.g. Nathan Rosenberg's (1976) studies of the machine tool industry, and Eric von Hippel's (1988) studies of scientific instruments. The steel industry in Cleveland (UK), the steam pump engine in Cornwell (UK) and the American steel industry are also examples of collective invention, all from the nineteenth century. From an historical point of view, OSS is a particular type of innovation process which Robert Allen (Allen 1983) calls collective invention, and which he defines as: "...the free exchange of information about new techniques and plant designs among firms in an industry" (p. 2). In a collective invention process, competitors voluntarily reveal relevant information to each other about an innovation regarding solutions to important technical problems. This information is then used to make incremental improvements in the basic/underlying technical equipment (Nuvolari 2003). These activities also pave the way for professional meetings, associations and journals, where detailed and formerly protected knowledge is shared.

Thus, a group of commercial entities combine resources for the free exchange of relevant information and knowledge to help solve a technical problem. The involved parties gain new knowledge and insights from participating in this type of inter-organizational co-operation, which happens in a rather informal way. This can be illustrated by the case of the nineteenth century machine industry[2], which is discussed in more detail below.

[2] Unfortunately, it has not been possible to get access to several of the original US sources, as they are not allowed to be sent out of the US.

In the United States in the 1820s, it was still customary for users to produce machines for their own use on an ad hoc basis. This was followed, between 1840-80, by the emergence and growth of firms specialized in machine production (Rosenberg 1976). This process of machine production was thus part of the process of industrialization.

The diffusion of technical knowledge across individual manufacturers was made easier because most of the machinery produced by these firms involved a broadly similar set of problems and skills (Rosenberg 1976). According to Rosenberg, the learning process underlying this problem-solving and diffusion of technical knowledge was made possible because the parties involved possessed only similar, and not identical, knowledge, skills and problems. This left more room for learning. Thus, skills acquired in solving one problem were transferred and used to solve other problems, e.g. in the production of different types of machines (ibid.).

In the nineteenth century, the machinery and metal-working sectors used common processes and operations based on similar skills and techniques (Rosenberg 1976). This not only made it possible to use decentralized sources of power, but also had the effect of making different/unrelated industries closely related technologically. The machine tool industry also had the role of "a transmission center in the diffusion of the new technology", in that "it dealt with processes and problems common to an increasing number of industries" (p. 19, Rosenberg, 1976).

An interesting example is the development of the universal milling machine in 1861. The Providence Tool Company used twist drills to make holes in that part of the gun known as the nipple. The company's superintendent, Frederick W. Howe, shared this information and knowledge with Joseph R. Brown of the Brown and Sharpe Company, which used similar drills to make sewing machines. This sharing of information had a direct effect on the development and production of the universal milling machine (pp. 432-433, Rosenberg 1963). Howe and Brown shared their experience and information on the types of milling machines previously designed for Robbins & Lawrence and the Newark Machine Co. This helped Brown realize that what he needed was a machine for cutting spirals. Thus was born the idea of building a machine suitable for both the specific task of grooving twist drills and general utility in machine shops (Roe 1914; Sharpe 1949).

However, the first machine tool built by Brown & Sharpe was a turret screw machine, which predated the universal milling machine. Frederick W. Howe and Joseph R. Brown often shared and compared notes regarding mechanical matters. At the same time, Howe was closely associated with the Robbins & Lawrence Company of Windsow, Vermont, in connection with the turret screw machine (Sharpe 1949). Thus, the creation of a turret screw machine was based on *inter-organizational* information sharing among different companies in the same industry. The users were companies and the participation took place in an informal, unregulated and voluntary manner. This type of co-operation can be characterized as inter-organizational, as was the case with Allen's (1983) collective invention. It is here termed unregulated, because co-operation between the companies was not regulated by any kind of legal measure.

4.2 The regulated open source innovation strategy

Here, regulation means the existence of legal measures, such as licenses, which ensure that the underlying critical knowledge cannot be restricted in any way, e.g. by patents, etc. Here, the term *open-source innovation* refers to "innovative agency to which the innovator has a priori waived the right to protect the innovation" (Ulhøi 2004).

As in the former case, from the point of view of sharing, open-source innovation is a rather "pure" form of OIP strategy. However, whereas the former (i.e. unregulated collective invention) used means, e.g. industrial journals and associations (Meyer 2003) to "reach" potential users, regulated open-source innovation assumes that the user will have to search for the relevant OIP-related project himself. The notion of property is inverted in open-source innovation, or, as Weber (2004) puts it: "Property in open source is configured fundamentally around the right to distribute, not the right to exclude" (p. 228). Open-source communities are non-profit communities consisting of contributors who are also users participating voluntarily in the development work. The products are accessible and available for everyone to use. The best-known example of open-source innovation is open-source software, e.g. Linux, Apache, Debian, etc., which has been thoroughly analyzed and described elsewhere (e.g. Hars and Ou 2002; Franke and Von Hippel 2003; Hertel et al. 2003), and will therefore not be discussed in detail here. Hence, this chapter looks at this type of approach strictly from the organization's point of view, i.e. in this case, the point of view of the open-source software project, not of the participant's.

The idea behind open-source software is that programmers can exchange files, ideas, and adapt and modify the source code (i.e. work freely on it). This results in faster development and improvement of the software than in the traditional, closed model of innovation. Having access to the source code allows users to adapt and customize software to their own needs, fix their own bugs, write their own code, as well as greatly reduce potential supplier lock-in (Weber 2004).

The boundaries of open-source software projects are very open, with users/contributors being granted access to the source code in return for keeping the modified code open. Open-source software projects are formal entities[3], which users/contributors join voluntarily and make contributions to, as well as utilize the developed software according to their own needs. Thus, co-operation with (and among) users, as external sources of knowledge, takes place at the intra-organizational level in the sense that the users enter the network (project) independently. Their "innovation (...) gets incorporated into more complex systems when and if it improves the performance of the whole" (p. 233, Weber 2004). Thus, participation is voluntary, although formal, due to parameters such as project membership and licenses.

4.3 The combined open/closed innovation model

Another variant of a user-centred innovation process resembling open-source innovation is the combined innovation approach, which allows a closed model to coexist side by side with ad hoc open business models. This is the approach being taken by a few well-positioned companies which supplement their proprietary software with open-source software, such as IBM with Apache web server, Linux and Eclipse. This innovation approach thus adopts the perspective of the company which is applying it. IBM, which started using Java in 1995 and Linux in 1999 (Schadler 2003), is one example of an existing company which chose to combine its previously exclusively proprietary business model with a non-proprietary one. In spring 2000, IBM set up its own version of a collaborative open-source development service, which was a major integrated strategy around open-source software. Its commitment to open source has since spread throughout the company, with its major mainframes and servers, as well as all of its major enterprise applications, being built around a Linux platform (Weber 2004).

In an open-source software project such as Apache, IBM is both a participant in and contributor to the project on the same terms as other contributors. On the other hand, the Apache Foundation is itself an example of a regulated open-source innovation approach. However, from IBM's perspective, participation in Apache is part of the company's combined open/closed approach.

IBM divides software solutions into two parts, one which can be open source, while the other stays in a proprietary form. The commercial incentives emphasized here are the sale of support and of the other part of

[3] Open-source software projects are considered formal since they set parameters for voluntary relationships among independent actors.

the solution, which represents the proprietary form. Even though the improvements in open-source software are not allowed to be commercialized, commercial companies can benefit through complementary proprietary segments (Lerner and Tirole 2001). IBM earns profit by selling computer servers with open-source software pre-installed, i.e. by selling the complement of computer hardware (von Hippel 2005).

In the case of open innovation, the boundary of the firm has certain openings in order to attract user contributions. These are conceptualized non-proprietary parts of the company's product offering, and serve several purposes, including getting fresh ideas from outside the company, i.e. exploiting external sources of knowledge, complementing a revenue stream, shifting competitive advantage to another architectural layer, enabling communication with and through its communities, getting closer to users, etc (West 2003). There is, therefore, a two-way communication where both users and the company learn through interacting with each other. Moreover, this co-operation, based on hybrid strategies inspired by open-source innovation, is also organized around the property regime that characterizes open source. Thus, this particular strategy is both regulated and formalized. The difference, compared with the former approach, is that contributing to the development of open-source software is only one part of IBM's strategy and activities, while an OSS project is mainly focused on creating and distributing open-source software.

4.4 The boundedly open innovation strategy

Bounded attempts to open up the innovation process at the intra-organizational level, i.e. within a commercial company, are based on principles of co-operation similar to open source. A company opens a few communication channels in order to get in touch with users and involve them in product development at an early stage, albeit under different conditions than the other archetypes of open source. This is in fact a simulation of open-source innovation at a mainly intra-organizational level. It lacks, however, significant elements of open source, hence the term boundedly open innovation.

The main element that is missing is the fact that this co-operation is not organized around the same property regime as open source innovation.[4] Furthermore, there is an imbalance in the two-way communication between

[4] Weber (2004) emphasizes this difference regarding other examples of what he calls the overuse of open source as a metaphor, e.g. "open-cola" alternatives to Coke and Pepsi, "openmusic" registry, "openlaw" project, etc. (p. 267).

the company and users, in that information mainly goes one way, i.e. to the company. To a large extent, the user assumes the role of informant, while the company is more of a recipient, letting ideas flow into it. This differs from open-source software development, where the critical knowledge component, i.e. the source code, is shared, and where users themselves can develop the software for their own use. However, as is often the case with open innovation, users are unable to manufacture the products on their own, since this would require other kinds of resources than those needed for developing software, e.g. different types of materials, manufacturing facilities, machines, tools, technical skills, etc.

Notwithstanding, empirical research from different sectors shows that users actually often develop prototypes of new products of commercial importance (Freeman 1968; Shaw 1985; von Hippel 1988). Furthermore, it has been argued that, the more effort a company puts into the early product development phase, the lower the costs of the development process as a whole (Boehm 1981).

Philips is one example of a company that has chosen to organize its innovation processes around users. In an interview, Josephine Green, senior director of Trends and Strategy at Philips Design[5], told how inspiration from the humanities, psychology, anthropology and ethnography had motivated Philips to involve users in the innovation process by creating a better understanding of people in their everyday life (Petersen 2005). The company uses ethnographic methodology to acquire an insight into customers' everyday life by letting them relate to and comment on different phases in the innovation process, or by testing prototypes (ibid.). They have thus taken the step of involving end users in analysis, design and evaluation.

Josephine Green emphasizes the necessity of being where people actually live (ibid.), thus making sure that Philips is "adapting technology to people, not the other way around" (p. 15, Breisford 2005). In this example of open innovation, it could be argued that, since Philips goes to users, the latter are not initiative-takers in the way they are in open-source innovation (e.g. software development). Furthermore, Philips looks for users with new and/or unfulfilled needs. This is a strategy used to identify innovative users that has been described as promising in the literature (Urban and von Hippel 1988; Herstatt and von Hippel 1992). The company becomes involved in the everyday lives of these users through such different tools as diaries, video and digital cameras, drawings, etc. (Petersen 2005). Philips thus goes

[5] Philips Design is a creative force of some 450 professionals and more than 25 nationalities. It operates as an autonomous unit within Philips Electronics and provides a full range of design services to a highly diverse portfolio of clients (http://www.parispwn.net/lunches/speaker_bio/speaker_greene.html)

outside the company to acquire local information from users. One part of the information is embedded in the way users live, work and behave in everyday life. It has been argued that information about users' needs and preferences can sometimes be difficult to transfer (i.e. coding, transfer and decoding) (Dougherty 1990). However, Philips tries to overcome this by observing the everyday lives of users, applying ethnographic methods, and involving users in product development. Philips HQ is actually located in a region, the Aachen-Leuven-Eindhovben region, which is the location for a €5.5 billion project focussing on (i) increased co-operation, (ii) open innovation, (iii) advanced networking, and (iv) zones of opportunities (http://www.pdc-office.org).

However, information may also be difficult to transfer because of the tacitness of the information, or because of the provider's mode of interaction and attributes of information-seekers or providers (von Hippel 1994). Furthermore, many users are not aware of their needs in connection with new products, and are often unable to articulate them. The subjectivity of product usability, functionality, reliability, aesthetics, etc., is one of the reasons for user involvement throughout the process of product development (Buurman 1997).

5. DISCUSSION AND IMPLICATIONS

5.1 Strategies for Opening up the Innovation Process

The four archetypes of OIP-related activities emerge and exist in different contexts and under different conditions. They can be characterized as four general forms of OIP strategies of organizational design, where each strategy has a different purpose. These archetypes are based on user co-operation, and one of the main things they have in common is that they all take into account the heterogeneity of user preferences, albeit for different reasons. In some cases the objective is faster development and product improvement, while in others it is the possibility of adapting products to one's own needs, reducing potential supplier lock-in (as, for example, in open-source software), consolidation of reputation and furthering career prospects (as, for example,(e.g. in the cases of collective invention, Ulhøi 2004). In yet other cases, user participation is used as a way to determine tacit preferences and needs, and maximize company value through bringing adapted, improved, customized, as well as new products to the market (e.g. open innovation in Philips). In boundedly open innovations, a company seeks external input (e.g. user innovation) and exploits it in a value-creation process. While this motive of creating business value is not a driver of OIP-related activities, it does play an important role with regard to the variety of OIP strategies. Thus, user involvement is employed for different purposes and in different degrees.

In the figure below, these four archetypes of open source are placed on a continuum to demonstrate their differences with regard to the extent of "openness", as well as the private-collective dimensions (figure 1).

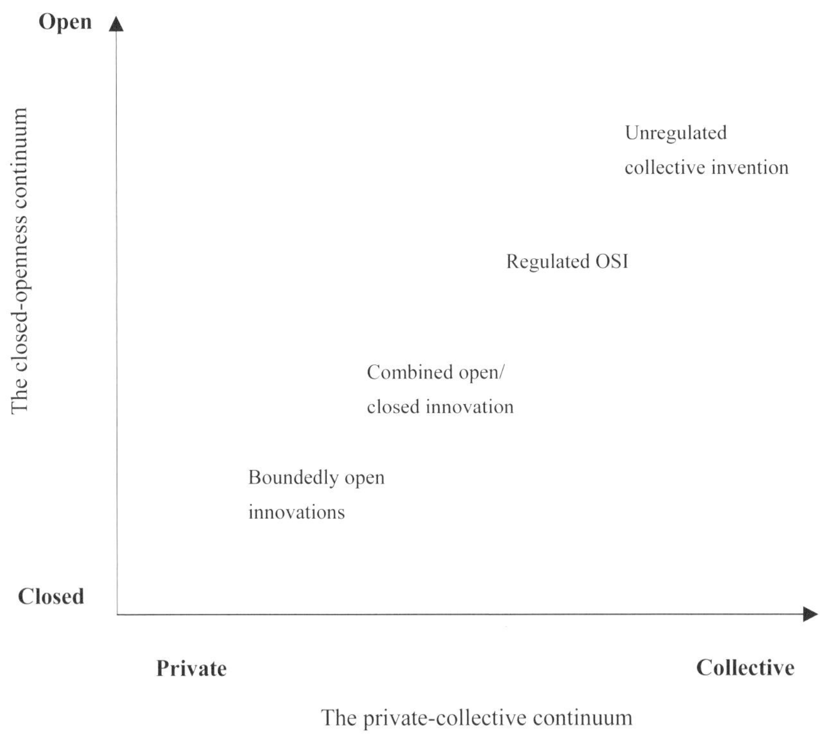

Figure 1. OIP strategies

Openness is here defined as the extent to which unrestricted access to the underlying knowledge is possible, i.e. the extent to which users are drawn into the innovation process and product development, as well as the extent of innovation disclosure. In figure 1, unregulated collective invention is placed very close to the collective model of agency, since it is represented by examples of the public disclosure of technical information and disclosure between competitors. Regulated OSI-related activities, represented by open-source software projects, are placed next to unregulated collective invention, since this form of product development/innovation process is accessible to everyone and the source code is open. The rights to intellectual property are thus voluntarily relinquished. Boundedly open innovation, on the other hand, is the archetypal manifestation of open source that is farthest away from the unregulated collective invention model. This is because users are drawn into the innovation process, though the company does not assume the same property regime, i.e. the rights to the intellectual property are not relinquished. In between the boundedly open innovation and regulated OSI are cases of the combined open/closed innovation strategy, where different combinations of open-source property regimes and proprietary property regimes can be found.

The four proposed archetypes of OIP strategies can be seen as different strategic means of involving users in the product development process. However, since users participate in different ways, it could be presumed that these archetypes involve different kinds of users. In regulated open-source innovation, e.g. open-source software projects, it could be argued that user participation takes place at users' initiative, whereas in the case of boundedly open innovation a company involves users through specific methods (e.g. ethnographic methods, research on people, cultures and societies[6]). It could also be argued that, in boundedly open innovation, users do not need to be the same kind of sophisticated users who are able to develop and/or produce the product themselves. In other words, they do not necessarily possess the required technical skills and knowledge, as with users of open-source software (open-source innovation). In the case of open innovation, experts are often used as moderators.

Table 1 summarizes some of the differences and/or similarities between users in each of the four archetypes. Key characteristics of organizations' roles with regard to innovation and product development processes in these archetypes are also identified. By the term *organizations* is meant entities which employ the principles of open source, whether they are open-source software projects, commercial companies, etc. The characteristics of co-operation in the archetypes are also reviewed.

[6] c.f. http://www.philips.com/assets/Downloadablefile/Philips_AnnualReview2004_2-13731.pdf

Table 1. The characteristics of users, organizations and co-operation in the four archetypes of OIP strategies.

	1. The unregulated collective invention strategy	2. The regulated open-source innovation strategy	3. The combined open/closed innovation strategy	4. The boundedly open innovation strategy
Users	Users are commercial entities experiencing the same (technical) problem	Independent, self-initiated development work	Independent, self-initiated development work	The "informant" role; involved in product development from an early phase
Organization	Makes resources available for joint problem-solving	"Mediator" of innovation sharing	"Mediator" of innovation sharing & participant/ contributor	The "recipient" role
Co-operation	Voluntary, informal participation and sharing of relevant information; sharing of innovations	Organized around open-source property regime; freely shared innovations	Partially organized around open-source property regime; freely shared innovations	Innovations are offered as products for sale (not shared)

On the user level, the four strategies differ in that users in the first strategy, the unregulated collective invention strategy, are commercial entities, e.g. a group of firms. In the other three strategies, users are individuals who have different roles. In the regulated OSI strategy, users are individuals who initiate development work in, for example, OSS projects. These individuals can either be doing the work for private[7] purposes or on behalf of a company[8] which employs them. Users in the combined open/closed innovation strategy are also individuals who join OSS projects, whose software is part of a particular company's product strategy. Finally, in the boundedly open innovation strategy, users have more of an informant role.

7 Private in this context means that they are *not* working on an OSS project on behalf of a company in which they are employed.

8 It is common for companies to have employees whose task is to contribute with development work on OSS for different purposes, e.g. to develop a piece of open-source software the company is using itself. One example is IBM, which hires contributors to Apache development groups (Lerner and Tirole, 2002).

Organizations in the first strategy (a group of firms) make their resources available for joint problem-solving, while organizations in the second strategy, e.g. open-source software projects (OSS projects), mediate innovation and information sharing between many different individuals taking part for various purposes. The same applies to organizations (commercial companies) in the third strategy. Moreover, they also participate actively in OSS development (developing OSS that they use as part of their open/closed strategy). In the fourth, boundedly open innovation strategy, the organization (commercial company) has a recipient role, in that the information goes mainly one way, from users to the company.

Co-operation in the four approaches is characterized by different degrees of free innovation/information sharing. In the first approach, technological information is voluntarily shared by making it public. In the second approach, regulated OSI strategy, OSS projects mediate innovation-sharing both through the way they are organized (online) and through the open-source property regime that characterizes them. In the third approach, the combined approach, co-operation is partly based on open-source property regime (the part that concerns the OSS the company is using), the other part being proprietary. In the final approach, co-operation results not in sharing, but in selling the products.

It is worth noting that, from an organizational point of view, extra-organizational resources play an increasing role during innovative activities. In a horizontal user-innovator network, a complex social exchange of information, experience and needs is taking place. Kanter (1988) argues that organizational complexity facilitates the generation of new ideas, and thereby stimulates innovation. Among other things, this complexity involves links to users and outsiders, openness to the environment, diversity and breadth of experience and multiple communication links (p. 183). OIP strategies seem to resemble these characteristics.

Conventional market research wisdom presumes that a particular product already exists or that users are aware of their needs beforehand. OIP strategies are not only about giving users what they want. By employing, for example, the boundedly open innovation strategy, organizations can create opportunity and capacity for understanding users' needs in a non-traditional way before even users themselves are aware of them. In this way, organizations lead product development and innovation towards new functionalities and products. Thus, organizations have the possibility of being both customer-led and leading customers.

5.2 Implications for Organization Design

Our discussion of the four archetypes and their individual characteristics suggests additional research regarding: (i) the purposes/motivations of embracing user participation, (ii) the degree of openness to the external sources of knowledge specific to each archetype, and (iii) the types of users and user participation involved in innovation activities in the four different settings. Moreover, it would be useful to determine when one archetype is preferred to another. In future studies, it might also be relevant to investigate in more detail which kind of innovation would benefit from being developed under a more open innovation strategy.

Being part of an ongoing open-innovation project is likely to be affected by the development level of the project and by the technical literacy of the contributor. Moreover, there is a need to investigate the extent to which the underlying motives and related costs of the proposed strategies to open up the innovation process vary across the choice of strategy, as well as the point in the entire development process at which users/developers join.

It would also be relevant to look at the relationship between the number of contributors to an open innovation project and the productivity of that project, i.e. to uncover the importance of mechanisms of co-ordination in relation to critical mass.

In addition, it may be useful to carry out comparative studies of information and knowledge sharing and exchange during different OIPs vis-à-vis traditional proprietary innovations. One study suggests that total organizational learning decreases during the total knowledge production process (Hatch and Mowery 1998). It would be relevant to investigate whether the same pattern emerges during OIPs.

The empirical studies of OS-based software innovations mapped out a couple of essential co-ordinating and structural mechanisms that depict a fundamentally different approach to innovation and business development, where, for example, the commercial focus should be directed away from the innovation farther up the value chain towards new, related support functions.

Involving users in product development and innovation activities reflects porous external boundaries. At the same time, it has interesting implications for organization design, since users play an active role in shaping the design of organizations. This type of change, however, is likely to influence lines of authority and job responsibilities, and hence also control mechanisms. Thus, by selecting an OIP strategy, organizations reflect a more flexible approach to coordinating activities. What is worth noting in these organizational strategies is that mutual benefits and interdependent relationships characterize the interaction and exchange between the organization and the users to a higher degree than is the case in traditional organizational hierarchies.

6. CONCLUSION

This chapter discusses alternative strategies for coordinating innovation activities, in which sharing and co-operation between the interacting parties play a critical part. Four archetypal strategies have been identified and classified according to the type of user involvement and the organizational level at which co-operation with external sources of knowledge takes place.

Acquiring extraorganizational knowledge may affect organizational design, since it will involve social interactions external to the organization and thus introduce new social patterns of human interaction to replace and/or complement existing patterns. Depending on the selected OIP strategy, adjustments and/or changes of organizational design may therefore be required. For the sake of clarity or simplicity, this paper has outlined and discussed four archetypal strategies. This is not to say, that only such archetypes are valid options – rather it is to be expected, that variations thereof or multiple hybrid strategies are possible options.

REFERENCES

Allen, R. C., 1983, Collective invention, *Journal of Economic Behavior and Organization,* **4**: 1-24.

Barki, H. and Hartwick, J., 1989. Rethinking the concept of user involvement, *MIS Quarterly 13*, **1**: 53-63.

Boehm, B., 1981, *Software Engineering Economics*. Upper Saddle River, NJ: Prentice Hall.

Breisford, C., 2005, The user in the driver's seat, *Password - Philips Research technology magazine*, **22:** 14-17.

Buurman, R. D., 1997, User-centred design of smart products, *Ergonomics* **40(10)**: 1159.

Chesbrough, H. W., 2003, The Era of Open Innovation, *MIT Sloan Management Review* **44(3)**: 35-41.

Chesbrough, H. W., 2003, *Open Innovation - The New Imperative for Creating and Profiting from Technology*. Boston: Harvard Business School Publishing Corporation.

Christensen, C. M., and Bower, J. L., 2001, Customer power, strategic investment, and the failure of leading firms. In Burgelman, R. A., Maidique, M. A. and Wheelwright, S. C., eds. *Strategic management of technology and innovation*, McGraw-Hill/Irwin, New York, NY, 428-446.

Cohen, W. M. and Levinthal, D. A., 2001, Absorptive capacity: a new perspective on learning and innovation. In Burgelman, R. A., Maidique, M. A. and Wheelwright, S. C., eds.

Strategic management of technology and innovation, McGraw-Hill/Irwin, New York, NY, 613-629.

Dougherty, D., 1990, Understanding new markets for new products, *Strategic Management Journal* **11**(1): 59-78.

Franke, N., and Shah, S., 2003, How communities support innovative activities: An exploration of assistance and sharing among end-users, *Research Policy,* **32**(1): 157-178.

Franke, N., and Von Hippel, E., 2003, Satisfying heterogeneous user needs via innovation toolkits: the case of Apache security software, *Research Policy,* **32**(7): 1199-1215.

Freeman, C., 1968, Chemical process plant: Innovation and the world market, *National Institute Economic Review*, **45**: 29-51.

Hars, A. and Ou, S., 2002, Working for free? Motivations for participating in open-source projects, *International Journal of Electronic Commerce*, **6**: 25–39.

Hatch, N. W. and Mowery, D. C., 1998, Process innovation and learning by doing in semiconductor manufacturing, *Management Science,* **44**(11): 1461-1477.

Herstatt, C. and von Hippel, E., 1992, From experience: developing new product concepts via the lead user method: a case study in a "low tech" field, *Journal of Product Innovation Management,* **9**(3): 213-221.

Hertel, G., Niedner, S. and Herrmann, S., 2003, Motivation of software developers in open source projects: an Internet-based survey of contributors to the Linux kernel, *Research Policy*, **32**(7): 1159-1177.

Hirschhorn, L. and Thomas, G., 1992, The new boundaries of the "boundaryless" company, *Harvard Business Review,* **70**(3): 104-115.

Ives, B. and Olson, M. H., 1984, User involvement and MIS success: a review of research, *Management Science,* **30**(5): 586-603.

Kanter, R. M., 1988, When a thousand flowers bloom: structural, collective, and social conditions for innovation in organization, *Research in Organizational Behavior*, **10**: 169-211.

Lanzara, G. F. and Morner, M., 2003, The knowledge ecology of open source software projects.

Lerner, J. and Tirole, J., 2001, The open source movement: Key research questions, **45**: 819-826.

Meyer, P. B., 2003, Episodes of Collective Invention, *working paper 368,* U.S. Department of Labour, Bureau of Labour Statistics.

Nobelius, D., 2004, Towards the sixth generation of R&D management, *International Journal of Project Management,* **22**(5): 369-367.

Nuvolari, A., 2003, Open source software development: Some historical perspectives, Eindhoven Centre for Innovation Studies, Eindhoven University of Technology, The Netherlands.

Petersen, M. K., 2005, Open innovation - mere praksis, mindre buzz. *Fremtidsorientering*, **1**.

Pfeffer, J. and Salancik, G. R., 1978, *The External Control of Organizations: A Resource Dependence Perspective*. Harper & Row, New York.

Roe, J. W., 1914, Early American Mechanics - Robbins and Lawrence Shop, *American Machinist*, **41**.

Rosenberg, N., 1963, Technology change in the machine tool industry, 1840-1910, *Journal of Economic History*, **23**: 414-446.

Rosenberg, N., 1976, *Perspectives on Technology*. Cambridge: Cambridge University Press.

Schadler, T., 2003, IBM's open-source stance. *CNET News.com*, http://news.com.com/Commentary:+IBM's+open-source+stance/2009-1069_3-981484.html.

Shah, S., 2000, Sources and patterns of innovation in a consumer products field: Innovations in sporting equipment, *MIT Sloan School Working Paper #4105*, Cambridge, MA.

Sharpe, H. D., 1949, A measure of perfection: the history of Brown & Sharpe, *Excerpts from an address to the Newcomen Society of England.*

Shaw, B., 1985, The role of the interaction between the user and the manufacturer in medical equipment innovation, *R&D Management*, **15**(4): 283-292.

Tidd, J., Bessant, J. and Pavitt, K., 1997, *Managing innovation: integrating technological, market and organizational change*. John Wiley & Sons, Chichester, England.

Ulhøi, J. P., 2004, Open source development: a hybrid in innovation and management theory, *Management Decision,* **42**(9): 1095-1114.

Urban, G. L. and von Hippel, E., 1988, Lead user analysis for development of new industrial products, *Management Science*, **34**(5): 569-582.

von Hippel, E., 1988, *The Sources of Innovation*. New York: Oxford University Press.

von Hippel, E., 1994, "Sticky information" and the locus of problem solving: implications for innovation, *Management Science,* **40**(4): 429-439.

von Hippel, E., 2002, Horizontal innovation networks - by and for users. *MIT Sloan School of Management*.

von Hippel, E., 2005, *Democratizing innovation*. Cambridge, MA: MIT Press.

Weber, S., 2004, *The Success of Open Source*. Cambridge, MA: Harvard University Press.

West, J., 2003, How open is open enough? Melding proprietary and open source platform strategies, *Research Policy*, **32**: 1259-1285.

Chapter 9

DOING A WHILE HOPING FOR B?

A STUDY ON ORGANIZATIONAL INNOVATION IN THREE LARGE ORGANISATIONS

Kaisa Henttonen

Technology Business Research Centre, School of Business, Lappeenranta University of Technology

Abstract: The study reported in this chapter was undertaken in order to find out why large organizations, despite their efforts, do not seem to be achieving their official targets to become more innovative. The paper builds on teleological and dialectical elements. A review of the literature on innovation management reveals contradictory tensions concerning the innovation phenomenon, or innovative activities, thus suggesting a range of tensions. The case study reported is qualitative in nature and was based on focus groups comprising 118 stakeholders in three large companies in ICT and the paper industry. The implication is, surprisingly, that the case companies are practicing exploitation but are aiming at results gained through exploration. The results therefore show that they seem to be doing A while hoping for B. In terms of practice, the findings suggest that organizations aiming to be more innovative should examine their official and operational goals (see Kerr, 1985) in the light of the interpretive framework put forward in this study, and see if they match.

Key words: Innovation, dualities, dialectics, large and mature firms, exploration, exploitation, ICT and the pulp & paper-industry.

1. INTRODUCTION

Sustained innovation has been considered particularly difficult for organizations with long histories of stable operations, and it is proposed that it would require them to fundamentally change their ways of operating (Dougherty and Hardy 1996). Furthermore, the practitioners interviewed for this study said that innovation had been on the agenda for years, but in many ways it had not led to concrete actions that would have engaged the whole

R.M. Burton et al. (eds.), *Designing Organizations*, doi: 10.1007/978-0-387-77776-4_9,

organization. Hence, the starting point for this study was the question *why large organizations, despite their efforts, do not seem to be achieving their official targets to become more innovative.*

Innovation is seen here as the creation of new value and not just of new things. In essence, it usually means change in the organization and in the economic situation (Afuah 1998). Many influential managerial frameworks, however, encourage individuals to think only in a way that fosters stability. The management literature features many rational and influential frameworks that are based on teleological thinking, which is concerned with determining if something "is" or "is not" (Ford and Ford 1994). According to Calori (1998), for example, the "positioning school" advises managers to choose a generic strategy, whether it be cost leadership or differentiation, but not anything in-between (Porter 1980). The more widely used framework, SWOT analysis, is also organized in dichotomies; strengths/weaknesses and opportunities/threats (Calori 1998). These frameworks represent teleological thinking.

On the other hand, Matthews (2006) in his recent book implicitly supports dialectics and argues that managers should master two broad managerial behaviors: strategizing and economizing. He claims that concentrating purely on economics leaves us without the tools to search for something new or improved, or to become involved in risky, challenging undertakings. Nevertheless, it does provide frameworks for cutting costs, improving productivity, and maximizing profits (Snow 2007) There is no doubt that the above-mentioned dominant frames of top-management thinking guide innovation and change in the organization. An examination of these may reveal the conscious or unconscious biases built into its innovative activities (Ford and Ford 1994).

In order to identify possible innovation-related framing the question was first asked whether the literature reported any contradictory tensions concerning the innovation phenomenon or innovative activities, and if so what types of framing were used. Some studies on innovation have already hinted at contradictions and tensions (see Galbraith, 1982 on innovating and operating types of organization; Bouwen and Fry, 1991 on market-orientation logic and theory-oriented scientific work; Leonard-Barton, 1992) on core capabilities and core rigidities, and Fryxell, 1990 on the dialectical nature of innovation cultures; Katila and Ahuja, 2002 on problem search and solving in new product development; Cule and Robey, 2004 on the process theory of organizational change; Gilsing and Noteboom, 2006 on the relation of exploration and exploitation). However, relatively little attention has been paid to the possibilities offered by tensions, oppositions and contradictions in explanations addressing the same phenomena (Poole and Van de Ven 1989).

A further aim of this study was to give empirical support to a relatively rare dialectical approach to studying the dynamics of innovation in large organizations. The case study is intended to serve as an empirical illustration of this approach. It is suggested that different frames of thinking may have an impact on the companies' goal definitions and their ability to change and to produce innovations. According to the results, the case companies are experiencing conflict between their official and their operational goals: the former define the source of monetary funds and prioritize the various targets, while the latter are more general and vague (see Kerr, 1985). It was also found that the exploration mode in innovation activities was the official goal in these organizations. However, operational goals could be described more as exploitation (see March, 1991). The implication is that sustained innovation in large organizations depends on both exploration and exploitation. Moreover, it seems that the case companies are doing A while hoping for B.

In what follows it is first suggested that this may be due to the competing frames of thinking in the literature on innovation management as well as in managerial tools and frameworks in general. Section 3 discusses the research design and methodology. The case study is described in section 4, and offers insights into how the case companies do not seem to realize that their official and operational innovation-management goals do not match. Dialectical thinking is put forward as a solution. This is discussed in more depth in section 5, and sections 6-8 conclude the paper with a discussion of the implications for the theory and practice of organizational design.

2. THE TELEOLOGICAL AND DIALECTICAL APPROACHES TO INNOVATION MANAGEMENT

As mentioned earlier, innovation, at heart, implies change. This paper is rooted in two change-oriented approaches, the teleological and the dialectic (Van de Ven and Poole 1995). The teleological approach relies on the normative assumption that some social state is preferable to another. (deRond et al. 2004), and this type of duality has been described as "either/or" thinking (Ford et al. 1994). It does not necessarily support innovation, however, nor it is likely to lead to smaller and incremental changes (Johannessen et al. 1999). What it may do is to simplify organizational innovation to some extent. Organizations are complex entities, shaped by the mindsets and dynamics of the individuals in them as well as by goals and strategies (deRond and Bouchhikhi 2004; Cule and Robey 2004).

Dialectics, on the other hand, represents contradictory teleological forces and allows contrary tensions, and could be characterized as "both/and" thinking. It occurs when individual teleological forces collide (Van de Ven and Poole 1995; Cule and Robey 2004), and illustrates how the conflicting interests of individuals create organizational change (Benson, 1975, 1977 cif. de Rond and Bouchhikhi 2004).

The goal-seeking behaviors of individuals are likely to be guided by their frames of thinking. Apparently, a certain type of thinking easily becomes the norm in organizations and among people, which means that underlying assumptions are mainly accepted as such. When these assumptions become rooted in the organization they are rarely questioned or scrutinized. (Ford and Ford 1994) These types of generally accepted frames shape our world and we may not even realize it.

2.1 Competing frames of thinking in innovation management

The literature on innovation seems to represent slightly contradictory frames of thinking. I refer to these here as exploration and exploitation because there appears to be a resemblance to the famous and classic exploitation vs. exploration dilemma described by James March (1991). According to this, exploration is more generally about long-term orientation and creating new capabilities and skills, while exploitation is to do with taking advantage of current skills and capabilities in the short term. The following table summarizes the findings of the literature review. It presents the interpretative framework used in the study, which contains the basic categories and assumptions guiding the investigation. The implication is that the pure exploitation mode gives managers the mind-set of productivity improvement, cost cutting and profit maximization, which apparently reflects a teleological approach to innovation and change. Similarly, the pure exploration mode represents the teleological approach, focusing on finding new, different things to do and engaging in inherently risky and challenging enterprise such as innovation. These two modes together are considered here to reflect the dialectical approach to innovation and change.

Table 1. A review of the literature concerning the seemingly contradictory frames of thinking in relation to the innovation phenomenon.

EXPLOITATION		EXPLORATION
Quality and costs Cost control and cost reduction is the name of the game (Porter 1985;Williamson 1991); improving existing products (Leifer et al. 2001); customer focus and understanding their needs, the notion of a lead-user (von Hippel 1986); putting the product in a total business concept incl. services and distribution (Miller and Morris 1998); the role of R&D is to streamline new technology development (Miller and Morris 1998); entry barriers (Porter 1980)	< >	***(Incremental and radical) innovations*** Acquiring new knowledge and turning it to new products, services etc., value-creating through continuous innovation with the help of networks (Ghoshal et al. 1999; Miles et al. 2000; Kim and Mauborgne 1999)
Integrated R&D Integration as a success factor in the product-development process aiming at speed (Cooper and Kleinschmidt 1995); project management controls the innovation efforts (i.e. portfolio and project-management techniques) (Miller and Morris 1998); the idea of the internal customer (Miller and Morris 1998); cross-functional integration (Mote 2005); "heavyweight project teams" (Clark and Wheelwright 1992); "rugby teams" (Nonaka and Takeuchi 1995); the integration of R&D, operations and production (Olson et al. 2001); to gain more speed (Cooper and Kleinschmidt 1995; Zahra and Ellor 1993)	< >	***Networked innovation/R&D*** Focus on collaboration with competitors, suppliers, distributors etc. (Rothwell 1994); the involvement of the whole company network (Blomqvist et al. 2004); the important role of collaboration (Miles et al. 2000); the need to collaborate to share the large investments (Rothwell 1994); global network organizations (Miles et al. 2005); the virtual organization (Wiesenfeld et al. 2001); fostering informal relationships (March 1991; Starbuck 1992; Cohen and Levinthal 1990); the role of hubs incl. idea hunters and gatherers, internal venture capitalists (Leifer et al., 2001)
Innovation as a supplementary activity Porter (1980); activity that is not linked to the on-going business operations (Burns and Stalker 1961); separate venture units (Dougherty 1995); focus on new technology development (Rothwell 1994)	< >	***Innovation embedded in all operations, key activity*** in the whole organization (Kim and Mauborgne 1999); a structure that allows slack (Damanpour 1991); spin-off innovations as ventures (Christensen 1997); a focus on modularity and flexibility in product designs and organizational designs (Sanchez and Mahoney 1996)

Internal combination of knowledge and search (Dougherty 2001); problem-solving types of activities (Cormican and O' Sullivan 2004); protecting knowledge (Kogut and Zander 1992); learning cycles inside the organization (Nonaka 1994)	< >	***Internal and external knowledge creation*** the external search for knowledge (March 1991); knowledge transfer inside and across internal units (Gulati et al. 2000; Cohen and Levinthal 1990); learning (Eisenhardt 1989); absorptive capacity (Cohen and Levinthal 1990)
Optimizing present resources (Williamson 1991); valuation and budgeting (Dixit and Pindyck 1995)	< >	***Creating (knowledge) options*** (McGrath 1997); the idea of dynamic efficiency (Ghoshal et al. 1999)

According to exploitative frame of thinking, the source of customer value lies in *quality and cost cutting* (e.g., Porter 1980), and control and more static efficiency (Williamson 1991). A variety of techniques, including total quality management, continuous improvement, process engineering, monitoring and imitating competitors (see Ghoshal and Bartlett 1999), and building entry barriers to the markets (Porter 1980) have been targeted to serve these goals. On the other hand, in the world of converging technologies and markets, innovations can change the operating landscape fairly quickly - hence the need for the value-creating logic of *continuous innovation* (Ghoshal and Bartlett 1999; Miles et al. 2000).

The emphasis in the integrated R&D approach is almost entirely on the single firm and the importance of linking together production, R&D and marketing (see e.g., Olson et al. 2001) in order to speed up product development (Cooper and Kleinschmidt 1995; Zahra and Ellor 1993) through the use of tools such as "heavyweight project teams" (Clark and Wheelwright 1992), "rugby teams" (Nonaka and Takeuchi 1995), portfolios, and project-management techniques (Miller and Morris 1998). The focus is almost solely on the perspective of just one firm. On the other hand, the more explorative *networked innovation/R&D* stresses the need for collaboration with third parties, i.e. alliances, interaction, and formal and informal knowledge exchange between firms, research institutes, universities and other institutions. It seems to stress the more holistic, ecosystem view of innovation. Organizations following this approach are even trying to take on a virtual-organization (see e.g., Weisenfeld et al., 2001) or even a global-network strategy (Miles et al., 2005).

The exploitation frame of thinking also allocates a more or less *side or supplementary role to innovation in everyday activities* (e.g., Porter 1985; Burns and Stalker 1961), the focus being on the development of new technology (see Rothwell 1994) in new-venture units, for example

(Dougherty, 1995). The exploration mindset, on the other hand, places innovation-related activities at the *heart of the whole organization* (see Kim and Maugborne 1999).

Again, exploitative thinking in knowledge creation seems to focus mainly on *the role of internal networks* in the search for new combinations and capabilities (see e.g., Dougherty 2001; Nonaka 1994 on internal cycles of knowledge creation). The protection of knowledge is also considered a key issue (Kogut and Zander 1992). On the other hand, explorative thinking is based more comprehensively on the knowledge-based view of the firm (KBV), which advocates value creation through knowledge creation and innovation. The new thinking calls for a *broad external search for knowledge* (e.g., March 1991), as well as for *knowledge transfer inside and across internal units* (see e.g., Gulati et al. 2000; Cohen and Levinthal, 1990). Furthermore, there is an emphasis on learning (Eisenhardt 1989) and absorptive capacity (Cohen and Levinthal 1990: 128) rather than on the problem-solving types of activities (Cormican and O' Sullivan 2004) that are typical of exploitative thinking.

Furthermore, exploitative thinking emphasizes the *optimizing of resources* through the development of valuation and budgeting techniques, for example (see Dixit and Pindyck 1995 cif. McGrath 1997). The aim is to be efficient and to take advantage of the existing economic options (see e.g., Williamson 1991). On the explorative side, on the other hand, the focus is on tackling the turbulent knowledge economy and on the *need to create options for knowledge creation* (McGrath 1997). Ghoshal et al. (1999) consider dynamic efficiency to be a result of creating both new options as well as new resources.

In sum, the transition from efficiency towards innovation would seem to be strongly reflected in the frames of thinking that are evident in the relevant literature.

3. METHOD

I started the research process by asking practitioners how they saw the innovation challenges they were facing. During this phase I conducted an extensive literature review covering the factors that hampered and enhanced innovation, and it was on this basis that the focus-group questions (see Appendix 1) and the questions addressing each of these seven categories were created. The review established that the qualitative literature on antecedent factors generally focused on issues related to *management, internal and external networks (e.g., culture, processes, rewards, communication and information, and resources). Management* means goal-oriented activities guiding the operations to meet the shared visions and targets, including planning, organizing, and monitoring activities. *Processes* concern described workflows and operation models, methods and tools that support organizational operations. Processes may be formal or informal. *Culture* is related to the common values, shared vision, beliefs, and traditions and is fundamentally a question of wrong and right. *Rewards and incentives* concern compensation for exceeded goals, new ideas, and best practices, for example. They increase the involvement of the personnel in the organization and motivate them to work more intensively. *External networks* are relationships between the organization and its partners, customers, and suppliers that support its operations and performance. *Internal networks* are relationships between the individuals, departments, and business units in the organization, *while resources* define its limits in terms of human resources and capabilities, and tangible and intangible assets for securing its operations and performance. Finally, *Communication* concerns the information flow between individuals, departments, business units, customers, suppliers, competitors, and partners. This may be formal or informal, and is supported by different communication devices including meetings, documents, and instructions.

3.1 Data collection and focus groups

Focus groups (FGs) were used as a data-collecting method in this study. The participants of the 25 groups from three large ICT enterprises (two companies) and the pulp & paper industry (one company) were selected on the basis of their individual characteristics related to the topic of enquiry (Langford and McDonagh 2003). The companies are hereon named Company A, Company B and Company C.

The selected companies also had to have innovation as one of their strategies. There is, hence, an underlying assumption that organizations are considered to benefit from creating innovations and managing the existing product/service/process performance simultaneously. Furthermore, companies were selected from different businesses because heterogeneity provides rich information for exploratory research. In an attempt to ensure heterogeneity in terms of insights and opinions the interviewees were chosen so as to represent different occupational groups and hierarchical levels. However, each of the 25 interviewed groups was internally occupationally homogenous.

The company representatives chose the 118 focus-group participants: around 58 per cent of them were from the two ICT companies and the rest were from the pulp & paper company. The groups comprised representatives from management, supplier interface, university interface, customer interface, worker groups, innovation experts, "white-collar" workers and trade-union officials. Each one was considered to reflect the social realities of a certain organizational level and context: neither managers nor employees are able to describe the full "truth" of how their organization functions or can function (Westenholz 1993: 38-39).

The focus-group method is a facilitated interactive group-interview process based on open-ended questions (Morgan and Scannell 1998) that are intended to enhance knowledge of the everyday world in order to give meaning to phenomena and on-topic issues (Edwards and Stokoe 2004; McLafferty 2004; Parent et al. 2000). The researchers acted as moderators (Morgan 1996) who asked the questions and sought elaboration. Each session lasted between two-and-a-half and three hours, and was digitally recorded. A total of 60 hours' worth of material was recorded during the 25 sessions, and over 700 pages of written data were collected.

3.2 Data analysis

Seven researchers (including the author) and two assistants participated in the different focus groups as moderators, and also coded the sessions. The same research team also conducted the analysis of the data to ensure direct contact with it. The main question during the primary coding phase was: "*What are the factors enhancing and hampering innovation in your organization?*" We looked for repetition, differences and regularities in the analysis, and excluded factors that were not clearly presented and needed further interpretation. All the interviews were analyzed using ATLAS.ti software.

4. FINDINGS

The following briefly illustrates how the five patterns of dialogue between exploration and exploitation were reflected in the three large case organizations according to the interviewees.

4.1 Quality and costs vs. incremental and radical innovations – what is the source of competitiveness?

The interviewees typically talked about constant savings, and about streamlining activities, saying that it was often the cost efficiency that mattered. Additionally, sticking to the old successful business area and adopting an "innovations are not our business" attitude seemed to slightly dominate the thinking in all the case companies. In the view of many, the quartile-economy approach to planning and decision-making inhibited innovation activities to some extent. Others thought that there were forces striving to maintain the status quo, which is not always conducive to innovativeness given the need to compromise and to make the "old, existing way" work.

Table 2. Exemplary quotations referring to contradictions characterizing the different innovation debates.

Quality and costs		**Incremental and radical innovations**
"At this point of time our company is in the "cost-cutting and back-to--basics" mode. The upper management has sent a clear message that innovativeness is not our number-one priority today." "...if it does not pay off in this quartile, we will concentrate on things that do pay off…" (Company A)	< >	"…but they [management] still mention innovativeness in their speeches…" "… if you get to the price races it's very shortsighted and you can't compete with prices and there's a need to try something else..." (Company A)
"We are constantly in the saving-costs mode. " "…savings everywhere….now we have this productivity mentality and now the thinking involves how to get the production going with less people…" (Company B)	< >	"Innovativeness is generally discussed all the time in many texts and speeches. The word 'innovation' is also present all the time." (Company B)
"…we have fairly strict processes….We also get certain budgetary frames for half a year and we have to operate inside the frame." "This means that we work in an environment where certain frames for operations are given and they don't leave much room for development or for being innovative.." (Company C)	< >	"Our management talks about innovation in their speeches. It [innovation] has been on the agenda for years. Innovation is something the management speaks about." "I think management is trying to promote the spirit that we are an innovative company that wants to deliver "humane" technology and integrate it into everyday lives. " (Company C)

This type of struggle between the old and the new is a typical tension in relation to learning (see Lewis 2000). In general, it seemed that the quality and costs approach was stronger in the case companies than the focus on incremental and radical innovations.

4.2 Integrated R&D versus networked innovation/R&D – where do the ideas come from?

In-house R&D was no longer considered adequate in any of the case companies. In general, when the focus is on efficiency the more redundant relations have to be cut out. As a result, the network is likely to become less dense given the reduced need for variability and the development of new combinations. Hence, the aim is towards specialization and stability. Another strategy would naturally be to differentiate. This could be pursued within existing network relations as it mainly involves applying what is known/has been done to a new context. It is also likely to lead to incremental innovations, however. Radical innovations need support from dense, informal networks of suppliers, competitors, customers, partners, universities, and research centers.

Table 3. Exemplary quotations referring to contradictions characterizing the different innovation debates.

Integrated R&D		Networked innovation/R&D
" this type of silo thinking…in our unit functions work quite independently and there are clear boundaries between units…" "We should get rid of this silo thinking that 'stay away, this is my area'…" "…our research center also serves the whole company…" (Company A)	< >	"..these external relationships -they bring added customer value to our innovation process. They allow us to gain new ideas and capable people. And we can build networks and benefit from the knowledge of people from outside our organizational boundaries..." "…this network – thinking …" (Company A)
"We have a strong product focus and product silos, which cause challenges to innovative ideas. As soon as an innovative idea crosses the product silos, the 'breaks will be hit' and the innovativeness and ideation are slowed down." "If customers have needs, ideas or solutions to problems, we would need to tear down the silos and then we could find someone to carry them out." (Company B)	< >	"I think that radical ideas can be found when suppliers tell you that something does not work and then it leaves you with an incentive to find a new direction and a new way of doing things." "We have a large network of customers, partners, research centers and universities."(Company B)
"We can partnership internally. And this is very central. It is one of our strengths." "We have strong project-management protocols and IPR processes." "They have so much bureaucracy that you need a lot of effort, time, coffee and cigarettes to take the idea through. Many innovative people give up when they see its impossibility." (Company C)	< >	"We are quite networked. It's hard to work here if you don't know people from the organization or from other organizations. You don't know who to call. If you know people you can call them and ask for help and ask them if they know anyone who could help. This enhances innovation, among other things." (Company C)

The collaborative networks are likely to result in longer-term future collaboration, but require all parties to share the risks of uncertainty. To conclude, the case companies seemed to be more in the integrated R&D mode, although there was some effort at networked innovation/R&D.

4.3 Innovation as a supplementary activity vs. innovation embedded in all operations – who is the legitimated innovator?

The general discussion seemed to culminate in the issue of who is the innovator, i.e. who has the legitimated role to create new ideas and who has the power to decide and to carry them through. This was typically reflected on as follows: *Person A: "Where are our Gyro Gearloose-type of people?" Person B: "Well, everybody thinks they're at our research center."* (Company C) Innovation could, first and foremost, be considered an "invention". This type of discussion suggests that it is the individuals at the research centers and the venture and incubation units who are the innovators. Indeed, the impression sometimes given in the interviews was that these units were seen as innovation fortresses, and it was here that innovations and innovativeness were considered to reside. The "entrepreneur" in Schumpeter's theory, the "Schumpeterian" entrepreneur (Schumpeter 1942 and 1934), represents this type of thought.

Table 4. Exemplary quotations referring to contradictions characterizing the different innovation debates.

Innovation as supplementary activity		**Innovation embedded in all operations**
"People are often encouraged to take care of their own jobs. People have not been encouraged to be innovative." "Innovative people are also often a different species. They ask difficult questions and they have been seen as distracting and disturbing as they bring up incomprehensible issues." (Company A)	< >	"... we should get the employee groups mixed...so that people from different professional groups would work together and we would get more ideas..." (Company A)
"We launch a development project and isolate it and then wait and after three months the project members provide us with a solution." "...and people then do not dare to innovate much because when the next round comes you need to show what you have done and if you have done this sort of thing [innovation] then you don't have anything to show them." (Company B)	< >	"Collaboration is the way to do these things [innovations, ideas]. Concentrating on this collaboration is really [essential]." "I would see that our strength would be to make the different people work together, exchange experiences, and think about new things and make new combinations."(Company B)
"The innovativeness, we think, comes more from the research unit." "And when it comes to innovativeness, we have ventures, a research center and other units that do incubation, venturing and innovate." "We think that our research centre is the basis for everything and everything comes from there [innovations] and they are spilled out of there [to the other parts of the organization]." (Company C)	< >	"We have the possibility to post notices concerning the ideas we have come up with."(Company C)

To conclude, the case companies aimed at innovation embedded in all operations. However, their processes and organizational arrangements still supported the view of innovation as a supplementary activity .

4.4 The internal combination of knowledge versus internal and external knowledge creation – how are the ideas created?

The interviewees described their innovativeness more or less in terms of problem solving. They also stressed the importance of listening to their customers more carefully in order to gain new ideas, and of trying to adapt accordingly. This type of thinking was inherent in the values of the organizations, but it was not so easily realized in the day-to-day work due to the restrictions imposed by the internal structures and the lacking contacts with the most important external interfaces, such as customers.

Table 5. Exemplary quotations referring to contradictions characterizing the different innovation debates.

Internal combinations of knowledge		**External and internal combinations of knowledge**
"I guess the learning comes into the picture when one would need to leave one's own playground and widen the territory and do other jobs." "There's a general opposition to everything new and so learning, learning new things, is difficult and unlearning is also difficult." "Always somebody refers to the fact that things have been going well the prevailing way so why to change it." (Company A)	< >	"Are we also allowed to fail? Because not all the ideas can lead to great success. One should allow and support experimenting even though it doesn't always turn out a success. One would, however, learn something and things would develop. " "Internal and external training has also been organized on topics we have wanted. I think this [education, training] creates a lot of [innovation] potential."(Company A)
"New people will have a hard time if people are always required to conform to a certain format. " "I have tried to get external courses and other schooling, and I was hoping the firm would support it but they didn't." "It [knowledge, ideas] does not flow to us. It [organization] is kind of closed." "Then I think that some people are keeping the information to themselves"…"in silos." (Company B)	< >	"Nobody creates the innovation alone in his/her head. Interaction is needed. " "Organizations should consist of people with a variety of professional backgrounds; humanists, engineers, sociologists, economists." "Breaking down the silos…is central." "This is in all our values but in practice it doesn't show." "Some years ago lower-level employees were also involved [in innovation]. It was good." (Company B)
"Our innovativeness is on another level. It's all about problem solving." "Innovations from customers and taking other outsiders along -it may be easily forgotten" "And sometimes it's [involving external actors] hard because of all the non-disclosure agreements. Also inside our firm this [involving various actors] is difficult. It gets more difficult when we go outside the organizational boundary."(Company C)	< >	"One of our values is continuous learning and continuous renewal. They would enhance innovation and innovativeness [if put to practice]." "If you have the courage to share your ideas with someone they will improve. " (Company C)

Argyris and Schön (1978) described the type of learning that was taking place in the case companies as "single-loop learning", which occurs when organizations compare their results with existing standards and then make improvements if needed. It is about having a single objective, but striving towards increasing virtuosity (Miller 1993). Double-loop learning, on the other hand, would require the organization to reconsider and question the standards or other technical specifications it may have (Argyris and Schön 1978). The need for changes may arise due to customer reaction, for example (Miller 1993), as it did in the case companies.

To conclude, the importance of internal and external combinations of knowledge was recognized in the case companies. However, the companies were still very much in the "single-loop learning" mode with internal partners.

4.5 Optimizing current resources versus generating options –how is the networked collaboration managed?

It appears from the interviews that the focus is on optimizing current resources, which may be a reflection of the carefully planned cost-cutting mode in which the organizations seem to be engaged. There is not much desire to create new options, and thereby to take risks that might ruin the well-planned cost-cutting efforts. This type of orientation also works against long-term planning. Furthermore, it seems to lead into situations in which there is not even "*small elbow room*" and not much scope "*to work and manouver*", because everything has been set for the year. It was a state of affairs that seemed to worry some of the interviewees, who realized that their companies (as big players) needed to create options for the future by teaching other players to play and not just to concentrate on short-term survival. They considered creating options important because they knew that their organizations could not by themselves create and maintain all the knowledge and skills that would be required in the future, regardless of their large size. In their view, this was how a business ecosystem worked. To conclude, the case companies were mainly in the optimizing-current-resources mode.

Table 6. Exemplary quotations referring to contradictions characterizing the different innovation debates.

Optimizing current resources		**Creating (knowledge) options**
"The aim is to organize all the units so that they operate in a homogenous way and this prohibits creating ideas." "This global way of operating - we don't get much information on what our role in the big picture is and where we're going." "And all the experiments [they are making with products]. It seems that they're becoming more and more secret or classified. " (Company A)	< >	"If we could find the most capable suppliers …those who could help us to develop into the kind of company we want to be…then we would also benefit from the innovativeness of those companies because they know their businesses are the best and can bring something new…We shouldn't disperse our resources.." (Company A)
"We also have certain functions that centrally define the optimal ways of doing things and the processes. Living with these processes and ways of doing things often isn't very innovative, but the effort is in trying to streamline 'the machine' [the organization] to give it an optimal shape." "We have certain product portfolios and programs and we need to work accordingly."(Company B)	< >	"I think innovativeness should show everywhere, marketing, customer service, in our own processes and everywhere. If we think about our success in business - it isn't ultimately all about fine technical gadgets but that we're able to do many things in an innovative manner." "Innovativeness should reside everywhere and all the time."(Company B)
"We should be able to react to changing situations and create solutions faster. However, now we already have decided what to do for the rest of the year and now it's the beginning of the year. " "Also we can't take on projects and do them any other way, if we're locked into certain ways of doing things." "We have given company-wide responsibilities to some suppliers. Then we have given them more freedom and innovative goals to develop the collaboration in practice and doing it so that it would include mutual benefit. " (Company C)	< >	"It brings continuity to our suppliers. We kind of know that there's continuity in certain areas for years. There's work. We can only tell them that there is work for half a year, but they can guess that it will continue. And therefore they may invest in development and innovate." "When we make contracts with the suppliers, we try to be fair so that something is left for the supplier as well. " " Some companies think that every move they make needs to bring profit. We first practice and see how it goes and in the future it may be beneficial. " (Company C)

In sum, the interviewees thought that there was too much concern with current business, with serving current customers, and with existing profit margins, and not enough attention given to conquering potential new markets with new ideas. Furthermore, even if the different patterns of dialogue between the exploration and exploitation modes are dealt with here one by one, they are likely to be dependent on each other.

5. DISCUSSION AND IMPLICATIONS

The focus in this paper was on the frame of thinking that lay behind the innovation activities in the three case organizations. Figure 1 lists these frames and shows how they lead to different goals, actions and results. Innovations are roughly categorized as incremental and radical (see e.g., Damanpour 1992: 561), and so that the point comes out more clearly the markets are classified as either old or new.

In general terms, it seems that the case companies are pursuing exploitation thinking but are also aiming at results gained through exploration. Naturally, this is not a strategy that is likely to end up with the desired results. Exploitation-oriented organizations are more likely to produce incremental innovations and changes, but if they apply exploration thinking they may be able to produce radical innovations. The main argument here is that the acceptance of dialectics-oriented, "both and", thinking may result in more imaginative combinations of both cost cutting and innovativeness, or of both incremental and radical innovations. Organizations using both thinking frameworks rather than teleological "either or" thinking may be able to exploit a wide variety of perspectives. They are also able to choose the situations in which it would be more useful to switch to the more permanent and stable exploitation frame such as when the decision to manufacture a certain product prototype has to be made.

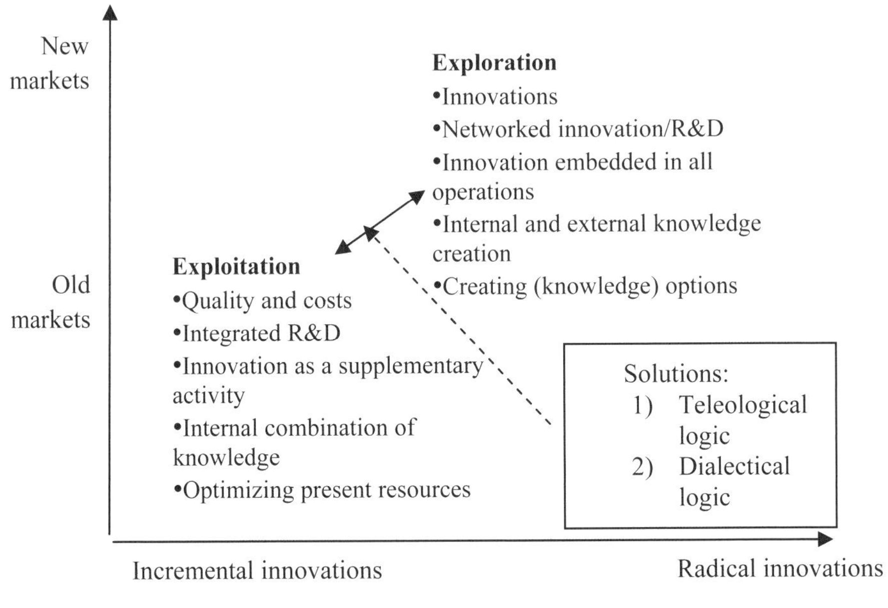

Figure 1. Juxtapositions between the two innovation frames of thinking; exploration and exploitation (based on the ideas of Smith and Tushman, 2005)

Figure 1 also demonstrates situations in which one type of thinking is more beneficial than another. Incremental process or product improvements are likely to decrease costs as well as to improve efficiency, and this type of thinking enables organizations to benefit from their existing products, technologies, and markets. Exploitation thinking enables them to make incremental changes and to make them rather quickly - partly because it does not necessarily require any changes in the current frame. Making incremental changes thus does not challenge the current thinking, which nevertheless might not be best suited to rapidly changing environments. The increasing rate of change presents great challenges to organizations that rely purely on the old, exploitation-type of thinking. Nevertheless, in recent decades firms have become skilful in conducting activities that enable them to hold on to much of their value and to allow very little to slip from their hands (see also Leifer et al. 2001; Ghoshal et al. 1999).

Exploration thinking, on the other hand, could be best suited to dynamic and uncertain operating environments in which innovation arises through a tension between the organization and the environment (Hamel and Prahalad 1996). In this case innovation is an interactive process involving all employees internally as well as the external operating environment. It is also acknowledged in the literature that radical innovations seem to arise in their time outside the organization's current strategic focus. It could be claimed that they may have often required a change in the current exploitative business thinking in a more explorative direction.

Hence, the processes of creating incremental and radical innovations seem to be distinct phenomena, and different conditions are needed to facilitate them. A suitable response to the pressure to innovate would seem to require the simultaneous application of both of the frames, exploration and exploitation: according to Smith and Tushman (2005) and Ghoshal and Bartlett (1999), long-term performance depends on the organization's ability to adapt and change through innovation (referred to here as exploration), yet to continue to perform in the short term (referred to here as exploitation). This paper does not, therefore, suggest that the case companies should engage in unlearning their current dominant way of thinking (exploitation), as they seem to be trying to do, but it does advocate making an effort to combine it with other frame(s) (i.e. exploration). Thus, there seems to be a need for the kind of capability that would facilitate such combinations.

I am aware that the data-collection method and the different participant groups may have highlighted the dialectical perspective. Additionally, focus groups do not permit the collection of as much in-depth information as semi-structured interviews, for example (Berg 2004). There may also have been instances of so-called "group think", and the more dominant group members may have imposed their strong opinions on the others. The strength of the groups, however, lies in their ability to provide a rich basis for further theoretical analysis of the innovation challenges facing large and mature firms, and in the avoidance of single-informant bias. The open-ended questions, the confidentiality and the interactive nature of the sessions nevertheless enabled relatively non-biased, truly company-originated innovation factors to emerge rather than a researcher-originated view. Furthermore, one cannot describe the "causal" conditions or processes driving the competing frames of thinking and their impact on changes on the basis of this data and the way it has been analyzed. However, it would be an interesting avenue for further research, of which this paper only marks the beginning.

6. INFORMING THE THEORY OF ORGANIZATIONAL DESIGN

The theory of organizational design alludes to the importance of creating organizational forms that enable both exploration and exploitation (see e.g., Siggelkow et al. 2003; Gibson et al., 2004). This literature seems to emphasize the balance between these forces, although March (1991: 5) notes that balancing is "a nice word", but "a cruel concept". However, the balance is likely to be affected by the managerial frames of thinking, for example.

Hence, it is argued in this study that conscious or unconscious frames of thinking affect the way organizations see themselves as well as their operating environments. In particular, the implication is that increased understanding and identification of these frames may enhance innovation management in that the actors concerned may be able to examine their own thinking critically and thereby avoid getting stuck in the status quo (see also Ford and Ford 1994).

It is further argued that innovation management in the context of contradictory forces is rooted in dialectical thinking, in other words in frames of thinking and processes that allow organizations to handle contradictions rather than to escape from them. Dialectics as an approach also remains rather underrepresented in the innovation literature, and it is in this context that this paper is intended to make a contribution.

It is therefore suggested that organizations applying dialectical thinking in innovation management are likely to be more innovative than those pursuing teleological logic. The ones that have been able to identify their thinking frames, the underlying assumptions and their influence on their activities may also be better equipped to respond to changes by taking actions such as adjusting their structures.

7. INFORMING PRACTICE

The study results give reason to believe that the dialectical view on innovation management, which fosters increased understanding of its complexity and challenges and of the organization of innovation activities, is also open to concrete advice.

Organizations that are aiming to be more innovative should examine their official and operational goals (see Kerr, 1985) using the interpretive framework suggested in this study, and then see if they match. They could identify in which mode (exploitation or exploration) their current operating is anchored, and try to expand their perspective towards the other one. On the individual level, organizations lacking innovativeness in their employees should reexamine their reward systems and/or staff-development policies, and decide whether these systems support the kind of behavior they are looking for. First, they would need to find out what innovation-related behaviors are being rewarded and encouraged. On the evidence of the case-study results it would seem that such an enquiry might provide surprising results. Companies could also investigate the processes or mechanisms that support innovative activities. It appears from recent research that managers understand the importance of innovativeness, but not many of them have paid attention to the means by which the innovations are created. Hiring people with the ability to adopt contradictory frames of thinking, training and rewarding them to do so, and setting up organizational processes that truly enhance the official goal, increased innovativeness, could also enhance organizational performance.

8. CONCLUSION

A major objective of this paper was to respond to the question why large organizations, despite their efforts, do not seem to be achieving their official targets to become more innovative. The case study was conducted in order to serve as an empirical illustration to support a dialectical frame of thinking in the innovation process. The aim was to find both theoretical and empirical support for this fairly rare thinking mode in organizational innovation. Additionally, despite the numerous studies on innovation, little is known about how organizations themselves perceive innovativeness and the factors affecting their innovative activities. Furthermore, not many studies take into account the fact that stakeholders may have differing perceptions of such factors. This multiple-respondent study was designed to avoid single-respondent bias, which makes it relatively rare (Ernst and Teichert 1998). A further aim was to apply less routinized methods to the examination of innovation: there are researchers (see e.g., Anderson et al., 2004) who claim that innovation research is becoming increasingly less radically innovative, and more routinized and cross-sectional. There is a clear need for more innovative approaches.

This would also imply that understanding innovative activities in organizations might well require the development of a new research paradigm, which would build on different ontological foundations. Innovation and innovative activities constitute a social process that involves a lot of contradictory tensions. It is not likely that they serve just one explicit or implicit purpose or goal as more traditional monistic approaches such as the teleological approach do. However, the continuous struggle between the opposing forces could be seen to create change, or innovation, in the organization. Dialectics would provide a new epistemological starting point for innovation research in departing from monistic assumptions such as homogeneity and teleology and advocating heterogeneity. (Van de Ven et al., 1995; Cule and Robey, 2004) It could provide valuable information on the dynamics of innovation and innovative activities in organizations both to academics and to practitioners. This paper only paves the way for the examination of innovation from a dialectics perspective.

Appendix 1. The focus-group interview questions

- Please introduce yourself briefly. Why is innovativeness of interest to you?
- Based on your experiences and insight, could you say what hampers innovativeness in your organization?
- Based on your experiences and insight, could you say what enhances innovativeness in your organization?
- Can you give some examples of successful and unsuccessful innovations in your organization?
- How is the intension to develop innovativeness visible in the daily activities of your organization? How is the intension to develop innovativeness visible in your own work? Could you please give some concrete examples.
- How would you measure the innovativeness in your organization? How should employees be rewarded for successful innovation?
- What would you do if you had all the power and resources to make your company the most innovative firm in the world? A) What would you do differently *in your work*? B) What would you do differently *at the organizational level*?
- Is there still anything you would like to add? Greetings to the management?

REFERENCES

Afuah A. (1998) Innovation Management: Strategies, implementation and profits, Oxford University Press, New York

Anderson N, De Dreu CKW Nijstad BA (2004) The routinization of innovation research: a constructively critical review of the state-of-the-science. Journal of Organizational Behaviour 25: 147-173

Argyris C, Schön DA (1978) Organizational learning, Addison-Wesley, Reading

Berg, BL (2004) Qualitative Research Methods for the Social Sciences. Pearson Allyn and Bacon, Boston, MA

Blomqvist K, Hara V, Koivuniemi J, Äijö T (2004) Towards networked R&D management: the R&D approach of Sonera Corporation as an example. R&D Management 34/5: 591-603

Burns T, Stalker, GM (1961) The Management of innovation. Tavistock, London

Calori R (1998) Essai: Philosophizing on strategic management models. Organization Studies 19: 281-306

Chase L, Alvarez J (2000) Internet research: the role of the focus groups Library & Information Science Research 22/4: 357-369

Christensen CM (1997) The Innovator's Dilemma. Harvard Business School Press, Boston MA

Clark KB, Wheelwright SC (1992) Organizing and leading "heavyweight" development teams. California Management Review 34/ 3: 9-28

Cohen WM, Levinthal DA (1990) Absorptive capacity: A new perspective of learning and innovation. Administrative Science Quarterly 35: 128-152

Cooper RG, Kleinschmidt EJ (1995) Benchmarking the firm's critical success factors in new product development'. Journal of Product Innovation Management 12: 374-391

Cormican K, O' Sullivan D (2004) Auditing best practices for effective product innovation management Technovation 24: 819-829

Cule, PE, Robey, D (2004) A Dual-Motor, Constructive Process Model of Organizational Transition. Organization Studies 25/2: 229-260

Damanpour F (1991) Organizational innovation: A meta-analysis of effects of determinants of moderators. Academy of Management Journal 34/ 3: 555-590

Damanpour F (1992) Organizational size and innovation. Organization Studies 13/3: 375-402

DeRond M, Bouchikhi H. (2004) On the Dialectics of Strategic Alliances. Organization Science 15/1:56-69

Dixit A, Pindyck RS (1994) Investments under uncertainty. NJ: Princeton University Press, Princeton

Dougherty D (2001) Reimagining the differentiation and integration of work for sustained product innovation. Organization Science 12/5: 612-631

Dougherty D (1995) Managing your core incompetences for corporate venturing. Entrepreneurship: Theory & Practice 19/3: 113-135

Dougherty D, Hardy C (1996) Sustained Product Innovation in Large and Mature Organizations: Overcoming Innovation-to-Organization Problems. Academy of Management Journal 39/5: 1120-1153

Edwards D, Stokoe EH (2004) Discursive psychology, focus group interviews and participants' categories. British Journal of Developmental Psychology 22: 499-507

Eisenhardt KM (1989) Making fast strategic decisions in high-velocity environment. Academy of Management Journal 32: 543-576

Ernst H, Teichert T (1998) The R and D/marketing interface and single informant bias in NPD research: an illustration of a benchmarking case study. Technovation 18/12: 721-739

Ford JD, Ford LW (1994) Logics of identity, contradiction, and attraction in change. Academy of Management Review 19/4: 756-785

Ford J, Backoff R (1988) Organizational Change in and out of dualities and paradox. In: Quinn, R, Cameron K (eds.) Paradox and Transformation. Ballinger Publishing Company, Cambridge, pp 81-121

Fryxell GE (1990) Managing the culture of innovation: the synthesis of multiple dialectics. In: Comez-Meijia LR, Lawless ML (eds), Organizational issues in high technology management. Jai Press, Greenwich, pp 37-55

Galbraith JR (1982) Designing the innovating organization. Organizational Dynamics 10/3: 5-25

Ghoshal S, Bartlett CA, Moran P (1999) A new manifesto for management. Sloan Management Review 40/3: 9-20

Gibson CB, Birkinshaw J (2004) The Antecedents, Consequences, and Mediating Role of Organizational Ambidexrity. Academy of Management Journal 47/2: 209-226

Gilsing V, Noteboom B (2006) Exploration and Exploitation in innovation systems: The case of pharmaceutical biotechnology. Research Policy 35:1-23

Guba EG, Lincoln YS (1994) Competing paradigms in qualitative research. In: Denzin NK, Lincoln YS (eds) Handbook of qualitative research. SAGE Publications, Thousand Oaks, pp. 105–117

Gulati R, Nohria N, Zaheer A (2000) Strategic Networks. Strategic Management Journal 21: 203-215

Hamel G, Prahalad CK (1996) Competing for the future. Harvard Business School Press, Cambridge

Johannessen J-A, Olaisen J, Olsen B (1999) Managing and organizing innovation in the knowledge economy. European Journal of Innovation Management 2: 116-128.

Katila R. Ahuja G (2002) Something Old, Something New: A Longitudinal Study of Search Behavior and New Product Introduction. Academy of Management Journal 45:6, 1183-1194

Kerr S (1985) On the folly of Rewarding A While Hoping for B. Academy of Management Journal 18/4: 769-783

Kim WC, Maugborgne R (1999) Strategy, value innovation and the knowledge economy. Sloan Management Review 40/3: 41-54

Kogut B, Zander U (1992) Knowledge of the firm, combinative capabilities, and the replication of technology Organization Science 3/3: 383-397

Langford J, McDonagh D (2003) Focus groups, Supporting Effective Product Development. Taylor & Francis, UK

Leifer R, O´Connor Colarelli G, Rice M (2001) Implementing radical innovation in mature firms: The role of hubs. The Academy of Management Executive 15/3: 102-113

Leonard-Barton D (1992) Core capabilities and core rigidities: A paradox in managing new product development. Strategic Management Journal 13: 111-125

Lewis MW (2000) Exploring paradox: Toward a more comprehensive guide. Academy of Management Review 25/4: 760-776

Lievens A, Moenaert RK, Jegers RS (1999) Linking communication to innovation success in the financial services industry: a case study analysis. International Journal of Service Industry Management 10/1: 23-48

March JG (1991)Exploration and exploitation in organizational learning. Organization Science 2/1: 71-87

McGrath GR (1997) Real options logic for initiating technology positioning investments. Academy of Management Review 22/4: 974-996

McLafferty I (2004) Focus group interviews as a data collecting strategy. Journal of Advanced Nursing 48 /2: 187-194

Miles RE, Snow CC, Miles G (2000) The Future.org. Long Range Planning 33: 300-321

Miles RE, Miles G, Snow, CC (2005) Collaborative entrepreneurship: How communities of networked firms use continuous innovation to create economic wealth. Stanford Business Books, Stanford California

Miller WL., Morris L (1998) Fourth generation R&D. Wiley, New York

Miller D (1993) The architecture of simplicity. Academy of Management Review 18/1: 116-138

Mohamed ZM, Tudor R (1996) Assessing and comparing the innovativeness and creative climate of firms. Scandinavian Journal of Management 12/2: 109-121

Morgan DL (1996) Focus Groups. Annual Review Sociology 22: 129-152

Morgan DL, Scannell AU (1998) Planning focus groups. Sage Publications, Inc., London

Mote JE (2005) R&D ecology; using 2-mode network analysis to explore complexity in R&D environments. Journal of Engineering and Technology Management 22: 93-111

Nonaka I (1994) Dynamic theory of organizational knowledge creation. Organization Science 5: 14-37

Nonaka I, Takeuchi H (1995) The Knowledge Creating Company. Oxford University Press, Inc. New York, USA

Olson EM, Walker OC Jr, Ruekert RW, Bonner JM (2001) Patterns of cooperation during new product development among marketing, operations and R&D: Implications for project performance. The Journal of Product Innovation Management 18: 258-271

Parent M, Gallupe BR, Salisbury D Wm, Handelman JM (2000) Knowledge creation in focus groups: can group technologies help? Information & Management 38: 47-58

Poole MS, Van de Ven AH (1989) Using Paradox to Build Management and Organization Theories. Academy of Management Review 14/4:562-578

Porter ME (1980) Competitive Strategy: Techniques for analyzing industries and competitors. Free Press, New York

Porter ME (1985) Competitive Advantage: Creating and Sustaining Superior Performance. Free Press, New York

Rothwell R (1994) Towards the fifth-generation innovation process. International Marketing Review 11/1: 7-31

Sanchez R, Mahoney JT (1996) Modularity, flexibility, and knowledge management in product and organization design. Strategic Management Journal 17: 63-76

Schumpeter JA (1934) The Theory of Economic Development: An Inquiry into Profits, Capital, Interest, and the Business Cycle. Harvard University Press, Cambridge, Massachusetts

Schumpeter JA (1942) Capitalism, socialism, and democracy. Harper & Brothers, New York

Siggelkow N, Levinthal DA (2003) Temporarily Divide to Conquer: Centralized, Decentralized, and Reintegrated Organizational Approaches to Exploration and Adaptation. Organizational Science 14/ 6: 650-669

Smith WK, Tushman ML (2005) Managing strategic contradictions: Top Management Model for Managing Innovation Streams. Organization Science 16/5: 522-536

Snow CC (2007) Book review: Strategizing, Disequilibrium, and Profit by John A. Matthews. Academy of Management Review 32/1: 308-309

Starbuck WH (1992) Learning by Knowledge-Intensive Firms. Journal of Management Studies 29/6: 713-740

Van de Ven AH, Poole MS (1995) Explaining Development and Change in Organizations. Academy of Management Review 20/3: 510-540

Von Hippel E (1986) Lead users: a source of novel product concepts. Management Science 32/7: 791-805

Westenholz A (1993) Paradoxical thinking and change in the frames of reference. Organization Studies 14/1: 37-58

Wiesenfeld BM, Raghuram S, Garud R (2001) Organizational identification among virtual workers: the role of need for affiliation and perceived work-based social support. Journal of Management 27/2: 213-229

Williamson OE (1991) Comparative economic organization: the analysis of discrete structural alternatives. Administrative Science Quarterly 36: 269-296

Zahra SA, Ellor, D (1993) Accelerating new product development and successful market introduction. *S.A.M. Advanced Management Journal* 58/1: 9-15

PART IV: FIRM PERFORMANCE

Chapter 10

WILL MODULAR PRODUCTS AND ORGANIZATIONS IMPROVE LEAD-TIME IN PRODUCT DEVELOPMENT?

Kirsten Foss
Center for Strategic Management and Globalization, Copenhagen Business School, Porcelænshaven 24, 2000 Frederiksberg, Denmark

Abstract: It is of great competitive importance for firms to improve lead-time in product development. This paper explores the economic rationale behind the idea that firms can improve lead-time by designing modular products and modular product organizations. The important characteristic of modular products is that there is a low technical interdependence among components so that these can be improved relatively independent. The contingency literature on organizational design indicates that this should have a major influence on organizational design in the direction of what can be termed a "modular organization" that is organizations with narrowly defined tasks, simple information structures and high degree of autonomy within units. I examine how improving lead-time as an organizational goal influences the way in which tasks and information structures in product development activities should be defined. The conclusion is that if a firm pursues a strategy of modular product design, it can more consistently implement those definitions of tasks and information structure that improve lead-time compared to a firm that pursues a strategy of integral design. Moreover, this will lead to the implementation of what some authors have termed a modular product development organization. However, this conclusion is reached under the assumptions that the architecture of the product is well specified and will not have to be altered, and that there are no fixed assets that needs to be shared among tasks/teams.

R.M. Burton et al. (eds.), *Designing Organizations*, doi: 10.1007/978-0-387-77776-4_10,

1. INTRODUCTION

Many benefits have been attributed to the modular product development strategy as compared to the integral product development strategy. These range from greater mass customization, easy upgrading of products, less need for market surveys, economics of substitution and increased lead-time (Feitzinger and Lee, 1977; Ulrich, 1995; Pine, 1993; Garud and Kumaraswamy,1995; Sanchez, 1996;).

Some of these benefits, such as greater mass customization, can mainly be attributed to the design of the product. Other benefits, such as improved lead-time, appear to be linked to the impact that the product design has on the organization of product development activities (Ulrich, 1993, Sanchez and Mahoney 1996, and Schilling 2000).

This paper is concerned with the relationship between improved lead-time, product development strategies and organizational design. I contrast the organizational implications of a modular product development strategy with those of an integral product development strategy. The aim is to examine if the combination of a modular product development strategy and a modular product development organization is an efficient choice when the aim is to improve lead-time. In doing so the paper adds to the literature on product development and the literature on organizational design.

Modularization[9] is a product development strategy that is based on a product architecture[10] that is defined prior to the detailed design activities, and where different functions of a product are implemented by different and relatively independent physical components. The definition of the interfaces is part of the definition of the architecture (Sanchez and Mahoney, 1996; Garud and Kumaraswamy 1993). This differs from an *integral* product development strategy, where the architecture emerges during the detailed design process, and where each function is implemented in many different components.

Modular product development organizations are characterized by rather independent and self-managing teams, the activities of which are

[9] It is difficult to rank product designs along a modular-integral spectrum because modular products may be defined by the architecture, the one to one mapping of functions to components, open/closed, standardized or customized interfaces, and the extent to which interfaces allow for easy mixing and matching of components (Mari Sako 2002). It should also be noted that products are rarely strictly modular or integral. In this paper the important characteristics are taken to be the definition of architectures and interfaces prior to detailed design and the one to one mapping of functions to components.

[10] An architecture can be defined as "(1) the arrangement of functional elements; (2) the mapping from functional elements to physical components; (3) the specification of the interfaces among interacting physical components" (Ulrich 1995, p.420).

coordinated by means of standardized interface specifications of product components (Sanchez and Mahoney, 1996; Sanchez 2000). Moreover, teams or tasks are narrowly defined and communication structures are simple.

The starting point for the arguments to be presented in this paper is that organizations are shaped by their purpose and by the coordination problem they face.[11] Product development organizations often have to fulfill many purposes such as minimize time spend on the development of a new product (lead-time), ensure accuracy in fulfilling design specifications, introduce new variants or radically new products that better fulfill customer wants or eases manufacturability. The different aims may introduce many different and sometimes incompatible organizational design principles thus requiring a trade-off between achievements of the different aims. For example, Sako (2002) argues that modules may look very different depending on whether the aim is to accomplish improvements in lead-time by easing manufacturability, or facilitate easy mixing and matching of components in products. Garud and Kumaraswamy (1995) point out that when the aim of firms is to realize economic advantages from reuse of components firms have to create incentive systems that supports design of re-usable components as well as information and knowledge sharing that ensures that designers in detailed product development know enough of the design of the components to re-use and upgrade these. Thus, managerial attention becomes very important and coordination cannot to the same extent be replaced by product interface specifications.

In this paper I fix the aim as being one of improving lead-time and investigate how the coordination problem facing organizations are influenced by a firms' choice between integral and modular product development strategies. The question asked is whether a modular product development organization is the efficient way of organizing modular product development when the aim is improving lead-time. Thus, a further contribution from this exercise consists in specifying the specific conditions under which modular products may produce modular organizations (Shilling & Steensma, 2001; Baldwin & Clark, 2000; Sanchez & Mahoney, 1996).

[11] From the contingency theory of organization theory (Lawrence and Lorsch ,1967; Thompson, 1967), we know that different types of technology, and especially differences in the nature of interdependencies between technological tasks are important contingencies in shaping organizations. In the product development literature it has been pointed out that the overall purpose of the product development effort influence organizational design. For example, Fujimoto (1989) has argued that the choice of strategy (volume producer or high–end specialist) shapes organizations. Moreover, Wheelwright and Clark (1992) point out that the organization of product development depends on whether the aim is to develop a totally novel product of to incrementally improve existing products.

The paper is structured as follows. Section II ("*Defining Key Concepts*") clarifies these central concepts. Section III ("*Defining Tasks to improve Lead-time in Product Development*") provides a perspective informed by economics on how to define tasks to improve lead time. Section IV "*Task Definition with Modular and Integral Product Development Strategies*" discuss how modular and integral product development strategies influence tasks definitions. In Section V ("*Informational Structures*") a team-theoretical and information process approach (Radner, 1992; Casson, 1994; Carter, 1995) is applied to understand how communication structures are designed to improve lead time and how these are influenced by modular and integral design strategies. Section VI (*Discussion: Will Modular Product Development Strategies Result in Modular Product Development Organizations?)* contains discussion of the results obtained from the analysis presented in the paper and compare these to some of the few empirical studies that exists of the link between modular product development strategies and organization of product development activities. Section VI ("*Conclusions*") summarizes the analysis with respect to the link between minimizing lead-time and modular organizations.

2. DEFINING KEY CONCEPTS

In the following, I use the terminology adopted by Ulrich and Eppinger (1995) to describe in more detail the different types of activities involved in product development. They group product development activities into five categories, namely 1) concept development, 2) system-level design, 3) detailed design, 4) testing and refinement, and 5)-production ramp-up. I shall limit my attention to the concept development, the system level and the detailed design phases, since many of the differences between modular and integral design strategies arise from the different ways of tackling the information processing and problem solving activities in these three phases. [12] The purpose of the concept development phase is to generate the product concept for the product.[13] At the system-level of design alternative concepts are evaluated and major sub-systems are defined. The detailed design activities consist of the development of the specific design solutions.

[12] This exclude the importance of the interdependencies between product design, production and marketing (Whitney, 1988).

[13] A product concept "... is an approximate description of the technology, working principles, and form of the product" (Ulrich and Eppinger, 1995, p.78). Ulrich and Eppinger use the word product concept in a different way compared to the general use in the marketing literature where a product concept is considered to be a unique package of functions.

There is no elaborate and precise definition of "a modular product development organization" in the literature. As described by Sanchez and Mahoney (1996) and Sanchez (2000), it is most easily characterized as a project organization of product development activities. Tasks are grouped into project teams rather than in accordance with functions or product developers' technical fields of specialization. Communication between teams are standardized and structured by the existence of technical interface standards that coordinate interfaces between projects. Finally, product development teams have a high degree of independence.

Independence between teams can be measured on a number of dimensions such as: whether design decisions can be based on information that is available within the team; the degree of freedom a team has with respect to design decisions; the degrees of freedom the team has with respect to the time frame for the project, budgets and use of other resources available in the organization, and the extent to which it is subdue to control of its activities from other members of the organization.

In this paper, I take the important characteristics of a modular product development organization to be a project organization, in which teams are independent in the sense that they:

1) can base design decisions on information that is available within the team, and
2) teams have high degrees of freedom in design decisions.
However, independence between teams along these two dimensions can, always be achieved by defining sufficiently large teams (Schilling, 2000) so another important characteristic is
3) that tasks/teams are narrowly defined so that there is a high degree of specialization in product development within tasks/teams.

Lead-time, which is the other important concept to be defined, is traditionally measured as the length of time from the initiation of a concept generation to market introduction (Clark, Chew and Fujimoto, 1987). In this paper I investigate only improvements in the time from concept generation to product design, rather than the time from product initiation to market introduction. This implies that I do not consider important issues such as design for manufacturability that may also improve the overall lead-time.

Lead-time in product development is perceived of as a very important variable in product development (Smith and Reinertsen, 1995; Meyer, 1993). Short lead-time makes a company able to respond fast to competitors moves in product markets, enables them to adjust fast to new customer requirements, and is also claimed to be a source of competitive advantage over less fast moving competitors. The latter may be grounded in the ability of a firm to earn quasi-rents on novel products because of the loyalty that customers may exhibit toward the first mover (Schmalensee, 1982; Shapiro, 1983; Klemperer, 1987).

Lead-time is influenced by many different factors. The literature on product development for example, mentions the level of ambition in the development project, the extent to which components can be reused and the competencies of those involved in the design activities[14]. Moreover, it is also suggest that lead-time is influenced by the way in which product development activities are organized and firms' choice of modular versus integral product development strategies. Cusumano (1997), for example, has argued that a modular product development strategy makes it possible to organize product development activities in ways that reduce the need for iterations of information between teams and enables a greater use of parallel product development activities. Both of these characteristics improve lead-time.

In order to better understand the link between lead-time, organizational design and product development strategies one must focus on the building block of organizations -that is the way, in which tasks are defined and allocated to teams.

3. DEFINING TASKS TO IMPROVE LEAD-TIME IN PRODUCT DEVELOPMENT

Defining tasks is one way of breaking up large-scale problems up into small scale problems that can be managed by small teams (Cusumano, 1997). There are many reasons why it is efficient to divide design activities of a large project among different individuals and an important one is that it may improve lead-time in product development. Tasks may loosely be defined as the partitioning of product development activities in a way, which delimit the activities that are carried out by one individual from those activities that are carried out by another individual.[15]

It will improver lead- time in product development most when tasks are defined in ways that simultaneously economize on bounded rationality, improve productivity and innovativeness all of which give rise to different

[14] In the following sections innovations are assumed to be incremental and invariant in type so that components cannot be used to a greater extent if a modular development strategy is chosen.

[15] I distinguish between activities, tasks and teams. Tasks may encompass one or more discrete separable types of activities. Teams are formed by grouping tasks.

criterion for task definitions.[16] However, as I argue in the following a modular product development strategy creates different opportunities for defining tasks and teams compared to an integral one, and these differences implies that there is less of a trade-off between the various criteria for task definition. Moreover, with a modular product development strategy the various criteria does to a large extent allow for a definition of tasks and teams in ways that are consistent with what I have take to be the important characteristics of a modular organization.

In order to focus on the differences in task definition that stem from the choice of modular versus integral product development strategies I have set aside the incentive issues so that the only coordination problem that emerges from task partitioning is that of aligning the activities among the various tasks. I have also set a side the problems of allocating a fix number of employees to fixed set of hours per day and fixed assets, assuming that there were no problems of sharing equipment and other facilities.[17] Tasks specification may be very different with a fixed number of employees, because it becomes important to ensure that all employees are fully occupied. The allocation of fixed assets and equipment among teams is another issue that impact on an organizational structure. When assets have to be shared among teams it may be very costly to have teams independently determine the use of these assets. "Negotiation costs" from independent actions may simply be high compared to the use of planning and authority. If equipment and facilities are shared among tasks and teams it may also be difficult to determine how much the operation of each of the teams contributes to the wear and tear of the equipment and facilities and an increased use of authority will be efficient for reasons of measurement costs (Barzel, 1989). Of course the interdependence between teams that arise for measurement costs reasons can be solved by introducing redundant equipment so that each team has its own equipment- a solution that may sometimes be very expensive.

[16] At one extreme, all task definition takes place at the very beginning of the product development project; at the other; it is part of the ongoing process of product development. Furthermore, task definition may be performed by the person(s) appointed as responsible for the entire project or it may be allocated to different broadly defined teams (Johne, 1984; Clark and Wheelwright, 1992; Lundquist, Sundgren and Trygg, 1996). However, the economic principles behind task definition remain the same. Innovativeness is the ability of an individual "... to retrieve a potentially useful piece of information from one's memory and then adapting that information to the problem in hand" (Ulrich and Eppinger 1995, p.88) – which is to recombine knowledge in new ways

[17] If the aim is to save on fixed costs tasks will be divided differently than when the aim is to improve lead-time (March & Simon, 1967)

I compare tasks definition in modular products where the architecture is well specified before detailed design with task definition in integral products where the architecture of the product is unspecified but emerge in the detailed design process. In the case of modular products I assume that the existence of technical interdependencies among components is perfectly known as are the range within which component changes influence these interdependencies. In the case of integral products I only assume that some of the technical interdependencies are known whereas the nature of the interdependency is unknown. Thus, the technical uncertainty differs in the two situations which is also one reason why task definition may differ. In the discussion section I take up the issue of how technical uncertainty in the design of the product architectures impacts on task definition and more broadly on organizational design.

3.1 Economizing with Bounded Rationality

One implication of bounded rationality is that there are sharply diminishing returns to problem solving, as problems become more complex. [18] This may show up as inferior solutions or as more than proportional time spent on problem solving (Alexander, Simon, 1969).

Decomposing design problems is a way of economizing with bounded rationality even if only one person is involved in problem solving activities (Simon 1969; Radner 1992). However, if different individuals solve different sub-problems, it may be possible to economize even more on bounded rationality and thereby improve lead-time. What sort of heuristics can then be used to define product development tasks? Within the sphere of social systems the solution proposed by Simon (1969) is to construct sub-systems and hierarchies by making a chart of who interact most intensely with each other. Then, Simon explains, "… the clusters of dense interaction in the chart will identify a rather well defined hierarchic structure" (ibid. p. 88). The underlying assumption is that task definitions, which economize on bounded rationality, are the ones that solve some of the coordination problem by reducing the need for communication the most.

In the context of product design, Eppinger, Withney, Smith and Gebala (1994) have suggested that the need of interaction between product-designers are strongly influenced by the type of technological interdependencies that designers encounter in the product design. Based on various case studies, they find that iterations between product development

[18] Complex in the sense that it is ".... made up of a large number of parts that interact in a non simple way" (Simon, 1969, p.86).

tasks are reduced most when tasks are defined on the basis of a chart of the interaction between the design parameters specified by designers.[19] Von Hippel (1990) has illustrated this point very well in an example of the development of an airplane, where the product development problem is subdivided in two different ways into two meta-tasks. In the first case one sub-problem consists of developing the rear end and the other sub-problem consists of developing the front end of the plane whereas in the second case one sub-problem is to develop the engine and the other to develop the aircraft body. If the design of the rear and front part is allocated to different teams, each team has to be fully informed about many more design variables and the way in which they are altered in product development than if the design of the body is allocated to one team and the design of the engine to the other team

To sum up, when specifying design tasks, one need to consider how to reduce the amount of design variables to be considered within in each task while at the same time reduce the amount of information each person needs to receive and communicate. The latter depends on the interdependencies in tasks. Technical interdependencies in the product design appear to be an important determinant of interdependencies in product development activities. This implies that the product development problem is best decomposed and allocated to task in accordance with these technical interdependencies.

If all technical interdependencies are well specified tasks should be defined to minimize the complexity in solving for the optimal design. The definition of tasks is different when interdependences are known to exist but are not specified. In that case product design entails experimentation in order to specify the nature of the interdependency and task definition must take into account the need for iteration between product development activities as well as making the complexity of problem-solving manageable to individuals. When there is technical uncertainty one also needs to take into account how task partitioning influences the speed with which designers discover solutions to incompatibilities in product designs. Improving innovativeness in this manner is the subject of the following sections

[19] Eppinger, Withney, Smith and Gebala (1994) mention that other factors beside information exchanges may also be of importance in defining tasks, for example, task duration and the degree of dependence with respect to "...task communication time, functional coupling, physical adjacency, electrical or vibration characteristics, parameter sensitivity, historical variance of task results, certainty of planning estimates, or the volume of information transfer" (p.4). These factors are particularly important when firms have a fixed number of designers employed in the organization.

3.2 Improving Innovativeness in Tasks

When it comes to improving innovativeness it seems that there is a rather complex relationship between a strong specialization of activities in tasks and innovativeness (Cohen and Levinthal, 1990). Improving innovativeness has much to do with being able to access the right knowledge at the right time. Bower, Langely and Simon (1983) and Simon (1985) argue that the possession of relevant knowledge and skills is what give rise to creative associations and innovation. In many phases in the product development process much of the knowledge that underlies what we ordinary refer to as skills is tacit. For example, designers may posses certain skills in concept generation and in the design and execution of experiments needed to test technical solutions. Moreover, the cognitive elements of tacit knowledge may create problems of communicating between specialist in area such as marketing, product design, and production functions.

Improving innovativeness within tasks seems to be subject to a trade-off between accumulating a certain depth of knowledge and accumulating a certain width of knowledge. On the one hand innovativness requires a certain "[i]ntensity of effort" and "....important aspects of learning how to solve problems are build up over many practice trails on related problems"[20] (Cohen and Levinthal, 1990, p.131). Moreover, in order for boundedly rational individuals to learn effectively from experience the complexity of the problems they solve will often have to be reduced by a decomposition of the problem and a rather narrow definition of the problem solving tasks (Levinthal and March, 1993). These factors call for a narrow definition of tasks.

On the other hand, a certain width of knowledge and therefore width in task definitions may also be important with respect to facilitating innovativeness. Cohen and Levinthal (1990) point out that "... in settings, in which there is uncertainty about the knowledge domains, from which potentially useful information may emerge, a diverse background provide a more robust basis for learning because it increases the prospect that incoming information will relate to what is already known" (p.131).

At the organizational level this problem could be remedied by employing experts of diverse backgrounds. However, the creation of new knowledge often requires interaction between different knowledge elements. When

[20] Much problem solving knowledge is cumulative in the sense that knowledge of prior advances within a field is necessary in order to assimilate information on new advances. In such cases the rate, at which new knowledge can be accumulated increases with the stock of existing knowledge (Cohen and Levinthal 1990).

experts only posse highly specialized knowledge, they may be unable to communicate with specialist in other sub-fields because there is not sufficient knowledge overlap. There are, as argued by Nonaka (1994), different means of facilitating communication between specialists in sub-fields. This implies that although a narrow definition of tasks create specialist knowledge containing tacit and explicit elements, these may be brought into contacts through various interactions, of which some require overlapping activities and close interaction.

To sum up, in order to enhance innovativeness in tasks it is important to distinguish between situations where new solutions most likely emerge from existing bodies of knowledge and where they most likely emerge from new bodes of knowledge. In the former case tasks should be defined to increase the depth of existing knowledge. This requires, some repetition or intensity of effort in the performance of the tasks is important, there has to be some relatedness between the types of problems that are to be solved in terms of the bodies of knowledge and, the complexity of the problem has to be manageable to individuals. In the case where there is great uncertainty with respect to what kind of knowledge is useful for problem solving knowledge accumulation have to be more extensive and tasks may have to be defined more broadly. [21] How broad tasks have to be defined depends on the extent to which the confinement from knowledge specialization can be overcome by the creation of knowledge transfer mechanism such as close links or overlapping teams in product development[22]

In the above I have been concerned mainly with product development as a unique problem solving activity. However, product development can also be viewed as an ongoing activity that consists of a number of recurrent activities. When viewed in this manner improving lead-time centers on improving productivity in product development by defining tasks to increase labor productivity.

[21] The importance of overlapping tacit knowledge between specialists can also explain difference in the size of teams. Schaefer (1999) has argued that low inter team communication cost will result in small and many teams whereas low costs of intra team communication will result in large teams at the expense of the benefits of division of labor. Low inter team communication costs may be attributed to relative few knowledge interdependencies between problems solving activities and low intra team communication costs to well established overlaps in the knowledge domains of specialists.

[22] In fact, the importance of knowledge sharing as a way of enhancing communication between specialists may explain the many recommendation of establishing close links between for example marketing and design or design and manufacturing (Clark and Fujimoto, 1987, Larson and Goblei, 1988, Clark and Wheelwright, 1992)

3.3 Improving Labor Productivity

Productivity gains arise from improved skills and time that is saved from avoiding having to switch from one task to another (Smith, 1776). In product development almost all activities have some element of skill. For example, designers use heuristics and technical insight to decompose design problems or to search for conceptual solutions. Skills may also consist in the ability to engage in creative processes when trying to conceptualizing new types of solutions or the care and accuracy, with which the problem solvers design and conduct experiments or use simulation models. Repetition of the same types of activities over and over is the key to accumulation of all these diverse skills (Cohen and Levinthal, 1990). To increase the rate of accumulation of skills, tasks will have to be defined around activities, which can be repeated by solving the same type of problems. This criterion for task definition may also lead to a reduction of "switching costs". In product development "switching costs" may arise when it takes time for an individual to change his mindset in order to perform a different type of activity. Such switching costs arise, for example, if one has to switch between market analysis activities and concept development activities or even if one has to switch between different types of components.

All this indicates that the more narrowly tasks are defined around repetitive activities the greater are the potential productivity gains within tasks. However, with very narrow definitions of tasks much more communication may have to be undertaken between product developers in order to ensure coordination of those activities that cannot be pre-planned. Thus, there is a trade-off between increasing productivity in individual product development tasks on the one hand and reducing time spend on communication between tasks on the other hand.

4. TASK DEFINITION WITH MODULAR AND INTEGRAL PRODUCT DEVELOPMENT STRATEGIES

Firms that pursue a modular product development strategy can decompose design problems and defined tasks differently from firms that follow an integral product development strategy. In a modular product each product function is implemented in the product by relatively independents components. For most incremental improvements of functions the important interdependencies between design variables to be explored are likely to be concentrated within components rather than between components. This implies that a definition of design tasks in accordance with the components that have to be developed most likely will be the one, which economize the most on bounded rationality.

A Modular product development strategy also implies that definition of product concepts and creation of a product-architecture are separated from detailed design activities. This indicates that tasks can be grouped round the repetitive activities of concept generation, architectural creation, and component design to enhance productivity without evoking a great need for communication.

Thus, with a modular product development strategy concept generation, architectural design and component designs can be undertaken as relatively independent projects in the sense that designers can mainly rely on information within the team in making design decisions. Defining tasks and teams around these activities ensures that the organization is able to economize on bounded rationality, and on costs of communications while achieving high productivity from learning by doing in component development and concept generation and architectural designs.

With an integral product development strategy there is no a priori obvious way of decomposing the product development problem unless technical interdependencies. Moreover, since the product has not been designed to reduce technical interdependencies it is likely that the design problem can only be decomposed to a lesser extent compared to that of the modular product. Finally, since many of the interdependencies will emerge during the design process it will call for extended communication or overlapping design activities between tasks/teams.

When firms follow an integral product development strategy it is more difficult to identify the repetitive activities because new interdependencies between the ways in which product functions are implemented emerge with the various product up-grades. Moreover, unforeseen interdependencies between technical solutions create a need for iteration in information exchange between the concept selection and detailed design activities. Thus, defining tasks around repetitive activities will not necessary economize the most on bounded rationality. Integral product development strategies thus, create a greater trade-off between achieving high productivity from learning by doing and independence in decision making.

Modular and integral product development strategies also require different types of knowledge accumulation in order to minimize lead-time. Sanchez (2000) points out that with integral product development strategies designers typically try to develop new technologies and new products at the same time whereas with modular product development strategies designers learning about "new technologies, new architectures and new components are intentionally decoupled" (p. 11).

This difference in the need for knowledge accumulation has implications for the way, in which tasks may be defined in order to enhance innovativeness. First, with a modular product development strategy and well-defined product architecture much of the uncertainty in problem solving is confined to the development of the individual components, which imply a definition of tasks and teams in accordance with the development of components. By defining tasks very narrowly around components one may increase the rate of accumulation of component specific knowledge. Thus, when the desire is to improve innovativeness in product development, tasks may be defined in a way that is fully in accordance with what is required for a modular product development organization.

Firms, with an integral product development strategy will often face more uncertainty as to what information is relevant for effective problem solving and innovativeness. This implies a wider definition of tasks or a wider definition of teams to create greater overlap in knowledge domains compared to that required of a firm pursuing a modular product development strategy.

Finally, firms that pursue either an integral or a modular product development strategy may be faced with a trade-off between defining tasks in way that maximize the accumulation of component/product specific knowledge and defining tasks in ways that maximize accumulation of technical expertise within sub-fields (such as various product technologies, marketing, production etc). This trade-off is often recognized in the debate concerning the functional organization of product development contra the project organization of product development (Weelwright and Clark, 1992; Larson and Gobeli, 1988; Allen and Hauptman, 1987). However, with modular product development strategies there is a higher probability that there is an overlap between specialization in component knowledge and specialization in sub fields within product technologies. So, at least the short run a modular product development strategy and a modular product development organization makes it possible to improve knowledge accumulation in ways that improve lead-time by defining tasks in accordance with components.

So far it has been argued that compared to an integral product development strategy a modular product development strategy makes it possible to greater extent to 1) economize on bounded rationality, 2) maximize repetition of similar activities as to increase productivity in tasks, and 3) increase innovativeness in component design. To realize the benefits from modular design strategies firms must define tasks in accordance with the interdependencies in product design so that each tasks can carried out relatively independent of all other tasks or be grouped into relatively independent teams. This was one of the major criteria of modular product development organizations.

With an integral product development strategy the decomposition of the product takes place simultaneously with the decomposition of the product development problem. If tasks are gradually defined in accordance with the decomposition that emerges one may economize on bounded rationality by reducing complexity and information exchange. Since interdependencies in the product design has not deliberately been kept at a minimum (as is the case of most modular product design) tasks most likely will have to be less specialized compared to the case of a modular product development strategy. It may also be difficult to ensure that the decomposition of the product allow for repetitive design activities when the product has to be upgraded. With changes in the product's functionality new interdependencies in the product design may emerge. All this implies that it is less likely that any task definition will simultaneously 1) economize on bounded rationality, 2) maximize repetition of similar activities as to increase productivity in tasks, and 3) increase innovativeness and one will have to choose between different criteria for defining tasks. Moreover, although some independent teams and tasks can be defined these are likely to be much less specialized in the activities they carry out compared to what can be expected with a modular product development strategy.

When design problems are not fully decomposable there will always remain some interdependencies in problem solving no matter how tasks are defined. These interdependencies have to be managed by creating efficient informational structures. In the following sections tasks definitions are taken as given and the informational structure is investigated assuming that tasks have been defined to improve lead-time. I argue that the design strategy influence the choice of efficient informational structures in a way that creates congruence between a modular product development strategy and a modular product development organization.

5. INFORMATIONAL STRUCTURES

Informational structure is defined as the procedures that are implemented in order to ensure proper communication of information between given tasks and teams.[23] From a team-theoretical, and information-processing perspective on organizations the efficient informational structures are the

[23] Galvin (1999) points out that in connections with product modularity the term informational structure is often used to denote only the type of product design information that is captured in what Baldwin and Clark (1997) call visible design rules. In team theory the term informational structure is used in a broader sense to cover the entire spectra of information required for decision making.

ones that economize most with information processing costs given the way tasks/teams are defined.[24]

Information processing cost consists of the costs of transmitting information, costs of investing in information channels, non-optimal decisions due to error in communication[25] or costs of obtaining information through investigations (Carter, 1995; Casson, 1994; Marschak and Radner, 1977). Many of these costs arise because time has to be spent on obtaining and transferring information or on correcting errors in decision making due to faulty communications. That is, time that adds to lead- time. The team-theoretical perspective therefore provides a basis, on which to identify informational structures which improve lead-time in product development.

The decomposition of the design problem and the way sub-problems are allocated to tasks/teams play an important role with respect to determining the design of informational structures since it is the interdependencies in problems solving that define the need for communication between tasks/teams. Three characteristics of the decomposed product design problem are important for choice of informational structures. The first important characteristic is what Casson (1994) refers to as "*decisiveness*", and the second important characteristic is what Radner (1992) refers to as "*associative operations*". Finally, it is also important to the choice of informational structures whether the decomposition of the product development problem requires that *tacit/sticky* knowledge be transmitted between tasks (Nonaka, 1994).

Decisiveness refers to a situation characterized by sequential interdependencies (Thompson, 1967) in activities, giving rise to a need for one-way communication. When a design problem is characterized by decisiveness, informational structures will to a greater extent be those that characterize a modular organization.

The *associative operations* refers to problem solving, where some of the information processing activities can be carried out completely independently of other information processing activities (pooled

[24] The team theoretical approach is an economic based information processing perspective on organizations. Some of the primary proponents of this approach are: Marchak and Radner (1977), Aioki (1986), Carter 1995, and Casson 1994. In the following analysis of efficient informational structures the standard team theoretical simplifying assumption of incentive compatibility is assumed to apply

[25] Errors in communication can, for example, be interpreted as a small probability that the wrong decision premises are communicated because tacit information is incorrectly encoded into memos, plans or interface standards (Carter, 1995).

interdependencies Thompson, 1967).[26] Associative operations greatly reduce problem solving time since it allows for the organization of parallel information processing.

Tacit or sticky information refers to the situation where costs of transferring information is high due to the way, in which it is encoded or due to the lack of " absorptive capacity" of receivers of the information (von Hippel, 1998). Receivers may, for example, lack an understanding of the context, in which the information is derived. Ulrich and Eppinger (1995) provide a fine example concerning the development of a fork for a mountain bike. The team who performed the market analysis identified customer needs as "easy to install". "For the team that performed the translation of customers needs into target specifications this was a too ambiguous statement, since it could be translated into a number of different technical specifications, such as "time to assembly" or "assembled by use of simple tools and simple movements". Such type of sticky information causes errors in decision taking and informational structures will have to be designed that reduce such errors.

In the following sections, I argue that a modular product design strategy creates design problems that to a larger extent are characterized by decisiveness and associative operations than is the case with an integral product development strategy. Moreover, much of the tacit knowledge is likely to be confined in tasks that are defined around the development of components. This allows for the use of more simple informational structures relative to firms that pursue an integral product development strategy.

5.1 Decisiveness and the use of Simple Informational Structures

One important aspect of design problems that determines the choice of informational structures is whether these are characterized by *decisiveness* with respect to the communication of information where "... [d]ifferences in decisiveness mean that some problems have a logical structure, which supports solutions without consultation and some do not" (Casson 1994, p.50). Natural decisiveness occurs when there is sequential interdependence (Thompson, 1967; Eppinger et al. 1994) between two decision takers (A and

[26] It should be noted that the logical structure of problems, which gives rise to natural decisiveness is different from those, which gives rise to associative processes. Decisiveness and associative processes do not preclude one another. In the case of associative processes there is no logical sequence to follow. However, the communication will be structured by the way, in which one has chosen to organize problem solving into an efficient hierarchical network (Radner, 1992).

B) and when decision taker B only needs to know the decision and not the premises for the decision reached by A (or vise versa). This is important when the premise for the decision is more costly to transmit than information about the decision that has been reached. For example, the concept generation process and the detailed design are characterized by decisiveness when the choice of a product concept can be carried out on the basis of information about customer preferences alone independent of information about the constraint set by knowledge about product technologies and design solutions. Moreover, the team that works on the system level design only needs information about the product concept chosen and not about the actual customer requirements.[27] A firm can also refrain from making inquiries into customer preferences or the state of technological knowledge or it can refrain from making investigation in either of the two teams. In such cases the firm will to an increasing extent use simple information structures. In the latter case decisions becomes entirely routine since no new information trigger new problem solving.[28]

When there is no decisiveness firms must implement more centralized or broader types of information structures. For example, firms can decide that all available information about customer preference and technological knowledge must be used in making the decision and that this information must be communicated to a central decision taker. Alternatively, all the information is communicated between the teams. The former is chosen when there are specialization advantages in decision taking while the latter is often chosen when information contains elements of tacit knowledge. For example, it can be important for designers of complementary components to know how a certain solution reacts to changes in test conditions rather than just to know that this solution as pointed out by Sanchez and Mahoney (1996), "... information and assumptions underlying upstream design decisions may not be transferred intact to downstream stages of development. Technical incompatibilities between interdependent components may actually be 'designed into' downstream components" (p. 69).

[27] The communication can be what Wheelwright and Clark (1992) has termed batch communication.

[28] One problem not dealt with here stem from the fact that often product developers do not know that they posses information that is valuable to other product developers. This creates what Hoopes and Postrel (1999) term "glitches" that are costly mistakes or costly duplications of work. According to Hoopes and Postrel such costs can be avoided though information integration mechanisms such as overlapping team activities. Those who have valuable information is likely to discover the need for communicating it to the relevant decision takers. This implies that in the choice of efficient information structure managers must take into account their ignorance of who poses what kind of valuable information.

Overlapping teams may be required when important tacit knowledge can only be transferred between teams through direct observations and co-development (Nonaka, 1992; Wheelwright and Clark, 1992). In the range between fully centralized and complete decentralized information structures is the use of a project manager who follows the project through some or all of the phases and accumulate much of the tacit knowledge about the project.[29]

In cases where, the design problem is not characterized by natural decisiveness it may sometimes be efficient to *impose* decisiveness on problems by dispensing with the communication of the decision premises. As an example the firm can choose to take customer preferences or technological knowledge as given and make that the "normal state". When an unusual state occurs (and is discovered) decisions will have to be made in a consultative manner otherwise it can be made in a sequential manner[30].

Modular and an integral product development strategy are to different extent characterized by natural and imposed decisiveness in product development activities. With a modular product development strategy the architecture and the interface specification of the product are determined independently of the development of the specific technological solutions that implement the various product functions. The interfaces specified in the architecture is the natural state of the environment which is to be taken for granted in the choice of the specific design solutions. Interface specifications simply eliminate changes in the decision premises caused by interdependencies between design solutions. When interface standards "freezes states" it creates informational independence between problems in a way that makes it possible to solve problems concurrently. One way communication, elimination of investigations of states, and concurrent design are all means of reducing lead-time relative to problem solving that require extensive consultation.

Decisiveness can be imposed on product development problems independent on whether firms pursue an integral or a modular product development strategy. However, with the decomposition of the design problem and the definition of tasks that characterize a modular design

[29] Clark and Wheelwright (1992) have identified three different types of teams, in which project managers are used. These are lightweight, heavy weight and autonomous team structures. These teams vary among other thing in the role and responsibility ascribed to project managers but they have in common the idea that a certain project manager is assigned to the project for at least some parts of the development process.

[30] Sequential decision-taking requires that the knowledge that has to be transferred is not tacit or sticky in the sense, that common experience is required in order to interpret the information.

strategy it is much more likely that important information will not have to be suppressed in order to achieve a simple communication structure.

Thus, with a modular product development strategy (and a well specified product architecture) it will be efficient to implement informational structures of a very simple kind since much of the information is "hidden" in interface standards. In other words it will be efficient to implement the informational structures that characterize a modular product development organization. The independence between tasks/teams that is achieved by defining interface standards may come at the expense of narrow constraints on the choice of design solutions within teams. However, in many cases interfaces can be specified in terms of functional requirements that the solutions have to live up to. This sometimes provides the designers with high degrees of freedom with respect to the choice of how these functional requirements are fulfilled.

With an integral product development strategy it is possible to implement simple informational structures by imposing decisiveness on problem solving. However, the uses of these more simple informational structures are likely to be limited compared to firms that pursue a modular product development strategy due to the greater importance of interdependencies among design activities. Lead- time can therefore not be improved to the same extent as with a modular product development strategy.

Another important way of improving lead-time is to make more extensive use of parallel problem solving. As will be argued in the following section integral and modular strategies also differ with respect to the extent to which lead-time can be reduced by parallel problem solving.

5.2 Associative Operations and Parallel Information Processing

The implementation of parallel information processes is eased when design problems have a structure that allows for what Radner (1992) calls "*associative operations*" such that problem solving activities can be organized into hierarchical structures of information accumulation.

Many of the activities that take place in product development can be characterized as associative operations. Linear information transformation and pattern matching are the two paradigm cases of associative operations. Linear transformation takes place when a set of information is transformed into another set of information by the use of some sort of algorithm. An example from product development is the transformation of customer statements into target specifications. Individuals with the same education and experience may employ some of the same tacit heuristics in performing this activity making it possible to allocate the activity to different individuals and have them perform the translation in parallel. Pattern matching takes place when a set of data is compared with a reference set of data in order to find the closest match. An example of this is the comparison of dimensions of many different design solutions to a specific design problem in order to find the one that matches a set of specifications.

Associative operations can be carried out by defining tasks so that groups of individuals compare sub-sets of solutions and each find the best solutions to the sub-sets problems. Sub-problems are synthesized by sequentially eliminating or transforming sub-solutions until a final solution is arrived at. Lead-time in for example, detailed design can be improved by having many teams working on discovering solutions to well specified detailed design problems[31] However, there are diminishing returns to this kind of parallel problem solving[32]. As argued by Nelson (1959) the costs of using several teams during the initial stage of design is small relative to the benefits that may accrue from the information gathering. Increases in teams add costs in a linear fashion while the probability of discovering a better solution increases in a hyperbolic fashion moving asymptotic toward 1 this determine an upper bound on the efficient number of teams (Arditti and Levy, 1980).[33]

Modular and integral product development strategies differ with respect to the extent to which parallel information processing is feasible. Both strategies allow for some activities such as concept generation and selection to be organized into parallel search activities each of which are hierarchically accumulated. However, with a modular product development strategy there is greater possibilities for parallel problem solving because the product is intentionally designed in a way that create relatively independent product development problems. This allows for a more extensive use of parallel development of components. The hierarchical

[31] There are also means of improving lead-time that can be used when problems are characterized by greater interdependence (as will often be the case with an integral product development strategy). For example, in cases of sequential interdependencies one team ideally have to await the results of the other teams. However, the "downstream" team can make an early involvement in the decisions of the upstream team in order to better predict the choice of solution (Wheelwright and Clark, 1992). In theses cases the use of parallel problem solving come at the expense of implementing very simple information structures.

[32] Parallel information processing may also be employed as a way of creating more variety in solutions as the number of solutions increase by having different individuals engaged in the transformation processes.

[33] Based on a study of two different design projects Marples (1961) finds that parallel search for design solutions are most likely to occur when organizations have sufficient manpower and when the problem is not felt to be so difficult that a number of feasible solutions seem improbable.

structure of a product-architecture provides the information as to how the individual solutions are to be aggregated into an overall solution.

5.3 Will Modular Product Development Strategies Result in Modular Product Development Organizations?

When the aim is to improve lead-time we should expect modular products strategies to improve lead-time more compared to integral product strategies and we should expect modular product strategies to result in organizations with narrow task specialization, simple information structures and high degrees of autonomy within tasks/teams. The main reason for this is that modular product designs are more simple compared to integral ones and that the specification of interfaces serves as a means of replacing managerial or inter-team coordination with pre-planning. Tasks and teams can be specified narrowly around architectural and component design while communication to coordinate the remaining problem solving-interdependencies is kept at a minimum. [34] The need for investigation and communication is suppressed because the architecture and the interfaces are defined as the normal state. Firms can use one-way communication from designers of the product architecture to designers of components and designers of components can hierarchically aggregate design solutions into product solutions. Moreover, when the architecture of the product is fully specified tacit and sticky information is to a large extent confined within tasks. This also implies that there will be little use of overlapping tasks/team activities. All of these are important characteristics of modular organizations as defined in section II.

An important assumption in this paper is that the technical uncertainty in product development is low. More specifically, I have assumed that with a modular product the product architecture is well specified in the sense that interdependencies between components are known to designers and that the rage within which component design variables can change without altering component interfaces is also fully known. All this implies that there is no need for adjustment of technical solutions as long as they fulfill interface specifications and that there is no need for changes in the architecture. If technical uncertainty increase such that designer do not know the rage at which component design variables critically change component interdependencies it alters the efficient definition of tasks and information structures. Teams working on different detailed design solutions will either have to make local adaptation through the use of intensive communication or authority or they may have to broaden teams and tasks to encompass more of the expected interdependencies (Dessein and Santos 2006).

However, the extent to which product designers realize the influence of component designs on product architecture depends on the way in which product development is organized. According to Henderson and Clark (1990), modular product development organizations will not provide the organizational structure conducive for such discoveries. They point to three main reasons for this. First information channels reflect how designers initially perceived of the physical interdependences in products and will not ensure communication about new important interdependencies. Second, technicians filter out information about components/materials that are not considered important to developments in focal component and finally, designers typically search for solutions build on prior experience with the product architecture. What designers need is to adopt new ways of searching for solutions and this may require that managerial authority is exercised to create new patterns of interaction in the organization.

When technical uncertainty is increased as the case is when firms do not know the architecture of the product firms need too engage in extensive discovery processes. Schaefer (1999) (see also Simon 1957 and, Perrow 1972) argues that a "preliminary modularization" of products is an effective way of reducing the time of experimentation needed to achieve an understanding of interdependencies between design variables. The project development group can perform a sort of controlled experiment by solving some sub-problems and trace the effects of the changes on the working of all other sub-problems. To improve lead-time in product development firms also need to organize the product development organization in ways conducive for carrying out an extensive discovery process. This entails a trade-off between centralization and decentralization as firms on the one hand need to search broadly for the interdependencies and on the other hand need to coordinate across their interdependent activities. Using an NK-search model Siggelkow and Levintahl (2003) argue that interdependencies in product architectures makes it efficient to initially use a decentralized structure which is centralized after a while to achieve coordination. This result holds even if the problem of searching for the optimal architecture is fully decomposable. What firms must do in order to benefit from the decentralized search is to create interdependencies among organizational units by decomposing the problem in ways that creates organizational interdependence. Thus, firms should use modular decentralized structure (with suppressed interdependencies among units) which is replaced with a centralized structure after some period of initial experimentation with the product architecture. However, if firms have only a short period in which to search for a product architecture and if that search is highly interdependent firms will do better with a centralized compared to a decentralized structure. However, too much decomposition of the search process may also be inefficient. Ethiraj and Levinthal (2004) have explored the implication on organizational design when designers do not know if the initial decomposition of a problem is the "right one". In an NK-search model they examine the consequences of too little and to much decomposition of problem solving with nearly decomposable problems and they find that to little decomposition results in prolonged search and a possible lock-in to discoveries of inferior architectures whereas too fine grained decomposition limits the organization's ability to adapt the architecture and posses even greater performance penalties to firms. Thus, from an information processing perspective we should expect firms to implement less modular organizations when they are faced with great architectural uncertainty unless they are also under sever time pressure. This conclusion is substantiated if we also take into account how the different organization structures influence knowledge accumulation.

5.4 Knowledge as a Substitute in Coordinating Product Development Activities

In the discussion I have focused on the exchange of information as a means of coordinating but exchange of information and preplanning can to some extent be substituted with the accumulation of knowledge of how to overcome technological interdependencies by inventing around these (Postrel, 2002). Moreover, communication costs (errors and time spend on communication activities) are likely to be influenced by the level and type of knowledge accumulated in firms (Puranam and Jacobides, 2006). When knowledge and information acts as substitutes in the coordination of product development investing in knowledge creation is an alternative means of improving lead-time in product development.

Postrel (2002) argue that in order to adapt and coordinate firms need to types of knowledge which calls specialist capability and trans-specialist understanding. Specialist capability effects problem solving in specific areas whereas trans-specialist understanding facilitates coordination across different domains of knowledge. Trans-specialist knowledge is "the means by which members of one specialty assess how effective another speciality is likely to be when faced with a given problem" (p.306). In product development trans-specialist understanding ensures that the specification of design concepts meets critical values to satisfy consumer needs, that interface standard are sufficiently detailed to ensure coordination and that the locus of problem solving is allocated to the speciality best equipped to handle the problem. Specialist capability refers to the ability of the experts in a given domain to solve problems in their domain.

Postrel (2002) argues that the two bodies of knowledge can be substitutable in problem solving activities. For example, if teams in detailed product development have much trans-specialist understanding they select solutions that take into account the impact on design solutions on other teams whereas if they have much specialist knowledge they are better able to invent around the problems imposed by the design solutions selected by other teams (as pointed out by Leonard-Barton 1992).

Two implications can be drawn from the arguments presented above. First, design interdependencies among team/tasks are dependent on the physical properties of the design *as well* as on the amount of specialist knowledge firms have accumulated. With unbounded levels of specialist knowledge each product development team can work relatively independent without receiving or transmitting much in formation as in modular organizations. There will also be less need for strict interface specification between components to reach a certain level of product performance since each team is capable of inventing around the restrictions implied by the choices made by other teams. Second, trans-specialist knowledge implies that there are boundaries between bodies of knowledge. These boundaries need not coincide with component interdependencies in products but when knowledge is accumulated through process of learning by doing the boundaries between knowledge bodies will gradually be influence by the way firms choose to create task/team specialization around components. If firms decompose product development tasks in accordance with the technical interdependencies in the product they create narrow specialization of knowledge since designers only know relatively few design parameters. If firms instead decompose the product development task such that interdependencies and the amount of design parameters that each designer needs to know are increased they will create a higher trans-specialist knowledge in teams because there will be greater sharing of knowledge about the same design parameters within teams.

When the two bodies of knowledge are not fully substitutable firms are faced with an important trade-off between investing in specialist capabilities and trans-specialist knowledge and therefore also an important trade-off between strictly modular organizations and less modular organizations. What determines the optimal trade-off depends on the problem solving properties of the two bodies of knowledge and the difference in costs of accumulating these two bodies of knowledge. Because of the advantages of prior related knowledge the costs of accumulating specialist knowledge is decreasing more rapidly than cost of accumulating trans-specialist knowledge. However, trans-specialist knowledge allows firms to better exploit different bodies of specialist knowledge. Thus, modularity of the organization is influenced by the optimal trade-off between accumulation of specialist capabilities and exploitation of knowledge through the accumulation of trans-specialist knowledge. When firm need to accumulate trans-specialized knowledge they need to define broader tasks to increase the knowledgebase, rotate employees, create cross-component development projects etc. all of which are deviations from a very strict modular product development organization.

Firms encounter a similar trade-off between accumulation of knowledge that allow them to explore new product architectures and knowledge them to effectively exploit old product architectures. Henderson and Clark (1990) argues that firms' ability to modify and identify product architectures is influenced by the knowledge they have accumulated and that modular product development organization increase the rate of accumulation of component specific knowledge at the expense of accumulation of architectural knowledge. That is, knowledge about ways, in which components are integrated and linked together, and the kind of deep knowledge of core design concepts and their implementation, that is required for radical innovations.

When firms are faced with very high levels of technical uncertainty they may for example know a few of higher level technical interdependences in a hierarchical decomposable design problem (Clark 1985) but need to discover all the lower level interdependencies in order to create product architecture. There are two ways in which firms can organize their search for the product architecture that lead to accumulation of different bodies of knowledge. They can decompose product development tasks as narrow as possible with regard to the design parameters that each needs to know making use of their knowledge of the identified interdependencies or they can define task to encompass many design parameters. According to Puranam and Jacobides (2006) the former increases the rate of learning of specialist knowledge (capability), and reduce the need for communication while the latter increases the rate of learning of trans-specialist (systemic) knowledge as well as the rate at which teams reduce costs of extensive communication of rich information. Based on simulation of problem solving in environment characterized by different degrees of technical and environmental uncertainty they conclude that it is efficient to build trans-specialist (systemic) knowledge when firms are uncertain about the nature or importance of the interdependencies they have discovered or when these interdependencies change over time. Thus, when firms have long time horizons, when learning is context specific and when firms are faced whit great technical and environmental uncertainty they should implement organizations that are as little modular as possible during the process of problem decomposition..

It appears that the conclusion on how modular organizations should be when faced with great uncertainty depends on the assumptions regarding the extent to which knowledge is context specific, how much specialized knowledge can substitute for more generic knowledge, the time horizon and the extent to which external chocks (such as new technical solutions) create competence destroying changes in what has been learned about the interdependencies and their nature. Firms have to expend some of the benefits of the modular product development organization in order to create innovativeness in architectural designs.

5.5 Modularization and the Boundaries of the Firm

Much of the debate on modularity is on whether modular product designs result in outsourcing of component development activities. In fact, one could argue that the ultimate modular product design organization is one, in which all component development activities are carried out by separate firms (Fine 1998) - all though such an arrangement cannot really be categorized as an organization (Sako, 2002). The debate on outsourcing does, however, set focus on other important dimensions such as the transaction specific investments that may have to be undertaken by the component developing firms or the loss of architectural knowledge (Henderson and Clark, 1990)

The empirical investigations on outsourcing and modularity does not give a clear- cut answer to the extent to which modularity create independence between firms. Baldwing and Clark (2000) examined the computer industry and found an increase use of modular products. They also found evidence for the relationship between modular products and organization with IBM´s development of the System/360 computer. However, their longitudinal study does not hold constant a number of factors other than product development strategies that would lead to less integrated organizations.

Shilling and Steensma (2001) also found that modular product designs were associated with more modular organizational forms at the industry level. This could in particular be attributed the increase use of industry product standards.

Hoetker (2006) examined modular and integral product development activities by note bookmakers and their decisions to retain or move component supply outside firm boundaries. He found that modularity in products does not help firms move activities out of hierarchy. However, firms engaging in modular product development were more inclined to reconfigure their supply chain because prior transaction mattered less when considering who to buy from.

The relative independence between design activities could be expected to result in an extended specialization across firms. Brusoni and Prencipe (2001) have observed the emergence of such patterns of specialization among producers of aircraft engines and among chemical plants. Also, they observed some specialization between architectural developers and components developers in the two industries. Their study do, however, reveal that developers of new product architectures typically had a wide technology base, a good understanding of customer needs and undertook some detailed design in particular critical components. Moreover, they coordinated development work across firms through highly interactive types of informational structures.

Sako (2002) points out that the use of supplier parks and modular consorita indicates that "... outsourcing of modules goes hand in hand with the development of a more "integral" organization, with geographic proximity facilitation much interaction and communication" (p.11). Her investigation of the auto industry also reveals that OEMs that outsource component design to suppliers often undertake "shadow engineering" that is they to engage in the same design activities as the suppliers. An important reason for this according to Sako is that OEMs do not want to loose their ability to integrate the systems.

The latter two studies indicate that it is important to take into consideration if a product architecture is fully specified. Firms will have to maintain integrative capabilities when they introduce new product varieties that require a redesign of the architecture, or if innovations in components introduce interdependencies in design decisions. This in turn requires an organization that is more integral than what is required for "ordinary" design activities –those, for which modules and interface standards are well specified. Moreover, technologies may sometimes shift from modular to integral and firms that have implemented a modular organization may because of organizational inertia be trapped in what Chesbrough and Kusunoki (1999) have called the modularity trap. To avoid such traps, firms may adopt less modular organizations. In sum, the uncertainty with respect to the architectural innovations that may be required in the future may lead firms to adopt less modular organizations.

Organizations have a very large number of dimensions, on which they can be characterized. The debate on modular organizations is mainly concerned with the issues of project organization and the informational structure of organizations. This makes it difficult to categorize real organizations as modular or non-modular, since it is unclear what characterize modular organizations along such dimensions as incentive structures and the use of central planning and authority. Judging from the writing on new organizational forms including modular organizations (Lewine et al. 1999a and b), these are characterized by very little use of authority and central planning. This, however, does not seem to be compatible with the central planning of the architecture and interfaces that is an important characteristic of modular product development organizations. If central planning and the use of authority in setting controlling and enforcing constraints on development activities were not centrally carried out, the informational structures would have to be much more elaborated to ensure compatibility between activities. The lack of more a more precise characterization of modular organizations makes empirical work difficult. Finally, organizational inertia may make it very difficult to adopt the organization to the requirements of the product development activities. This may also imply that firms that pursue modular product development activities have not implemented a modular organization.

6. CONCLUSION

The main purpose of this paper was to investigate how modular designs and organizations improve lead-time in product development. A secondary purpose is to provide an economic rationale behind the proposition that modular products result in modular product organizations. In the product development literature it is often implicitly assumed that modular products produce modular product development organizations. However, the efficiency of different organizational designs cannot be assessed without considering the aim the constraints facing members of the organization. I have taken the improvement of lead-time in product development to be the primary aim of the organization, and the interdependencies in product designs along with costs of communication to be the main constraints facing product designers.

The analysis of the link between modularization in products, lead-time, and modularization of organizations has been pursued in three steps. The first, step was to investigate how to design tasks and informational structures to improve lead-time. The second step was to investigate the influence of modular versus integral product development strategies on definitions of tasks and informational structures. Finally, I discussed whether it was efficient to implement modular product development strategies by means of what some writers in the area of new product development have termed modular organizations.

Based on the analysis presented in this paper it is reasonable to assume that organizations pursuing a goal of improving lead-time will exhibit differences with respect to definitions of tasks and informational structures depending on whether their product development strategy is an integral or a modular product development strategy. Moreover, the differences in the organization of product development stem from the differences in the interdependencies between design decisions.

Firms that pursue a modular product development strategy can improve lead-time with more narrowly defined product development tasks and with the implementation of informational structures that rely on less information gathering, greater independence in decision taking and more parallel information processing compared to firm that pursue integral product development strategies. These are the characteristics of modular product development organizations

The analysis pursued in this paper has not systematically taken into account the nature of the knowledge and information interdependencies between architectural innovations and modular innovations in components. But it has been indicated in the literature (Clark and Henderson, 1990; Chesbrough and Kusunoki 1999) that a less modular organization may be needed in order to facilitate trail and error learning processes and cross-component knowledge accumulation, required for architectural innovations. Moreover, organizational inertia and interdependencies other than informational ones may causes organizations to be less modular than one would expect from the analysis presented in this paper.

REFERENCES

Aoki, M., 1986, Horizontal vs. Vertical Information Structure of the Firm, *American Economic Review*, **76**, (5), 971-983.

Alexander, Christopher, 1979, *Notes on the Synthesis of Form*, Harvard University Press: Cambridge Mass.

Allen, Thomas J. and Hauptman, Oscar, 1987, The Influence of Communication Technologies on Organizational Structure, *Communication Research*, **14**, (5), 575-578.

Arditti, Fred and Levy, Haim, 1980, A Model of the Parallel Team Strategy in Product Development, *The American Economic Review*, **70**, (5), 1089-1097.

Baldwin, Carliss Y., and Clark, Kim B., 2000, *Design rules: The power of Modularity*, Cambridge, MA: Harvard Business School Press.

Baldwin, Carliss Y., and Clark, Kim B., 1997, Managing in the Age of Modularity, *Harvard Business Review*, (5) 84-93.

Barzel, Y., 1989, *Economic Analysis of Property Rights*, Cambridge University Press: Cambridge.

Bower, Gordon, Langely, P., and Simon, Herbert, 1983, Studying Scientific Discovery by Computer Simulation, *Science*, **222**, 971-975.

Brusoni, Stefano and Prencipe, Andrea, 2001, Unpacking the Black Box of Modularity: Technologies, Products and Organizations, Industrial and Corporate Change, **10**, 179-205.

Carter, Martin J., 1995, Information and The Division of Labour: Implications for The Firms' Choice of Organization, *The Economic Journal*, **105**, (429), 385-397.

Casson, Mark, 1994, Why are Firms Hierarchical?, *Journal of the Economics of Business*, **1**, (1), 47-77.

Casson, Mark, 1997, *Information and Organization*, Oxford: Oxford University Press.

Chesbrough, H. and Kusunoki, K., 1999, The Modularity Trap: Innovation, Technology Phase-Shifts, and Resulting Limits of Virtual Organizations, in Nonaka and Teece, D. (eds) *Managing Industrial Knowledge*, Sage.

Clark, Kim B., 1985, The Interaction of Design Hierarchies and Market Concept in Technological Evolution, *Research Policy*, **14** (5), 235-251.

Clark K. B., Chew, W. B., and Fujimoto, T., 1987, Product Development in the World Auto Industry, *Brookings Paper on Economic Activity*, **3**, 729-781.

Clark, Kim B. and Wheelwright, Steven C., 1992, Organizing and Leading 'Heavyweight Development Teams, *California Management Review*, **34**, (3), 9-28.

Cohen, Westley M., and Levinthal, Daniel A., 1990, Absorptive Capacity: A New Perspective on Learning and Innovation, *Administrative Science Quarterly*, **35**, (1), 128-152.

Cusumano Michael A., 1997, How Microsoft Makes Large Teams Work Like Small Teams, *Sloan Management Review*, **39,** (1), 9-20.

Dessein, Wouter and Santos, Tanos., 2006, Adaptive Organizations, *The Journal of Political Economy*, **114** (5), 956-995.

Egidi, Massimo, 1992, Organizational Learning, Problem Solving and the Division of Labour, In: Simon, Herbert; Massimo, Egigi and Robin Maris (eds.), *Economics, Bounded Rationality and the Cognitive Revolution,* Aldershot: Edward Elgar.

Eppinger, Steven D., Whitney, Daniel E., Smith, Robert P., and Gebla, David A., 1994, A Model-Based Method for Organizing Tasks in Product Development, *Research in Engineering Design*, **6,** 1-13.

Ethiraj, S. and Levinthal, D., 2004, Modularity and Innovation in Complex Systems, *Management Science*, **50** (2), 159-173.

Feitzinger, Edward and Lee, Hau L., 1997, Mass Customization at Hewlett-Packard: The Power of Postponement, *Harvard Business Review*, **75,** (1), 116-121.

Fine, Charles H., 1998, *Clockspeed: Winning Industry Control in the Age of Temporary Advantage.* New York: Perseus Books.

Fujimoto, Takahiro 1989, *Organizations for Effective Product Development: The Case of the Global Automobile Industry*, Unpublished D.B.A. Thesis, Harvard Business School.

Garud, R., Kumaraswamy, A., 1993, Changing Competitive Dynamics in Network Industries: An Exploration of Sun Microsystems' Open System Strategy, *Strategic Management Journal*, **14**, (5), 351-369.

Garud, R., Kumaraswamy, A., 1995, Technological and Organizational Designs for Realizing Economics of Substitution, *Strategic Management Journal*, **16 (Special Issue)**, 93-109.

Galvin, Peter 1999, Product Modularity, Information Structure and the Diffusion of Innovation, *International Journal of Technology Management,* **17**, (5), 467-479.

Henderson, Clark 1990, Architectural Innovation: The Reconfiguration of Existing Product Technologies and the Failure of Established Firms, *Administrative Science Quarterly*, **35**, (1), 9-30.

Hoetker, Glenn 2006, Do Modular Products Lead to Modular Organizations?, *Strategic Management Journal*, **27**, (6), 501-518.

Hoopes, David G. and Postrel, Steven 1999, Shared Knowledge, "Glitches," and Product Development Performance, *Strategic Management Journal*, **20**, (9), 837-865.

Johne, Fredrick A., How Experienced Product Innovators Organize, *Journal of Product Innovation Management*, **1**, (4), 210-223.

Klemperer, Paul 1987, Entry Deterrence in Markets with Consumer Switching Costs, *Economic Journal*, **97**, 99-117

Langlois, Richard N, Robertson, Paul L., 1992, Networks and Innovation in a Modular System: Lessons from the Microcomputer and Stereo Component Industries, *Research Policy*, **21**, (4), 297-313.

Langlois, R. N. 2002, Modularity in Technology and Organizations, *Journal of Economic Behavior and Organization,* **49** (1) 19-38.

Larson, E. W. and Gobeli, D. H., 1988, Organizing for Product Development Projects, *Journal of Product Innovation Management,* **5**, (3), 180-190.

Lawrence, P.R. and Lorsch, J., 1967, *Organization and Environment*, Homewood, Illinois: Richard D. Iwing.

Levinthal, Daniel A. and March, James G., 1993, The Myopia of Learning, *Strategic Management Journal,* **14**, (8), 95-112.

Lewine, Arie, Henk, Y., Volberda, W., 1999a, Prolegomena on Coevolution; A Framework for Research on Strategy and New Organizational Forms, *Organization Science,* **10**, (5),519-535.

Lewine, Arie, Long, Chris P., and Caroll, Thimothy N., 1999b, The Coevolution of New Organizational Forms, *Organization Science*, **10**, (5), 535-551.

Lundquist, Mats, Sundgren, Niklas and Trygg, Lars, 1996, Remodularization of a Product Line: Adding Complexity to Project Management, *Journal of Product Innovation Management*, **13**, (4), 311-324.

Marples, David L. 1961, The Decisions of Engineering Design, *The Transactions on Engineering Management*, 55-71.

Marchak, J., and Radner, Roy, 1977, *Economic Theory of Teams*. New Haven: Yale Univeristy Press.

Meyer, C. 1993, *Fast Cycle Time*. New York: The Free Press.

Nelson, Richard, 1959, The Economics of Invention: A Survey of the literature, *Journal of Business*, University of Chicago, **32**, 101-127.

Nonaka, Ikujiro, 1994, A Dynamic Theory of Organizational Knowledge Creation, *Organization Science*, **5**, (1), 14-37.

Pine, II, Joseph B., 1993, *Mass Customization: The New Frontier in Business Competition*, Boston Mass.: Harvard Business School.

Postrel, Steven, 2002, Islands of Shared Knowledge: Specialization and Mutual Understanding in Problem-Solving Teams, *Organizational Science*, **13**, (3): 303-320.

Radner, Roy, 1992, Hierarchy: The Economics of Managing, *Journal of Economic Literature*, **30**, (3), 1382-1415.

Sanchez, Ron, 1996, Strategic Product Creation: Managing New Interactions of Technology, Markets and Organizations, *European Management Journal*, **14,** (6), 121-138.

Sanchez, R., 2000, Modular Architectures, Knowledge Assets, and Organizational Learning: New Management Processes for Product Creation, *International Journal of Technology Management*, **19**,610-629.

Sanchez, Ron and Mahoney, Joseph T., 1996, Modularity, Flexibility, and Knowledge Management in Product and Organization Design, *Strategic Management Journal*, **17** (special issue), 63-76.

Schaefer, Scoott, 1999, Product Design Partitions with Complementary Components, *Journal of Economic Behavior & Organization*, **38**, (3), 311-330.

Schilling, Melissa A., 2000, Toward a General Modular Systems Theory and its Application to Interfirm Product Modularity, *Academy of Management Review*, **25,** (2), 312-334.

Schilling, M.A. and Steensma, H.K., 2001, The Use of Modular Organizational Forms: An Industry-Level Analysis, *Academy of Management Journal*, **44** (6): 1149-1168.

Schmalensee, Richard, 1982, Product differentiation Advantages of Pioneering Brands, *American Economic Review,* **72**, (2), 349-365.

Shapiro, Carl, 1983, Optimal Pricing of Experience Goods, *Bell Journal of Economics*, **14**, (1), 497-507.

Simon, Herbert A., 1969, *Science of the Artificial*, Cambridge Mass.: The M.I.T. Press.

Simon, Herbert A. 1985, What we Know about the Creative Process, In: R.L. Kuhn (ed), *Frontiers in Creative and Innovative Management*, Cambridge, MA: Ballinger.

Smith, Adam, 1776), *An Inquiry Into The Causes of the Wealth of Nations*, 1980 ed., Indianapolis: Liberty Press.

Smith, G.P. and Reinertsen, D.G., 1991, *Developing Products in Half the Time*, New York:Van Nostrand Reinhold.

Thomson, James. D., 1967, *Organizations in Action*, New Your: McGraw-Hill.

Ulrich Karl, T., 1995, The role of Product Architectures in the Manufacturing Firm, *Research Policy*, **24**, (3), 419-440.

Ulrich, Karl T. and Eppinger, Steven D.,1995, *Product Design and Development*, New Your: McGraw-Hill, Inc.

von Hippel, Eric, 1990, Task Partitioning: An Innovation Process Variable, *Research Policy*, **19,** (5), 407-418.

von Hippel, Eric, 1994, Sticky Information and the Locus of Problem Solving: Implications for Innovation, *Management Science*, **49,** (4), 429-439.

von Hippel, Eric and Tyre, Marice J., 1995, How Learning by Doing is Done: Problem Identification in Novel Process Equipment, *Research Policy*, **24**, (1), 1-12.

von Hippel, Eric, 1998, Economics of Product Development by Users: The Impact of 'Sticky' Local Information, *Management Science*, **44**, (5), 629-644.

Wheelwright, Steven S. and Clark, Kim B., 1992, *Revolutionizing Product Development*, New York: The Free Press.

Chapter 11

STRATEGIC PLANNING AND FIRM PERFORMANCE

The influence of organizational context

Bo H. Eriksen

Department of Marketing and Management, University of Southern Denmark, 55 Campusvej, 5230 Odense M, Denmark

Abstract: This chapter investigates the relationship between strategic planning and organizational performance and explores interactions between organization structure and planning in the determination of performance. The chapter provides an empirical analysis using moderated repression on a sample of 250 Danish firms. The results suggest that strategic planning influences performance positively but that the effect is moderated negatively by the extent that decision making in the organization is decentralized. The results suggest that planning effectiveness is limited by the organizational context.

Key words: Organizational effectiveness, organizational structure, strategic planning.

1. INTRODUCTION

One of the major premises in strategic management has been that strategic planning is an instrumental process for relating a firm to its competitive environment (Boyd and Reuning-Elliott 1998, Miller and Cardinal 1994, Pearce et al 1987). Strategic planning is associated with collection and interpretation of data that are important for aligning the firm with its competitive environment, and it follows that better alignment leads to better firm performance (Armstrong 1982). However, strategic planning processes take place within an organizational context that may influence the impact of strategic planning processes on organizational performance, as the organizational structure may strengthen or weaken the ability to implement these processes. As strategic planning deals with the long term management of the enterprise, a key issue is to balance organizational tradeoffs, such as

R.M. Burton et al. (eds.), *Designing Organizations*, doi: 10.1007/978-0-387-77776-4_11,

tradeoffs between differentiation and cost performance, exploration and exploitation, and similar conflicting demands in the organizational task environment. Managing tradeoffs is sometimes referred to as managing organizational ambidexterity (cf. Duncan 1976, Gibson and Birkinshaw 2004). Obtaining a alignment between strategic planning processes and organizational structures is important for the ability to manage organizational tradeoffs and misalignment may cause poor performance.

This chapter provides an empirical analysis of the planning-performance relationship that takes into account the effects of organizational structure, and thus address a weakness pointed out in prior research (Pearce et al 1987, Yasai-Ardekani and Haug 1997, Andersen 2000 and 2004). Specifically, since an organization's strategic planning process is nested in an organizational context, the chapter focuses on the potential moderating effects of organizational structure on the relationship between strategic planning and performance.

The chapter explores the possible moderating effect of four structural variables, namely formalization, specialization, decentralization, and integration. The results show that only decentralization moderates the planning-performance relationship, but that this effect is negative. The result has implications for strategic management and organization design, suggesting that centralized top management processes are difficult to align with decentralized organization structures.

The paper proceeds as follows. In the next section a brief review of the theory and empirical findings on the strategic planning – performance relationship is provided. The section concludes that strategic planning should be seen in its organizational context, and a useful theoretical lens for understanding strategic planning in its context is information processing theory (Galbraith 1973, Tushman and Nadler 1978). Following this, the notion of organizational information processing is discussed, and the assertion that it is appropriate to separate the organization structure from information processing is advanced, and consequently, effective information processing will be dependent on organization structure. The research design and methods used in the empirical analysis is presented followed by a discussion of the empirical results. In the concluding section the research and practical implications of the findings are discussed.

2. STRATEGIC PLANNING AND ORGANIZATIONAL PERFORMANCE

Strategic planning can be viewed as a process whereby the firm obtains and evaluates information about its competitive environment, its resources and capabilities, and other factors that are relevant to its strategic decision making (Armstrong 1982). The consequence of strategic planning is to improve knowledge about these factors, and thereby reduce decision making uncertainty in the firm. The benefits that can be obtained from strategic planning relate to the process for determining long term goals, generating and evaluating alternative strategies, and monitoring the level of goal achievement (Armstrong 1982). Strategic planning will therefore enable to firm to align its resources and capabilities with the environmental challenges it faces (Ansoff 1991) which is believed to lead to better organizational performance (Boyd and Reuning-Elliott 1998, Miller and Cardinal 1994, Pearce et al 1987).

The assertion that strategic planning is positively associated with performance has been hotly disputed. Proponents of strategic planning have consistently argued that formal planning leads to better decisions (Ansoff 1991) and that in turbulent environments this will be especially important because the benefits of uncertainty reduction are greater in such environments (Miller and Friesen 1983; Glick, Doty and Huber 1993, Miller 1987). Also, it has been argued that strategic planning aids large companies integrate and control diverse operations which will lead to greater levels of efficiency (Grinyer er al 1986, Vancil and Lorange 1975). In contrast, opponents of strategic planning have argued that planning is a bureaucratic feature that leads to rigidity and low capability for adaptation to changed environmental and competitive conditions (Mintzberg 1987, 1990). Eventually such rigidities lead to poor performance as failure to adapt to changed circumstances results in inefficiencies.

Despite its high importance as a theoretical construct within strategic management, the empirical evidence for a substantive relationship between strategic planning and performance has been less convincing (Pearce et al 1987), and there have a fair share of inconsistent empirical findings regarding the effect of strategic planning (Andersen 2004). Early empirical research on the strategic planning – performance relationship did not to provide evidence for a consistent relationship between planning and performance, partly due to methodological limitations, and partly due to lack of controls for important contextual factors (Pearce et al 1987). Failure to control for relevant contextual factors has been cited as a key reason why early empirical studies have failed to show a consistent and positive relationship between organizational effectiveness and strategic planning (Jemison 1981, Pearce et al 1987). In fact, Yasai-Ardekani and Haug (1997) find important contextual effects on strategic planning characteristics.

Another criticism that has been raised is that there is a lack of theoretical basis of the planning – performance link (Rogers et al 1999). Since the benefits of strategic planning relate to its importance in making strategic decisions (Armstrong 1982, Ansoff 1991), a possible candidate for a theoretical basis is information processing theory.

Building on early work by Thompson (1967) and Lawrence and Lorsch (1967), information processing theory maintains that organizations are information processing systems, and that matching information processing needs with information processing capability will improve organizational effectiveness (Galbraith 1973). From the perspective of information processing theory (Galbraith 1973, Egelhoff 1991, Tushman and Nadler 1978), information processing leads to reduced uncertainty – and reduced uncertainty leads to better decisions. Strategic planning is a type of information processing that will lead to reduction of uncertainty about internal and external factors that influence the alignment between the firm and its environment. Better decisions resulting from a strategic planning process will therefore improve organizational performance. This assumption about the role of strategic planning is consistent with its treatment in the strategic planning literature (cf. Armstrong 1982 and Ansoff 1991).

Hypothesis 1: Strategic planning influences organizational performance positively.

3. INFORMATION PROCESSING AND ORGANIZATION STRUCTURE

As asserted earlier, strategic planning can be viewed as a form of information *processing* in the organization. In contrast to processes, organizational structures represent state aspects of organizations (Miller 1987). Information processing, defined as a process variable (or set thereof), should therefore be viewed as different from organizational structure, defined as a state variable (Egelhoff 1991). In information processing theory, the structure of the organization has been argued to be instrumental for the organization's information processing capacity (Thompson 1967, Galbraith 1973, Tushman and Nadler 1978). Egelhoff (1991) argued that in the literature, the constructs that have been used to define and describe information processing have been treated as unobservable, and that generally, inferences have been made regarding the relationships between variables describing organizational structure and performance. This implies that a more complete model of the relationship includes both process variables relating to information processing and state variables relating to organizational structure.

If organization structure is viewed a state description of organization, its role in information processing theory is to regulate the flow of information in the organization (Scott 1992 chapter 4). This means that organizational structures influence how issues are framed, what events decision makers judge to be important, and how problems are solved. The organizational structure therefore functions as a filter for what the organization happens to perceive, and how the organization acts upon its perception (Miles, Snow and Pfeffer 1974, Leifer and Huber 1977, Normann 1977).

If the organizational structure regulates the flow of information in the organization, it becomes an enabler of strategic planning. If strategic planning is important for relating the organization to its competitive environment (as hypothesized above) the organizational structure will influence performance indirectly as a moderating effect. The key question remains whether the moderating is negative or positive, that is whether certain structural elements reinforce the strategic planning efforts or acts in a counterproductive manner.

Four variables have been used consistently in studies of organizational structures (see e.g. Miller and Dröge 1986): Formalization, integration, specialization and decentralization. The potential moderating effects of these four variables will be the focus of this chapter.

Formalization refers to the extent of use of standards for procedures, performance, and the designs of jobs (Miller and Dröge 1986, Inkson et al 1970, Khandwalla 1974, Pugh and Hickson, 1976). If formalization is high, monitoring activities and performance will be easier, and it is easier for the organization to produce highly reliable and standardized information for decision making, and to enforce the implementation of decisions (Duncan 1976). Formalization is therefore likely moderate the planning performance relationship positively.

Hypothesis 2: Formalization moderates the relationship between strategic planning and performance positively.

Integration is associated with the use of liaison processes and structures (Galbraith 1973, Lawrence and Lorsch 1967, Miller and Friesen 1984, Mintzberg 1979). Liaison processes and structures provide integration of organizational activities (Miller and Dröge 1986, Lawrence and Lorsch 1967). They are implemented to improve the interpretation of complex issues by bringing together different sources of experience, expertise, and information. These structural elements are therefore likely to support problems solving efforts where the organization confronts highly complex problems with substantial degrees of uncertainty about means and ends. Integration is therefore moderate the strategic planning performance relationship positively.

Hypothesis 3: Integration moderates the relationship between strategic planning and performance positively.

Decentralization is characterized by the degree of delegation of decision making authority where high degrees of decentralization mean that employees have discretion over decisions (Pugh et al 1968, 1969). When decentralization is high in the organization the organization may become more responsive to its environment (Andersen 2004), and its members will obtain more specific and timely information that will enable better interpretation of complex issues. On the other hand, decentralization of decision making authority may make it more difficult to achieve effective implementation of strategies as decisions are more difficult to coordinate in decentralized organizations. For example, conflicts may emerge between decentralized managers in the organization that can prove to be counterproductive in relation to the strategies determined by the top management in the organization. Therefore two competing hypotheses are proposed:

Hypothesis 4a: Decentralization moderates the relationship between strategic planning and performance positively.

Hypothesis 4b: Decentralization moderates the relationship between strategic planning and performance negatively.

Specialization characterizes the extent that labor is divided into specialized tasks, requiring workers with specialized skills (Van de Ven and Ferry 1980). Specialization has been associated with the ability to capture valuable information about the organizational environment (Cohen and Levinthal 1990), and increased specialization enables for example the capture of valuable technological knowledge. Therefore, higher degrees of specialization lead to better acquisition of relevant information for the strategic planning process and therefore enhance the effectiveness of strategic planning efforts.

Hypothesis 5: Specialization moderates the relationship between strategic planning and performance positively.

4. RESEARCH DESIGN AND METHODS

To analyze the hypotheses in the present paper, data were collected through a survey of CEO's from Danish firms with more than 100 employees. Survey research is the most feasible approach for empirical analysis of organizations in large scale studies since direct observation is quite costly and archival measures of organizational structure and process are difficult to obtain. The data were subsequently analyzed using moderated regression to test the hypotheses.

4.1 Data collection

The data employed in this paper was obtained from a survey of CEO's of Danish firms with more than 100 employees. I chose to sample relatively large organizations to avoid organizations with little structural complexity where structure is likely to matter very little. The sample was drawn from a publicly available business directory that contains contact information for firms and in some cases the name of the CEO of the firm. The number of firms listed in this business directory corresponds roughly to the population, and the initial list included 1,506 firms from all economic sectors. 115 cases had more than one record, and 10 firms were either bankrupt or not registered at the address in the database, bringing the sample to be contacted down to 1,381.

The first round of data collection was implemented in late March 2005. A personal letter was sent to the CEO with a request to fill out a web-based questionnaire. This yielded a total of 68 responses. I chose to include a paper version and a self-addressed envelope with the follow-up letter. After the second round 171 usable questionnaires in total had been returned which yielded a response rate of 12.4 % (171 divided by 1,381). Therefore, in late April, I sent out a third letter with an enclosed self-addressed envelope and a new copy of the questionnaire. After the third round of data collection, the total number of responses was 250 usable questionnaires, yielding a response rate of 18 %. The response rate is satisfactory and in line with expectations of prior published surveys of CEO's.

Since the sample size is relatively large, and since virtually all firms in the population of firms with more than 100 employees in Denmark were contacted, the problem of response bias is likely to be minor. The sample is of course biased towards large firms, thus limiting the extent that findings can be generalized to small entrepreneurial firms. The sampled firms report between 80 and 33000 employees with a median value of 237.5 employees.

Due to item non-response, the usable number of cases ranged between 229 (model 2 and 3 in table 2) and 238 (model 1 in table 2).

4.2 Methods

All the research instruments that are used in the analysis are previously validated instruments that have shown good validity in prior studies. All the scales except specialization exhibit sufficient scale reliability with Cronbach's alpha ranging between .76 and .85 (cf. Nunnally and Bernstein 1994). Specialization had an alpha of .59 which is generally considered insufficient. The measure was nevertheless retained in the analysis to achieve completeness in the analysis as the measure has been shown to be reliable in earlier research (cf. Van de Ven and Ferry 1980). Table 1 shows the descriptive statistics for each variable employed in this study and the sources for each instrument. All measures were measured on 5 point likert scales.

Organizational performance was measured using subjective measures of performance based on Venkatraman (1989) where the respondents were asked to assess their firm's performance in relation to their closest competitors. Prior studies have established good convergent validity between these and objective performance measures (Venkatraman 1989). Using subjective performance measures avoids the disadvantages associated with using accounting measures of performance such as distortions related to differences in accounting convention such as income smoothing, depreciation principles, and similar common accounting practices. It should also be noted that the majority of the companies in the population are privately held firms, and not listed on any stock exchange, and therefore market-based measures of performance are not available.

The remaining measures of strategic planning and organizational structure were gathered from diverse sources (which appear as a note to table 1), and have all been used successfully in prior studies (i.e. with sufficient reliability).

Table 1. Descriptive statistics

	N	Mean	Std.dev.	Alpha	1.	2.	3.	4.	5.
1. Growth[1]	238	3.81	0.59	0.77					
2. Strategic planning[2]	239	3.97	0.61	0.80	0.19				
3. Formalization[3]	243	3.73	0.84	0.85	0.10	0.41			
4. Integration[4]	243	3.94	0.78	0.76	0.08	0.45	0.25		
5. Decentralization[5]	238	3.66	0.55	0.78	-0.02	0.03	-0.07	0.18	
6. Specialization[6]	241	2.83	0.68	0.59	0.13	0.13	0.09	0.25	0.11

Sources: [1] Venkatraman (1989), [2] Boyd and Reuning-Elliott (1998), [3] Cardinal (2001), Aiken and Hage (1968), Dewar and Werbel (1979), Hall (1968), [4] Miller (1983), [5] Inkson, Pugh, and Hickson (1970), Pugh and Hickson (1976), [6] Van de Ven and Ferry (1980).

Inspecting the descriptive statistics in table 1 shows that the variables integration and formalization are positively correlated with strategic planning, and that specialization and decentralization are correlated with the other structural variables suggesting a more complex relationship than the one that is captured in the moderated regression analysis. Organization structure may influence the planning performance relationship in other ways that through moderation, for example indirectly through its effect on strategic planning, or perhaps configurations of strategic planning and organizational structures can be identified. This is, however, a task for future research to explore, and thus outside the bounds of this chapter.

5. RESULTS

Table 2 shows the results of the moderated regression analysis. The analysis was performed using fixed effects regression analysis with dummy variables used to control for industry effects on performance. The analysis of interaction effects used interactions between mean centered, standardized variables with a standard deviation of 1 and a mean of 0 to reduce problems associated with multicollinearity.

Across models, the industry effect showed a modest performance difference between industries, suggesting that external context influences organizational performance, an observation that is in line with expectations derived from multiple studies in strategic management (e.g. Rumelt 1991, McGahan and Porter 1997, Eriksen and Knudsen 2003).

In all model specifications strategic planning was positively and significantly related to performance, confirming the results of prior metastudies (e.g. Miller and Cardinal 1994). The only structural measure that was related directly to performance was specialization, providing a positive and significant effect in model 2 and 3.

In model 3, the results of the moderated regression are shown. Only the interaction between strategic planning and decentralization is significant. The effect is negative, providing support for hypothesis 4b. Alternative models that analyzed the moderating effects one by one were explored and provided results consisted with the ones presented in table 2. The negative interaction effect suggests that autonomous managers that can initiate strategic decisions may be in conflict with a centralized strategic planning process. This result points towards one key aspect of aligning the firm's strategy process with its organizational structure, namely how to coordinate strategies in structurally differentiated organizations. The results obtained herein indicate that this task provides a challenge for managers of decentralized firms and corroborates results obtained by Andersen (2000, 2004).

Overall, the results presented in this chapter suggest a modest moderating effect of organization structure on the relationship between strategic planning and performance. Only the extent of decentralization moderated the planning performance relationship while the remaining structural factors appear to be nil. However, as there are significant and strong relationships among the structural variables and the strategic planning variable, there may be alternative models and analytical techniques that may capture these in a better way.

Table 2. Regression results

	Model 1	Model 2	Model 3
Constant	2.99***	2.79***	2.80***
	(0.25)	(0.39)	(0.41)
Strategic planning	0.21***	0.22**	0.22**
	(0.06)	(0.08)	(0.08)
Formalization		0.01	0.00
		(0.05)	(0.05)
Integration		-0.02	-0.02
		(0.06)	(0.06)
Decentralization		-0.04	-0.03
		(0.07)	(0.07)
Specialization		0.12**	0.13**
		(0.06)	(0.06)
Strategic planning x formalization			-0.01
			(0.05)
Strategic planning x integration			0.01
			(0.04)
Strategic planning x decentralization			-0.10**
			(0.04)
Strategic planning x specialization			0.00
			(0.04)
Industry dummies F-value	1.88*	1.74*	1.75*
Model F-value	10.58	3.14	2.44
R^2	0.09	0.11	0.14
df	228	215	211
N	238	229	229

Standard errors in parantheses, *=p<.1, **=p<.00, ***p<.001

6. INFORMING THE PRACTICE OF ORGANIZATIONAL DESIGN

This chapter provides an empirical analysis of the relationship between strategic planning and performance, and the possible moderating effect that organization structure has in this relationship. The data analysis demonstrates that strategic planning is a useful means to an end – but that the extent of decentralization reduces this effect. The present study complements Andersen's (2000, 2004) studies in showing that the interaction between decentralization and strategic planning is negative. The results presented herein add further substance to the findings of Andersen.

While other studies have argued that decentralization provides benefits in terms of increasing adaptation, the results suggest that a paradox arises when the firm tries to simultaneously achieve centralized coordination and control through strategic planning and adaptation through local (decentral) responsiveness. This challenge appears to be related to the notion of ambidexterity where Duncan (1976) suggested that organizations should implement dual structures to deal with the conflicting pressures of innovation and efficiency. Recent empirical research shows that ambidextrous organizations appear to achieve better performance than organizations that specialize in either exploration or exploitation (Gibson and Birkinshaw 2004, He and Wong 2004, Jansen, van den Bosch, and Volberda 2006, Lubatkin, Simsek, Ling, and Veiga 2006, Sidhu, Volberda, and Commandeur 2004, Sidhu, Commandeur, and Volberda 2007). While ambidexterity may appear to be an appealing concept, its state of development is as yet modest (Lubatkin, Simsek, Ling, and Veiga 2006). Therefore, it may be premature to offer substantial advice to practicing managers, as it is not entirely clear which structural and processual mechanisms that managers should adopt in order to achieve alignment between strategic planning and decentralization.

6.1 Informing the theory of organizational design

The present study adds further knowledge about the structural influences on strategic planning relating to measures of strategic planning, integration, specialization, and formalization. However, the results suggest that the analytical strategy employed in this chapter is inadequate in terms of capturing the complex relations between strategic planning and organizational structure. Alternative conceptualizations based on e.g. configuration theory in organizational analysis (e.g. Meyer et al 1993) or alternative analytical methods such as causal analysis.

In terms of the substantive results, the chapter points toward a need for better understanding of the organizational paradoxes that appear when the organization pursues conflicting goals and activities, and when different activities or structures appear to be in conflict. Recently, research attention has been directed towards problems of this character under the heading of organizational ambidexterity, and the results obtained herein highlight the need for a better understanding of how to resolve organizational paradoxes.

REFERENCES

Aiken, M. and Hage, J., 1968, Organizational interdependence and intra-organizational structure.' *American Sociological Review* **33**, 912-930.

Andersen, T. J., 2000, Strategic planning, autonomous actions and corporate performance. *Long Range Planning* **33**: 184-200.

Andersen, T.J., 2004, Integrating decentralized strategy making and strategic planning processes in Dynamic Environments.' *Journal of Management Studies* **41**(8), 1271-1299.

Ansoff, H. I. 1991, Critique of Henry Mintzberg's The design school: reconsidering the basic premises of strategic management, *Strategic Management Journal* **12**: 449-461.

Armstrong, J. S., 1982, The value of formal planning for strategic decisions: Review of the literature, *Strategic Management Journal* **3**: 197 – 211.

Boyd, B. K. and Reuning-Elliott, J., 1998, A measurement model of strategic planning, *Strategic Management Journal* **19**(2), 181-192.

Cardinal, L. B. 2001, Technological innovation in the Pharmaceutical industry: The use of organizational control in managing research and development, *Organization Science* **12**(1). 19-36.

Cohen, W. M. and Levinthal, D., 1990, Absorptive capacity: A new perspective on learning and innovation, Administrative Science Quarterly **35**, 128—152.

Dewar, R. and Werbel, J., 1979, Universalistic and contingency predictions employee satisfaction and conflict, *Administrative Science Quarterly* **24**, 426-448.

Doty D. H., Glick, W. H., Huber, G. P., 1993, Fit, equifinality, and organizational effectiveness: A test of two configurational theories, *The Academy of Management Journal* **36**(6), 1196-1250.

Duncan, R., 1976, The Ambidextrous organization: Designing dual structures for innovation, In R. Kilman and L. Pondy (eds.), *The Management of Organizational Design*, 167-188. New York: North Holland.

Egelhoff, W. G., 1991, Information-Processing theory and the multinational enterprise, *Journal of International Business Studies* **22**(3), 341-368.

Eriksen B and Knudsen, T., 2003, Industry and firm level interaction - Implications for profitability, *Journal of Business Research,* **56** (3): 191-199.

Galbraith, J., 1973, *Designing complex organizations*, New York: Addison-Wesley.

Gibson, C. B., Birkinshaw, J., 2004. The antecedents, consequences, and mediating role of organizational ambidexterity, *Academy of Management Journal*, **47** 209–229.

He, Z. L. and Wong, P. K., 2004, Exploration vs. Exploitation: An empirical test of the ambidexterity hypothesis, *Organization Science*, **15**(4), 481-494.

Jansen, J. P., van den Bosch, F. A. J., Volberda, H. W., 2006, Exploratory innovation, exploitative innovation, and performance: Effects of organizational antecedents and environmental moderators, *Management Science*, **52** 1661–1674.

Inkson, J.H.K., Pugh, D. S., and Hickson, D. J., 1970, Organization, context, and structure, *Administrative Science Quarterly,* **15**, 318-329.

Jemison, D. B., 1981 Organizational versus environmental sources of influence in strategic decision making, *Strategic Management Journal,* **2**(1), 77-89.

Khandwalla, P. N., 1974, Mass output orientation of technology and organizational structure, *Administrative Science Quarterly,* **19**, 74-97.

Khandwalla, P. N., 1977, *The design of organizations*, New York: Harcourt, Brace, Jovanovich.

Lawrence, P. R. and Lorsch, J. W., 1967, *Organization and environment,* Boston: Harvard Business School Press.

Leifer, R., and Huber, G. P., 1977, Relations among perceived environmental uncertainty, organization structure, and boundary spanning behavior, *Administrative Science Quarterly,* **22,** 265-247.

Lubatkin, M. H., Simsek, Z., Ling, Y., and Veiga, J. F., 2006, Ambidexterity and Performance in Small-to Medium-Sized Firms: The Pivotal Role of Top Management Team Behavioral Integration, *Journal of Management,* **32**(5): 646 - 672.

McGahan A. M. and Porter, M. E., 1997, How much does industry matter, really? *Strategic Management Journal,* **18** (Special Issue Summer): 15-30.

Meyer A. D., Tsui, A S., Hinings C. R., 1993, Configurational Approaches To Organizational Analysis. *Academy of Management Journal*, **36** (6): 1175-1195.

Miles, R., Snow, C., Pfeffer, J., 1974, Organization-environments: Concepts and issues, *Industrial Relations,* **13**, 244-264.

Miller C. C. and Cardinal, L. B., 1994, Strategic Planning and Firm Performance: A Synthesis of More than Two Decades of Research. *The Academy of Management Journal,* **37**(6), 1649-1665.

Miller, D., 1987, Strategy Making and Structure: Analysis and Implications for Performance, *The Academy of Management Journal,* **30**(1), 7-32.

Miller, D., and Dröge, C., 1986, Psychological and traditional determinants of structure, *Administrative Science Quarterly,* **31**(4), 539-560.

Miller, D. and Friesen, P. H., 1983, Strategy-Making and Environment: The Third Link, *Strategic Management Journal,* **4**(3), 221-235.

Miller, D. and Friesen P. H., 1984, *Organizations: A quantum view*, Prentice- Hall: New Jersey.

Mintzberg, H., 1987, The strategy concept II: Another look at why companies need strategies, *California Management Review,* **16**(2), 44-53.

Mintzberg, H., 1990, The Design School: Reconsidering the Basic Premises of Strategic Management, *Strategic Management Journal,* **11**(3), 171-195.

Normann, R., 1977, *Management for growth,* New York: Wiley.

Nunnally, J. C. and Bernstein, I. H., 1994, *Psychometric theory, 3rd edition.*' New York , McGraw-Hill.

Pearce, J. A., Freeman, E. B., Robinson, R. B., 1987 The Tenuous Link between Formal Strategic Planning and Financial Performance *The Academy of Management Review,* **12**(4), 658-675.

Pugh, D. S. and Hickson, D. J., 1976, *Organizational structure in context*, Westmead, Farnborough: Saxon House.

Pugh, D. S. and Hickson, D. J., Hinings, C. R., and Turner, C., 1968, Dimensions of organizational structure, *Administrative Science Quarterl,y* **13**: 65-105.

Pugh, D. S., and Hickson, D. J., Hinings, C. R., and Turner, C., 1969, The context of organization structures, *Administrative Science Quarterly,* **14**: 91-114.

Rogers, P. R., Miller, A.,. Judge, W. Q, 1999, Using Information-Processing Theory to Understand Planning/Performance Relationships in the Context of Strategy, *Strategic Management Journal,* **20**(6), 567-577.

Rumelt, R. P., 1991, How much does industry matter? *Strategic Management Journal*, **12** (3): 167-185.

Scott, W. R., 1992, *Organizations: Rational, natural and Open Systems*, Englewood-Cliffs, Prentice-Hall.

Sidhu, J. S., Volberda, H. W., Commandeur, H. R., 2004, Exploring exploration orientation and its determinants: Some empirical evidence, *Journal of Management Studies* **41** 913–932.

Sidhu, J., Commandeur, H., and Volberda, H., 2007, The Multifaceted Nature of Exploration and Exploitation, *Organization Science*, **18**(1), pp. 20–38,

Thompson, J. D., 1967, *Organizations in action*, Oxford, Oxford University Press.

Tushman, M. L. and Nadler, D. A., 1978, Information processing as an integrating concept in organization design, *Academy of Management Review,* **3**(3): 613-624.

Vancil, R. F. and Lorange, P. 1975, Strategic planning in diversified companies, *Harvard Business Review,* **53**(1): 81-90.

Van de Ven, A. H. and Ferry, D. L., 1980, Measuring and assessing organizations, New York, John Wiley and Sons.

Venkatraman, N. 1989, Strategic orientation of business enterprises, *Management Science,* **35**(8). '942-962.

Yasai-Ardekani, M and Haug, R. S., 1997, Contextual determinants of Strategic Planning Processes, *Journal of Management Studies* **34**(5), 729-767.

Printed in the United States of America